Virgin australia

RINSMA/MANON
PNR: YMDVY6
FROM: BKK

0 1 0 5 3 9 9 9

Jetx

I0418335

PHUKET

RINSMA/MANON
WF SV2N
29DEC

SYD JQ202 29DEC 0720

RINSMA/MANON MRS

17FEB
09:35

PRG
PRAGUE

16FEB
10:55
T2

AY715

HEL
HELSINKI

AY096

Virgin australia

RINSMA/MANON MRS
PNR LBRRKA

SEQ- 01

F128
PERTH

F121

ZQN

QANTAS

06 DEC
QUEENSTOWN

05 DEC
SYDNEY

SYD

AKL JQ

tigerair

PP

HKG   (12DEC) 1305

AG: 01/15

HO 347331   NSMA/MANON MRS

JUNEYAO AIRLINES   捷

RINSMA/MANO

Jetx

MOSCOW SVO
SVO   LO675   11NOV 1
WAW   LO270   11NOV 0

PRINT DATE (GMT): 11NO

0790 1A 518591

17DEC 152

ALSO BY MANON RINSMA

13 Diamonds: Life Before Death from a Child's Perspective
A Memoir, 2018

MBOSSED: Leave Your Mark on the World by Being You
Self-discovery Journal, 2021

A FAR CRY FROM
Yesterday

MR

A FAR CRY FROM YESTERDAY

FINDING TOMORROW IN DISTANT LANDS

First edition, February 1, 2025
ISBN: 979-8-9909954-1-3

Inquiries: info@manonrinsma.com

All maps are abstract representations.

Cover Photo by Manon Rinsma Leonard *(Lake Baikal, Russia, 2015)*
Author Portrait Photography by Dustin Sheffield

FINDING TOMORROW
IN DISTANT LANDS

MR

For Lazlo,

a true friend
who encouraged me
to finish this story
for those of us
who get to live
will go experience
like he deserved to
but could not
may he rest in peace

Contents

Author's Note

Prologue

PART ONE

ENDINGS AND PINK TREES ON THE HORIZON | 5

PART TWO

A COLD TRAIN OF WANDERING THOUGHTS | 75

PART THREE

BREAKING POINT OF THE SOUL | 125

PART FOUR

DON'T WAIT FOR TOMORROW TO COME | 181

PART FIVE

EVERYWHERE BUT MOVING BACKWARD | 209

PART SIX

PAUSING LONG ENOUGH TO PROCESS | 267

PART SEVEN

CLEAR EYES ON THE ROOF OF THE WORLD | 291

Epilogue

Acknowledgments

Author's Note

In writing this book, I had to relive, re-remember, and dive deep into the depths of my soul and memories—all that was painful and all that was beautiful. To accomplish this, I drew extensively from my personal journals, documenting my experiences from my unique perspective. Alongside my written words, other invaluable resources included my abundant collection of photographs, videos and messages—both text and voice—from others, as well as journal entries and communications from individuals I encountered during my travels. I researched factual information where possible and consulted with several people featured in this book to ensure accuracy. Forgive me if sometimes the days were fuzzy —memory is a tricky thing, prone to both clarity and distortion, shaped as much by emotion as by fact. I am deeply grateful to all those I crossed paths with, who contributed to my story. On occasion, I chose to omit certain people and events—not to diminish their importance, but for the sake of narrative, or else this would have been a trilogy rather than a single book. To protect privacy, I have refrained from naming individuals, except for the friend to whom this book is dedicated and a few well-known public figures. In some instances, I altered identifying details and correspondence from others to maintain anonymity. There are no composite characters in this narrative.

Prologue

In the wake of loss, amidst the echoes of fury, my journey around the world began—a quest to reclaim solace, to unearth peace within the embrace of distant lands.

Now here I am, many months later, struck by breathtaking views of towering summits. I stand at the edge of the Wakhan Corridor, overlooking Afghanistan from the southern reaches of Tajikistan, the barren peaks instilling a calmness in my heart. I have covered my long blonde hair with a headscarf; the gentle wind swirls around me, lifting sand and making my dress dance along the heights of the mountain roads. I never imagined I would venture this deep into unfamiliar territory, places I had never even looked at on a map.

The past couple of nights have been a challenge. After backpacking through two dozen countries across four continents, I should have known better than to venture into the wilderness with nothing but a large pickup truck, a jerrycan of fuel and a few fellow travelers I had met at a hostel.

We struggled to find food and shelter in this remote region, and altitude sickness was a constant. The road was long and treacherous, and the threat of patrols kept us on edge. In the distance, I could hear the muffled sounds of what seemed to be military, hidden among the sheer walls of rock.

But as I stand on the rocky edge, looking down at the gorge, just a small figure in the midst of all this majesty, the fears from the previous nights start to fade away. My thoughts prompt flashbacks—anxieties, memories and pent-up pains flicker before my eyes. It's all in the past now, a different part of me. Instead of a hole, there's a wholeness in my heart.

Is this it? Have I pushed my boundaries enough? Crossed enough borders? Am I ready to reach the finish line, my finish line—that elusive feeling I have been searching for but can't quite put my finger on? To be *normal* again, rather than a citizen of the world roaming the globe looking for answers?

Questions swirl in my mind as my gaze stays fixated on the landscape. For months, I've searched for a sense of fulfillment, wondering if this journey would ever be enough, if it would ever lead anywhere. I recall the burning desire to change my life, to take a different path—but what path? The goal was never to figure everything out, but to understand who I am and what is truly important beneath the surface. Face the pain, push myself beyond my limits, reflect, learn, feel, see, envision and decide something—anything. Love myself even, for how could I ever love anyone else if I couldn't appreciate the spark that made me, *me*? And step away from the darkness that haunted me for so long, the feeling of never quite belonging, not anymore, not even in what I had always called home.

The light at the end of the tunnel that I envisioned never included Kalashnikovs in the hands of intimidating soldiers or clothes drenched in diesel fuel. But that's what life is—it's not a perfect arc with a beginning and an end; it flows with the tides—and sometimes the water catches you by surprise. Yet, here, on the edge, taking it all in, I am so close.

I see the landscape and feel the early morning sun; all else has disappeared. All I hear are the whispers of my journey, the whispers of the past. If this isn't the epiphany I was looking for, then what is it? What else could I possibly search for on this endless road?

I have been terrified I might never get that feeling—the one I knew I would recognize when it came, the feeling that would say, "enough is enough, this is what you're going to do."

"Manon? Are you ready to continue? We need to reach the next town before nightfall," a voice with a French accent breaks through my loud moment of silence.

"Yes," I reply, wondering what other choice I have but to keep moving forward.

One year earlier

PART ONE

ENDINGS AND PINK TREES ON THE HORIZON

Netherlands

As I stared into the lipstick-shaped mirror of my shoebox-sized studio in Amsterdam, I asked myself, *What do I have to lose?*

I had just returned from a weeklong university field trip to Marrakech, Morocco, where I had ridden camels in the hot North African desert, visited abandoned *Game of Thrones* film sets, and watched rattlesnakes dance to a flute in crowded marketplaces. But my mind had been elsewhere—I had a suspicion that my boyfriend of many years was cheating on me. It was that feeling of distrust, that sixth sense that something isn't quite right, amplified by a notification showing he just friended a random person on social media, and further fueled by his facial expression when he picked me up at the airport. Female intuition is a powerful force, and the strength of this force was confirmed when I had an unexpected moment alone with his phone a few days later while sharing a locker at an event. I was hesitant to look when it kept buzzing, but there it was, right on the home screen: "Don't you mind lying to your girlfriend about us?" and "Do you want to meet up at a parking lot this weekend?"

Everything was ending. My Master of Science dissertation was almost finished, which also meant I was about to lose my student housing in Amsterdam. And now I had kicked this cheating boyfriend out the door. Nothing I hate more than unfaithfulness—besides the woman in my father's life and gum. I really, really despise gum.

My apartment felt hollow and desolate. His belongings had been removed, I stayed to sort through the emotions. Anger, sadness and confusion swirled within me. And, strangely, a sense of liberation. I missed having someone to come home to, but I also realized I had the ability to replace this longing for something positive. I decided to take this opportunity to do all the things I had ever wanted to do, to take risks and make unexpected changes. It was time to take back control of my life.

So there I was, on my 23rd birthday, staring at myself in the mirror, reflecting on my life and all the possibilities that lay ahead, when suddenly, my phone rang. It was my father, calling from my hometown an hour and a half away.

"Happy birthday, my grown-up daughter! What would you like for your birthday?" he asked.

"Dad, I would love to have a backpack."

"A backpack for school? Aren't you graduating soon?" he seemed confused.

"Ha, no, a *backpack* backpack—like a real backpack—to travel the world!"

Two hours later, we were trying on backpacks in every shape and color. Step one was complete. The second step was to actually put the backpack to use. I had always dreamed of traveling the world—there were so many places to visit, cultures to explore, languages to learn, and foods to try.

I had always loved the coziness that a home represented too, but the truth was that I hadn't felt at home for a long time. Losing my mother to brain cancer when I was twelve left me feeling lost and uncertain about what the future might hold for me or where I belonged. There was a world of possibilities right out the door. I could go anywhere.

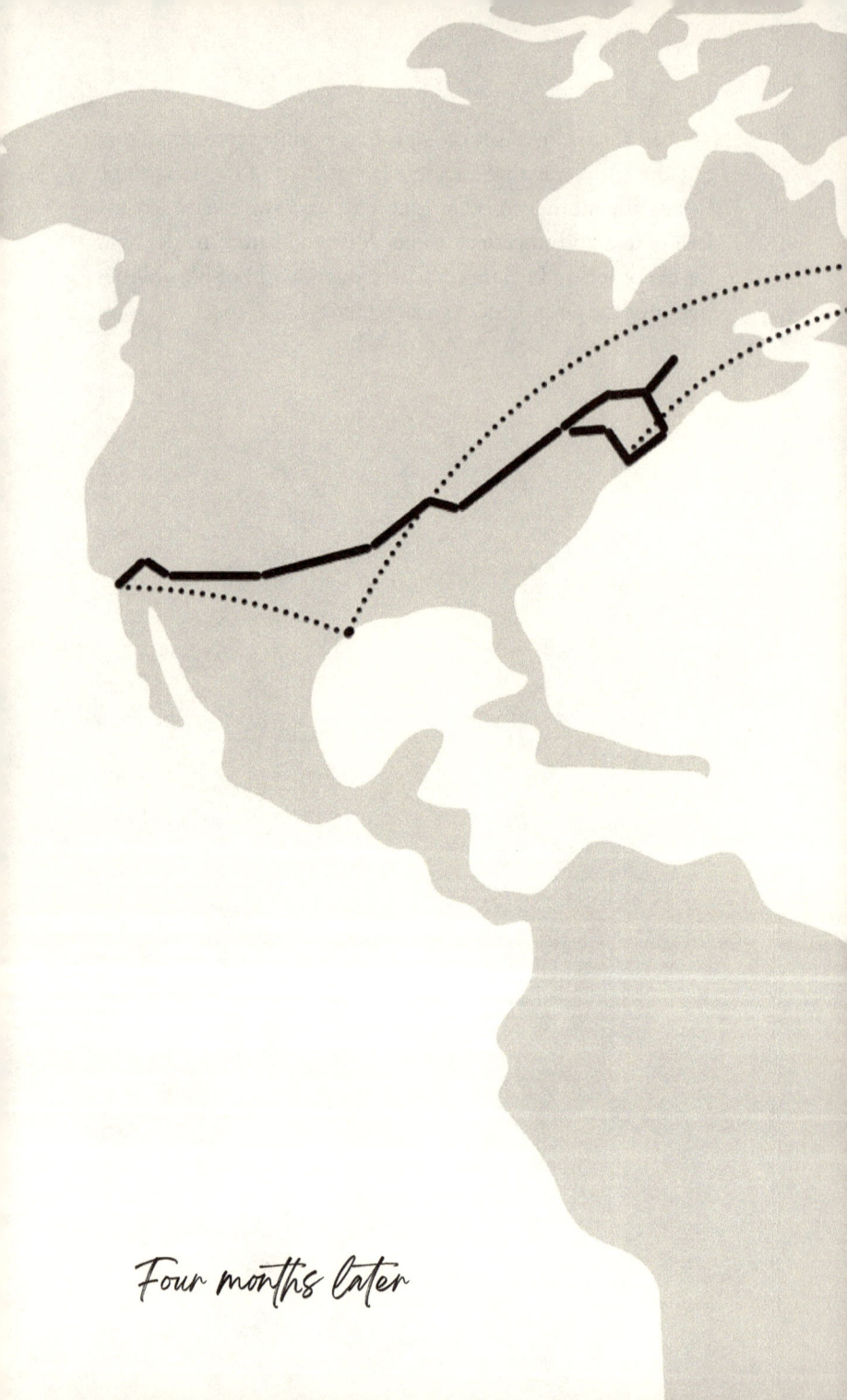

Four months later

United States

Friends and family gathered at Amsterdam Schiphol Airport four months after I made my decision to leave, the atmosphere heavy with emotion. Goodbyes are never easy, but this was more of a "See you later!" With every embrace, I could feel the love they had for me, yet their looks said something else: no way I would survive a North American road trip, alone, by Greyhound bus. This was my chance to prove everyone wrong, to show that I was not a lost little lamb needing care and protection. If anything, their doubt fed my hunger.

"Go now, my child," my father whispered in my ear as I held him tight.

"I will be back for Graduation Day," I promised, knowing I couldn't possibly rob my dad of the opportunity to watch me throw my cap in the air for receiving my master's degree.

As I walked over to the Passenger Only Zone, I knew this journey would be different from all others before. It was a test, a trial run for everything that year was going to be. I would return home in six weeks for a quick pit stop; after that, much bigger plans were on the horizon. I looked around one more time to catch a last glimpse of my people, and then I was gone. I was on my own now, ready to take on the world.

"Manon! You made it!" A familiar voice called out my name at the baggage claim at Los Angeles International Airport.

I was grateful to have J greet me on the other side. Three whole years had passed since I last saw him back during my summer at the University of California. Yet, upon meeting him again, it seemed more like three months.

As we drove away from the airport, along the Pacific Coast Highway, I rolled down the window and inhaled the sweet

California breeze: palm trees and ocean salt. It felt good to be back. This familiar scent filled me with zest; knowing I had friends I could count on bolstered my confidence. The iconic cinematic sights, the laughter of people enjoying the warm weather and the unmistakable anticipation of countless dreams all converged. I was ready to take on the city and push myself out of my comfort zone. I wanted to feel alive again.

"Have you ever been to WeHo?" J asked, his eyes widening with anticipation.

"We? Ho?" I furrowed my brow.

"West Hollywood, of course!" he exclaimed. "You haven't lived until you've been to The Abbey!" After a pause, he continued, "But you've tried AMF before, right?"

"Oh, I don't do drugs," I said firmly. "Ever."

"Drugs!" he laughed. "No, honey, it's a cocktail! You'll see, come along now!"

I had no idea what kind of cocktail it was, nor had I spent much time in West Hollywood. Besides, his cheeky laughter was infectious, I had to find out what this was all about.

Hundreds of people, buzzing with Friday night energy, marched up and down the streets of West Hollywood. Lights, music, food, unicorns and smiles filled the air. It felt like a magical place. As we entered the nightclub, a church-like building decorated with stained glass windows, a string of deep beats took control of my body. On the dance floor, four golden-skinned, muscular men in tight uniforms took the stage above the crowd. The partygoers cheered as dollar bills were thrown around, eventually landing in the muscular men's underwear.

"Yes, let's get you a drink!" J shouted against the music, pulling me to the bar with a mischievous glint in his eye. "Two AMFs please, bartender!"

I watched an exquisitely handsome—also golden-skinned and muscular—bartender gather the ingredients. Vodka, rum, tequila, gin, blue curaçao: an endless list of alcoholic beverages went into my glass, creating a fluorescent blue concoction that looked like a deadly poison. I was reluctant, but I was also curious and eager to let go and relax—for once.

"Here you go honey, your first AMF!" J said, handing me the cocktail.

"What does AMF stand for anyway?" I asked.

"Adios Mother—" he yelled back, slowly disappearing into the crowd.

I smiled, took a sip of my drink, and looked around. Surprisingly, I felt safe, like I could really drop my guard. People of all ages and backgrounds danced the night away, free from the worries and responsibilities of everyday life. As I watched their carefree bodies move, I felt the weight of past expectations and disappointments lift from my shoulders. I was in control of my own happiness.

No more drama, no more pain, no more... purse. *Why was my purse open?* A wave of panic rushed through me; the music faded and my heart pounded. I rummaged in my purse for my phone and wallet. I felt my iPhone, and sliding my fingers into one of the compartments, I touched my wallet. I took a deep breath. Slowly, my surroundings stopped spinning, the muffled sounds returned, and my heartbeat slowed down. *I probably just forgot to close it,* I thought to myself, realizing I had just dodged a minor disaster.

Wait! There was something else in that purse. *Oh no.* It was not there. It was really not there. I didn't feel it. My ears began to ring as I stumbled to the side of the dance floor in despair. I grabbed my friend by the arm.

"What's wrong?" he said, holding me up.

"My passport... It's gone."

My heart sank. I felt the panic rising within me. I never lost control, and this was the reason why. I had been planning this journey for weeks, visiting embassies and consulates to get my documents ready. China, Russia—they were not going to let me in without the visas. My dreams seemed to suddenly slip away. I had been foolish and let the excitement overtake me, now I was paying the price. I thought about my friends and family at Amsterdam Airport, the sympathy and skepticism in their looks. I had let them down; I had let myself down.

The ground beneath me felt unsteady, as if the floor was crumbling away. I glanced around, utterly befuddled, and spotted a security guard standing nearby.

"Ma'am, we got you," he said confidently. "We intercepted your passport an hour ago. The security team out front are keeping it for you."

A wave of relief washed over me. It was all so surreal, I could scarcely believe it. I was certain I would have to pull the plug, but now I was granted a second chance. With my passport in hand, I felt kind of reborn: the lights seemed brighter, and the steady thump of a bass reverberated around me. My journey wasn't over after all, it had only just begun. I zipped up my purse and hit the dance floor.

For the remainder of my time in Los Angeles, I made a conscious effort to take things easy. I returned to Santa Monica for an afternoon, a place that had held a special place in my heart since I first visited back in 2012 and fell in love with its iconic pier and dramatic sunsets. Running into the Pacific Ocean for the first time in three years, the cool, salty water brushing my skin, I couldn't help but smile. Could it be the untamed movement of the waters, the roar of the crashing waves, or the sight of dolphins leaping gracefully in the distance? Maybe it was the golden coast, where anything felt possible. The creativity, the perfect temperatures and the boundless opportunities gave me a sense of belonging I had been craving. Whatever it was, it made me feel grounded and profoundly happy. But I also knew there were many more places to explore. As the sun dipped below the horizon, painting the sky and everything around me with a beautiful pink and orange hue, I asked myself, *Oh, beautiful world, what other wonders do you have in store for me?*

Three days later, it was time to say goodbye to California— but not before one last unexpected challenge. The night before my departure, J had to vacate his apartment in Westwood, so I wandered aimlessly around UCLA's campus with my backpack, unsure of where I would sleep. Eventually, I encountered a group of friendly Swiss exchange students who kindly allowed me to stay at their summer school accommodation, located in Redondo Beach. Although it was a bit far south, I had the opportunity to meet wonderful new people—including E, a kind stranger at a coffee shop who would become a great new friend—and I saved fifty dollars on lodging. It's true, they could have been serial killers. Still, I was trying to have more faith in humanity.

After surviving the night, a Greyhound bus bound for Las Vegas awaited. I always had a soft spot for Greyhound. There was something inherently peaceful about long-distance bus rides: the steady hum of the engine, the rhythmic sway of the bus and the ever-changing scenery outside the window. It was a place where I could lose myself in thought, pretend not to understand a word of English, and let the landscape blur into a calming backdrop for my mind. When the bus pulled away, I took one last look at Los Angeles, confident that I would return one day.

•

Sin City, nestled in the desert of Nevada, presented its glistening skyline five hours later. Las Vegas evoked a sense of nostalgia in me: I had visited the gambling capital with a large group a few years earlier, but I had never ventured to the nightlife city on my own before. This time I would wander the infamous streets all by myself.

The bus dropped me off in Downtown, north of the renowned Las Vegas Strip, in the middle of the day; my hostel lay somewhere in between. With no internet access on my phone and only a screenshot of directions, I began my trek down Las Vegas Boulevard, watching how the barren desert enveloped the sprawling, multi-billion-dollar casinos.

Every so often, I would come across an abandoned shoe on the sidewalk or a piece of lingerie hanging from a tree branch. The twenty-eight-minute walk, weighed down by an overstuffed backpack and the scorching sun, felt like an eternity. This was the first time I considered the burden of unnecessary stuff, and realized I could—and should—have packed lighter.

Finally, the gates of Hostel Cat came into view—an impregnable fortress, with no visible entrance. Hostels were still new to me, so I wasn't sure what to expect. My thought was, I managed to get three nights for an incredible rate of eighteen dollars per night. How bad could it be?

"Are you searching for the hostel?" A side door that I hadn't noticed swung open and a friendly, bearded man gestured for me to come in.

Upon entering the compound, I was greeted by a lively, colorful sight: a handful of small, quaint cabins, adorned with different country flags, dotted a large courtyard, and in the central square, travelers, chatting away, gathered around a barbecue grill.

My cabin housed nine fellow wanderers from around the world. I immediately connected with a vibrant blonde from Brazil, who coaxed me to join the hostel pub crawl and meet everyone. By the time we were ready to hit the town, I had forgotten all my fears of being alone in a foreign city, sleeping in a room with nine strangers. This was what the adventure was all about—stepping outside my comfort zone, connecting with others, and becoming the person I knew I could be. As my mother used to say, "Carpe Diem." I was ready to seize the day. Fremont Street, here we come!

"Would you like to dance?"

The invitation caught me off guard; I wasn't in the habit of dancing with strangers. I hesitated for a moment. No one wanted to dance with me when I was younger, and when I clawed my way out of long-term relationships and my own shell later on, I became quite selective, screening potential partners thoroughly. But there was something about this dark and handsome foreigner that intrigued me.

Maybe it was the thrill of breaking out of my set ways or the opportunity to experience something new. Maybe for once I could deviate from my rigid path and take a chance on something spontaneous. Los Angeles had triggered something in me—it set something free.

"I am so much better at English than you are!" he said playfully in his German-Croatian accent.

There is always an instant spark of competition whenever a German and a Dutch are in the same room.

I doubt it, I said to myself, as my new Brazilian girlfriend mischievously nudged me, trying to encourage me to engage.

It was a refreshing change to feel desired, as if the fear of staying alone was temporarily lifted. Nearly half a year had gone by since things ended with my boyfriend, and after that, I had been cautious about opening up my heart to avoid pain and disappointment.

I had always taken relationships seriously. Ever since I was twelve, I had been trying to fill the void left by my mother's passing. Her absence created a longing for love, connection and stability that I was hoping to find through romantic entanglement. Yet even now, despite feeling desired, I couldn't shake the sense of incompleteness. Romance, in any form, would only distract me from what was truly important. Still, the allure of connection was hard to resist—I had nothing to lose. What if this guy was special? It seemed unfair to dismiss this possibility without giving him a chance first.

He took my hand and stepped closer, guiding me gently on what to do. His smile was disarming as he whisked my hair away from my face. Surrounded by dozens of people under a canopy of colorful lights, I scanned the crowd, wondering if anyone would judge me for lowering my defenses just this once. I caught a glimmer in his eye—something reassuring, something safe. Intrigued, I gave in to the moment.

When the others from our pub crawl were drifting away, we stepped into the warm night and began strolling down Las Vegas Boulevard. The breeze and his presence both kissed my cheeks softly. He spoke with a joyful hush as we giggled together until we reached the hostel, pausing across the street from it, where a wedding chapel stood illuminated in the night—a fittingly notorious Las Vegas backdrop. For hours, we lingered in each other's presence, hungry for more time.

He murmured, "I wish you could come to Colorado with me," knowing he had to leave in the morning.

"I wish you could stay here longer." I replied wistfully.

"Will you visit me in Germany then?" he asked, hopeful.

"I don't know. I will think about it," I said, trying to stay focused on the present and not get ahead of myself.

By dawn, I had meticulously analyzed every aspect of this person, delving into his motivations, aspirations and desires. In return, I shared a piece of my soul, cautiously opening up brick by brick. My mind was in control, trying to keep my emotions at bay and keep focus. But the German-Croatian from cabin seventeen proved to be a formidable opponent; he attempted to unravel me, seeing things in me I hadn't seen in myself.

In just one night, he had become a part of my story, and I a part of his—a paragraph in time, uncertain if it would ever become a chapter.

"Where are you going?" he asked when I distanced myself.

"I have to go," my voice barely above a whisper.

"What time is it?" he glanced at the brightening sky.

"6 a.m."

As I walked away through the crisp morning air, the sun slowly creeping up over the horizon, I imagined how life would be with someone like him by my side, veering off my planned path to have more time together. *Ah, silly me,* I thought, trying to shake it off after we had parted ways. My loyalty to commitment was unwavering and the very thought of entertaining the idea of deviation was foolish. Yet, I couldn't deny the rush of excitement I felt from taking that spontaneous leap of faith.

I made my way back to my room and collapsed onto my bunk bed, my mind still racing as the German-Croatian was packing his bags in his cabin. To quiet the thoughts, I needed to speak them aloud so I stepped out into the courtyard to call a friend. Shortly after, I hung up, catching sight of the still handsome—no longer a stranger—making his way toward me with quick, purposeful strides.

"Will I ever see you again?" he asked, his eyes searching mine.

"I don't know," I replied, feeling a twinge of unease.

"So, this is it then? Goodbye?" His gaze was intense, as if he was trying to see into the depths of my soul.

I offered an uncomfortable smile, and before I could say something, he leaned in and pressed his lips to mine. He then spun on his heel, hoisted his bags over his shoulder and walked away. I just stood there, watching as he disappeared through the gates.

The sound of laughter coming from my room broke my reverie. Las Vegas was an adult playground like no other. Perhaps some quality time with new friends was exactly what I needed. I found a kindred spirit in the Brazilian girl I had met the day before; her zest for life inspiring. Together, we threw ourselves into the glitzy strip of Sin City.

One after another, sparkling casinos rose before us, growing increasingly extravagant, colorful, grandiose, and simply breathtaking. My favorite of them all was The Venetian, with its Italian art and architecture, charming canals evoking Venice's enchanting atmosphere and painted blue skies. The night never truly fell there.

"Are we really going for it?" I asked, giggling.

"We have to live!" she squealed, giggling back.

We sneaked into the pool area of the luxury hotel without proper authorization. I could feel my heart pounding as we showed a business card—instead of a room key—to the security guard and quickly stepped into the elevator with an elderly couple. When the doors opened, we followed the couple out into the hallway and waited for them to walk away.

"We need a real room number," I whispered.

"Goodness, we do!" she nodded.

On the marble floor adorned with intricate rugs, we walked past richly colored paintings, blinding chandeliers and mirrors framed in gold that reflected the opulent decor, while elaborate floral arrangements filled the air with a sweet fragrance.

"This one?" I paused and pointed at a door.

"Yes!" she exclaimed. "And we're here with our parents, who are napping in the room, so we forgot to bring the key!"

This might actually work, I thought, heading back to the elevator and making for the pool deck.

Laying on a beach chair by the poolside, I took a deep breath and glanced at our surroundings. It was a lavish retreat, with Roman-inspired architecture, crystal-clear waters, lush greenery and elegant palm trees swaying gently in the breeze. The scene reflected timeless elegance, blending Mediterranean charm with modern luxury. I closed my eyes and enjoyed the moment. Finally, we could relax.

"Excuse me, ladies?" another security guard towered over us, blocking the sun.

I sighed inwardly and opened my eyes.

"Yes, sir?" I replied with a shaky voice.

"Would you like to join us as a VIP at TAO Beach Club?"

Surprised, I answered, "Yes, please..."

We couldn't believe how our impulsive plan had worked by just daring to take a chance. It felt as though we had stepped through a portal into a new world where anything was possible, leaving our mundane reality behind.

Adjacent to the main pool area, the beach club featured luxurious cabanas with billowing curtains and cushioned loungers under umbrellas, offering comfort amidst the desert heat. The ambiance was both serene and sophisticated, inviting us to unwind in luxury with complimentary beverages. With my feet dipped in the shimmering pool and a refreshing, icy drink in hand, I gazed up at the sky and wondered if life could get any better. It was beyond anything we could have ever imagined.

Among the people we met there were a group of friendly Danish travelers who invited us to a sumptuous dinner. As a long-term traveler on a tight budget, I had to be mindful of my expenses; the thought of splurging on a fancy restaurant was normally out of the question. However, Las Vegas had already proven that anything was possible—even a gourmet meal prepared by none other than Wolfgang Puck. Besides, they wouldn't take no for an answer. So, we hastened back to the hostel to change into the most stylish outfits we could muster.

Back in my room, I searched through my red backpack frantically. *Now, I wished I had packed more*, I thought to myself. Just as I was giving up hope on finding anything suitable, I heard a voice behind me.

"Here, take this!" a new roommate handed me a flowered skirt.

I thanked her again and again, got changed and went back to The Venetian.

The Danish group offered a fine bottle of wine and eagerly asked about my life, making me feel instantly at ease. It was invigorating to be surrounded by Europeans who felt like old friends; their warmth and curiosity comforting.

They ordered nearly everything on the menu, ensuring I experienced all the flavors. Their purpose was clear; they were having the time of their lives—just like I was. The man across the table shared their itinerary with me, each activity the promise of unforgettable memories: gambling, pool outings, fine dining and indoor skydiving.

"Indoor skydiving!" I exclaimed, unimpressed. "You guys are fit, young and adventurous, living life to the fullest in the city of Las Vegas. You should go skydiving for real."

The others around the table shook their heads vigorously, but the guy across from me lit up with excitement, as if he had just had a brilliant epiphany.

"If I'm jumping out of a plane, you're jumping out of a plane!" he declared, pointing at me.

Oh boy.

The evening progressed, but I was preoccupied. My pulse quickened and my appetite vanished. *I apologize, Wolfgang,* I thought to myself, trying to think of the desserts instead of jumping out of an airplane.

I should have considered my words more carefully, but then again, it's common for other people to make promises they don't intend to keep—or so it seems. Who knew if this guy was serious.

The rest of the night went by in a blur and the following day my phone buzzed loudly, indicating an incoming message at an early hour of 7:03 a.m. Confused, I groggily searched for my phone.

N:
MEET ME OUTSIDE IN 15 MINUTES.
WE'RE GOING SKYDIVING.

I shoved my phone under my pillow, trying to ignore it. But soon the words sank in, causing me to bolt upright in bed, fully awake. What do you mean, going skydiving in fifteen minutes?! As I fumbled out of my bunk bed, I wondered if he really meant it. But deep down, I knew I had to prepare myself just in case.

Dressing quickly in a pair of comfortable pants and a shirt, I made my way to the front of the hostel. My chest thudded with every beat. Soon, I saw a classic American muscle Harley-Davidson motorcycle approaching. The sound of the engine filled the air; the roar of the United States. A soft smile spread across my face.

"Good morning! Are you ready?" The rider stopped and handed me a helmet.

"Danish, is that you?"

"Yes, let's go! They are waiting for us," he shouted.

His calmness subtly reminded me of my oldest brother. Meanwhile, the situation made me think of my dad—he would kill me for getting on the back of a motorcycle with a semi-stranger. But I was here to challenge myself. And despite my reservations about jumping out of an airplane 10,000 feet above the ground, I was excited to see where this impulsive decision would take me. So, I climbed onto the back of the Harley-Davidson, took a deep breath, and fastened the helmet.

The city quickly disappeared behind us as we raced down the road, leaving only a cloud of dust in our wake. My hair tangled in the wind, my arms bare under the sun. I held on tight, but my whole body vibrated. The wind suddenly felt solid, pushing me back as we sped forward. I could hear nothing but the roar of the engine, encouraging me to embrace the thrill of the moment.

"Yeehaw! Isn't this amazing?!" N, now more friend than stranger, shouted back at me.

Eventually, an airfield appeared ahead of us. At the front desk, the receptionist walked us through the process and had us fill out a number of forms.

"If you don't succeed at first, skydiving is not for you," she concluded with a cheeky smile.

"Great," I nodded. "Sounds good."

I put on a bright blue jumpsuit with multiple straps and belts, then stepped into a PAC 750XL aircraft, a single-engine turboprop with a spacious cabin designed for skydiving. The door was still cracked open when we took off and while we continued to soar higher and higher, until we reached altitude.

"You ready?" my tandem-jump partner said after strapping me tightly to his harness.

Slowly, we shuffled to the now wide-open door. He remained calm and composed, not even flinching. I, not so steady. Although I had never had a fear of flying, the idea of jumping out of an airplane felt counterintuitive. I was placing my life in the hands of my tandem partner who, in turn, placed his life in the hands of a parachute. It was another leap of faith—this time literally.

"Don't you dare drop me!" I shouted against the jet engine, realizing that my last words should be more memorable.

For a fleeting moment, my life flashed before my eyes. My feet dangled from the aircraft, the world beneath me appearing hazy, intangible, unsteady. There was no escape; this was no time to falter. I braced myself. We took the leap.

The wind tugged at my cheeks. I grinned, kept on falling through the sky, and grinned some more. The earth approached at an alarming pace, but for the first time in a long time, I felt truly free. I spread my arms, pretending to be a bird soaring through the air—a gesture that reminded me of the days I used to gallop fiercely with my gelding through nature. This was what I had promised myself—daring to color outside the lines more, as my younger self always had been curious about but afraid to do.

Then, suddenly, the pull of the parachute yanked me to a halt. The whirlwind stopped, and Earth no longer raced toward me. Strangely, even if suspended high above the ground, I felt safe. I held on to that sensation; it would serve as a reminder that pushing my boundaries could lead to comfort and confidence. I savored that moment, grateful for the opportunity that was given to me. I gazed above, wondering if my mother could see me.

"Pull your legs up!" my tandem partner yelled, bringing me literally back down to earth.

After a rough landing in the dusty desert, my lack of athleticism barely fazed me: I felt invigorated, unstoppable, and bruised from victory, as though nothing could bring me down from the high of this incredible experience. I couldn't wait to call my family and tell them all about it, also feeling the urge to remind them just how much I loved them.

•

The Albuquerque County Fair was covered in Stars and Stripes, and the air was filled with the strangely mixed aromas of roasted corn, funnel cakes and hay bales. Livestock pens bustled with activity as proud farmers showcased their prized animals to curious onlookers while cowboys demonstrated their impressive roping skills. I navigated through crowds of families, their hands full of stuffed animals won at carnival games. The sounds of live country music echoed around us, and I tapped my feet to the rhythm.

I had taken the overnight bus from Las Vegas giving me nineteen hours to explore the surroundings before my next bus departed at 4 a.m.—just enough time to make the most of this layover with K, a dear friend from Amsterdam who was studying at the University of New Mexico.

"Are you guys going to the house party later on?" one of his fellow students asked.

"Do you want to go?" he turned to me.

I chuckled, "Sure! I have all night."

When night fell and we arrived at the party, the thumping bass of music greeted us at the door. Inside, a lively game of beer pong heated up, with cheers erupting after every toss, while clusters of partygoers laughed and debated in every corner. I quickly joined in.

"It doesn't matter where I leave you; I can always trust you to have a good time, even without knowing anyone," K said with a grin as he wandered off.

Hours later, I looked at my watch; time flies, and I had to start making my way back to the station.

"I've just met the most beautiful girl," he sighed deeply as we walked out.

This was something I began appreciating about life abroad: how much more malleable we become to chance encounters.

On our way to the bus station, he told me everything he had learned about the gorgeous Brazilian he had just met, while frantically trying to remember how he had saved her number in his phone. Visibly smitten, he rambled on while I wrapped an arm around his shoulders and gave him a teasing squeeze. Little did he know that that beautiful girl would become his wife.

•

The past few days had been full of escapades and thrill, but now there was only silence. The grueling, three-night bus journey through Amarillo, Oklahoma City, Tulsa, Springfield and St. Louis left every muscle in my body aching. I felt disoriented, drained. The views comforted me—stretches of road with nothing but endless wheat, soybean, corn, and cattle fields in every direction. It reminded me of home.

My mind wandered to my childhood, to the view from my bedroom window: the serene countryside—farmland and animals grazing—set against Rotterdam's skyline in the distance. Time had passed. So much had changed. My mother's touch was no longer there to warm the once cozy house and the recollections of my father's choices after her demise brought a twinge of sorrow to my heart. I closed my eyes. How did it come to this? I took a deep breath allowing painful memories to resurface.

In 2012 I traveled to Istanbul, Turkey, with a team of fellow students for a business competition as a representative of the Rotterdam University of Applied Sciences. Our challenge was to collaborate with international companies and present a marketing plan while competing against other universities. This event aimed to uphold the strong trade relations between Turkey and the Netherlands, in the presence of the Dutch crown prince and princess—now the King and Queen. During the competition, we were honored to hear some inspiring words from the royal couple and we won! Winning this competition with my team still is one of the proudest moments of my academic years. I had fought hard to be on the team. It was the beginning of a new awareness. I had a way to demonstrate my potential and to be taken seriously.

As my plane flew back to Amsterdam, I couldn't wait to show my dad the trophy. Throughout my childhood, we had been inseparable. He was my buddy, my role model, and my rock. Whether it was for picking me up at school or at the horse stables, he had always been there for me. He had promised to be at the airport—I could always rely on him.

"I have a surprise for you, daughter," I heard my father say on the other end of the phone after I had landed.

I couldn't have been more excited. Maybe he had arranged a celebratory welcome at arrivals?

As I walked through the exit into the arrivals hall, my eyes scanned the crowd. One by one, my fellow students were reunited with their families. Where was my dad? Then, I spotted two familiar faces off to the side—my godparents. I was overjoyed to see them! They were the kindest people on earth, and they had been like an extra set of parents, especially after I had lost my mother. I joined them and embraced them warmly.

"Where's dad?" I asked, my eyes still darting around the hall.

They looked at each other. Confusion flooded my mind. How could he not be there? He'd promised!

Seven years had passed since my mother died. Life had never been the same. The home we once cherished now felt dark and cold. The hand-spun Persian carpets had lost their allure. The French porcelain plates, once reserved for special occasions, now collected dust behind a glass cabinet.

My father had remarried—to my best friend's mother. Sadly, our friendship did not survive that union—and neither did the warmth in our home. My devotion to my father and our special bond continued, but now I had a competitor.

That new person moved in shortly after my mother's funeral. My father and I barely had any time together before she arrived. I do recall a trip we made to Florida to escape our misery for a little while. But when we returned, she was there, *waiting*. At least that's how I felt it.

After my mother disappeared in February, it didn't take long for her personal items to disappear as well. By the time the sun began to warm the chilly countryside, all her pictures were gone, and her closets empty.

An item I managed to save was a dress she had once sewn herself from curtains. The flower-pattern of the dress made it feel extra homey and comforting—a small piece of her that I could hold onto. Along with the dress, I managed to save some jewelry and a few scarves. Every time I wore any of these treasures, I felt my mother close to me, as if she was still there, guiding me through the days.

Winning this huge trophy in Istanbul was an incredible achievement, and I knew that my parents would have been so proud of me. But at the airport, I couldn't shake the disappointment that my dad wasn't there. I learned the other woman in his life had claimed him. They had a dinner reservation at someplace that evening, a reservation she had conveniently forgotten to mention earlier, and that they simply could not miss. It stung to know that my dad's commitment to this woman's plans had taken priority over my biggest moment.

Something told me that she was always intentionally going to undermine the important events in my life—and this day at the airport was a case in point. After I got home that night and cleared things with my dad, she knocked on my bedroom door and came in.

"Congratulations, Manon," she said with a smile that didn't quite match her eyes. Her tone was flat, devoid of genuine warmth or enthusiasm.

My heart raced. Was she really happy for me, or was this just another attempt at putting on a façade? I was confused.

"Your father simply had something else to do. I'm sure you understand." Her voice tinged with a hint of condescension. "The world doesn't revolve around *you*, Manon."

Her words stung like wasp venom. I tried to keep my composure. Was it so much to ask for? To be with my father on such an important occasion?

I replied with trembling hands: "Thank you..."

•

Concentrate. Where am I? I gradually opened my eyes again. Peering out the bus window, I spotted the *Welcome to Indiana* sign. I smiled. There's a sense of lightness and grounding when returning to a place one holds dear.

Over the years, it had become a sort of second home. When I first visited New Harmony in 2006, I was fourteen years old with big dreams of spending time in mighty America. As a young Dutch student in a town of about eight hundred souls, I was featured in the high school newspaper. A local boy recognized me in the library, and we became friends. I proudly referred to him as my "first American friend" for years to come.

Seven years later, I returned to live there for a few months while conducting independent research for my university. Before my arrival, he and I reconnected through social media, and it was surprising to see how openly and easily he welcomed me into his circle of friends. All of them soon became my friends, and I discovered how easy it was to create a brand new community for oneself, making me wonder how often I could replicate this, duplicate those feelings, if I mustered the courage to relocate somewhere else on the world map. It was a direct challenge to my difficulties to adapt to change and the belief that only my childhood home (when my mother was still alive) could be my true home. But that too was slipping away as my father intended to sell the house where I grew up.

"Manon! Over here!"

One of my girlfriends from Evansville, Indiana, was waiting for me at the bus stop. She drove me to her family home, where her parents had graciously offered me the guest room for a week. The constant adrenaline and numerous sleepless nights spent on the Greyhound had sapped all my energy.

Seeing a well-made bed covered with soft pillows and cozy blankets made me feel warm and safe. I was constantly on edge, and not knowing who to trust had made traveling alone rather difficult. Now, I could finally relax. I sank into the mattress and gazed at the ceiling for a moment. *How grateful I am for these wonderful people*, I thought before closing my eyes.

When I woke up a few hours later, there were several new text messages, of which many written by the German-Croatian I had met in Las Vegas, and who now seemed to think I was purposely avoiding him.

The German-Croatian:
YOU ARE JUST ENJOYING LIFE.

I guess I am, I said to myself while I continued to read.

I DON'T WANT TO GET IN THE WAY.

MAYBE I SHOULD LEAVE YOU ALONE.

DO YOU MISS ME?

IT WOULD HURT IF YOU WOULD FIND SOMEONE ELSE.

The messages kept coming, one after the other; at a cadence of only a few minutes apart. It overwhelmed me.

BUT YOU ARE A FREE WOMAN.

I AM NOT GOING TO HOLD YOU BACK.

NOT AFTER EVERYTHING YOU TOLD ME.

I AM NOT GOING TO STOP YOU.

YOU ARE PRETTY GOOD AT IGNORING ME...

I ALMOST DIDN'T NOTICE.

What was he saying? I cared for him deeply the moment I met him. He would have been exactly what I needed one year ago. He was thoughtful, considerate, kind, caring, witty and full of compliments. So why did I not share his feelings? Perhaps because my future was uncertain. My heart wasn't ready for this kind of commitment. I feared it would divert me from the purpose of this journey.

Still, I couldn't deny that he had become an intimate friend, a source of comfort and moral support. He was like a breath of fresh air and a welcome change after everything I had left behind in the Netherlands. Yet I didn't know how to deal with his feelings—it wasn't meant to be. Even if I could fancy doing wonderful things with him (should we choose to spend more time together), the only outcome I anticipated was heartbreak. And this time it wasn't going to be my heart breaking.

The next day I went straight to New Harmony to see my circle of friends there. They welcomed me back with the sound of a ukulele playing. Being among them allowed me to focus on the present moment. It was heartwarming to return to a place where time was at a stand-still and where friendships thrived despite the distance.

Nestled along the Wabash River, the town is small but rich in history. Originally founded in 1814 by George Rapp and his followers, a group of German immigrants seeking religious freedom, New Harmony later became a hub for intellectual and scientific pursuits under the leadership of social reformers Robert Owen and William Maclure.

Strolling through the quaint, colorful streets with many early 19th-century buildings, I also observed grand Greek Revival columns and pediments, as well as the ornate detailing of Victorian architecture. These styles mixed seamlessly with American vernacular structures, offering a glimpse into the practical designs of the town's early settlers.

With the ukulele still being played by one of my friends, it was impossible not to feel the echoes of the town's utopian past. That same morning I took in the scent of blooming flowers from the numerous public gardens, blending with the earthy aroma of the surrounding forests. The Roofless Church, an open-air sanctuary surrounded by a brick wall, invited contemplation and reflection, while the meticulously restored Rapp-Owen Granary stood as a reminder of the town's industrious beginnings.

My friends and I gathered at a small garden with a view of Main Street, from where the rest of the town was only a stone's throw away. Local artisans displayed their crafts in charming boutiques and golf carts were riding around everywhere—a preferred means of transportation.

"What'd y'all like to do today?" the strong-built, bearded friend, D, drawled, his accent laced with a hint of twang. "Y'all wanna go shoot some guns?"

"Shooting?" I perked up.

"You're gonna need some fuel," another friend chimed in as he reached his hand out. "Take one of these."

I looked down, unwrapping the curious confectionery called Twinkies. To my surprise, biting into one was like eating sweet sand filled with foam—terrible and delicious all at once.

"Alright, let's go!"

My friends jumped into three different vehicles—no one carpooled—as we drove to one of their family homes.

D parked his pickup truck diagonally along a vast grassy stretch that ended in a tree line with cardboard boxes hidden among the forest. After getting out, I followed him around his car filled with curiosity. I glanced at the truck bed and my eyes widened at the sight of a handgun, four rifles and a crossbow, lined up with care.

Holding an AR-15–style semi-automatic, I thought of the carnivals of my childhood and how good I was at shooting games. But these weapons were far more intimidating; their weight hinted at their sheer destructive power. I felt uneasy but also, somehow, curious and confident. It almost felt natural, reminiscent of playing the violin. With a deep breath and steady hands I took aim and fired, hitting each of the cardboard targets with precision. These boxes were no match.

I picked up a smaller handgun to compare and contrast, thinking smaller meant easier. But with a heavy caliber nothing was less true. I couldn't use my shoulder to assist when aiming, and after the successful use of a long gun I became overconfident. With my friend by my side, I stretched out my arms, bringing the handgun closer to its target and fired. I was trying to see if I had hit the mark when D swiftly and tactically swiped the gun from my hands, pointing the weapon in a safe direction before clearing the chamber.

"That could've been real bad," he muttered because the gun had misfired.

I looked at my empty hands. "What could have happened?"

"Kaboom," he said while handing me back the gun.

I was playing with fire, trusting my friends. These were no toys. Once again I rested my finger next to the trigger. In my grasp I held something that could take life away in a second—even my own. Yet it had the potential to save lives too. The magnitude of that duality was sobering, making me suddenly aware of the thin line between life and death.

As my stay in Indiana came to a close, the girl with whom I was staying invited me to a friend's wedding shower. How could I say no to that? I tagged along with the group of her girlfriends, moms and aunts on their trip to the French Lick Resort Casino and Winery—an elegant and tasteful getaway filled with love and family vibes.

We drove through fields of vibrant autumn colors and more quaint towns decked out in pumpkins and orange blooms, all celebrating the Halloween season. I marveled at the sight of charming farmhouses with white picket fences and old barns draped in warm hues. The more time I spent on the road, the more I began to notice the little details. I had become more comfortable trying new things and going with the flow.

On our arrival my phone started to vibrate.

The German-Croatian:
WHEN I WENT TO VEGAS, I NEVER THOUGHT I WOULD MEET THE ONE.

I tried to distance myself from matters of the heart, while celebrating the fruit of other people's love on this getaway to the French Lick Winery.

Determined to stay emotionally guarded, I tried wine tasting to drown out my feelings. However, my eyes kept gliding over the text on my screen. He called me *the one*.

"I will try the rhubarb wine, please."

The taste was delicious: a burst of tart and sweet that invaded my palette. But as I savored the wine, my phone buzzed again. The emotional demand from the messages clashed with my wish to feel free and follow the flow. Each text was a reminder of the connection I was trying to avoid—making it hard to fully immerse myself in the wine-drinking experience.

SHOULD I STOP TEXTING YOU?

I asked myself whether to reply, feeling the weight of the decision. The contrast between the lighthearted wine drinking at this cozy high-top bar surrounded by wooden barrels and the serious nature of that message was obvious. I put my cell phone away. I wanted to enjoy the event without being tethered to my phone in order to embrace the spontaneity and freedom I had come to cherish on my road trip. Yet the persistent vibration in my purse chained me to my unresolved feelings.

My fingers reached for my phone again, as if extending a hand, allowing the connection to continue.

WE WILL TALK LATER.

I PROMISE.

•

Leaving Indiana, I headed to Kentucky, where R, my oldest brother—a renowned scholar on the region's history—flew in from France, where he lived, to attend the annual Communal Studies Conference at Shaker Village of Pleasant Hill. His groundbreaking research was summarized in an encyclopedia-sized book he had spent many many years working on. Serendipitously, our schedules aligned, allowing us to cherish quality sibling time at the conference, where we shared memories and appetizing meals.

With a twenty-two-year gap between us, he was my grand academic example. His passion for history was infectious, and I found myself more engaged than ever. We stayed together in a comfortable guest room of the village inn. Its rustic charm with original hardwood floors provided the perfect backdrop for our serious conversations.

One night, as we sat on our beds, the soft glow of lanterns illuminating our faces, I confided in him about my recent adventures. I mentioned the new people I had met and the lessons I had learned along the way. He listened intently, offering insights about why he had decided to move to France, following his heart.

I nodded while absorbing his wisdom. "I've been trying to push myself more, even if it feels daunting. I want to live a life full of experiences, with no regrets."

"I know it's scary," he said, his voice calm and reassuring. "But remember, little sister, you are brave."

His belief in me made me believe in myself, and this unwavering support and love were the fuel I needed to keep on going.

He looked uneasy when he dropped me off at the Greyhound station in Louisville, Kentucky. I couldn't blame him: the station wasn't the nicest one I had seen. As the bus pulled in, my brother looked at me with his piercing eyes.

"Life doesn't always go as planned, little sister," he said while giving me a tight hug. "But what's important is that you never regret your decisions, no matter the outcome. Don't ever give up, and keep pushing forward—that's our strength."

"I love you, brother," I whispered back.

I hopped aboard and, with a deep breath, settled into my seat. As the bus turned the corner, I started to feel confused. All the familiar faces and places were behind me now, and I was truly on my own. With those occasional friendly faces and the kindness of strangers I had been relatively secure. But now, with no more planned visits, I wouldn't have any safety net until my flight to Amsterdam from New York City later in the month.

I had decided to head to Detroit, hoping to cross the border into Canada from there. With another long bus ride ahead of me, I began to feel more comfortable and pulled out my travel journal. I immediately started to write, trying to capture the thoughts and feelings that were swirling around in my head. Flipping back through the pages, my eyes fell on a message from one of my friends in Indiana: *forget about the freaky deaky Dutch*. It was ironic, really. It reminded me of how proud I am of my Hollander heritage, as well as the need to spread my wings and fly.

While traveling to new places, meeting new people, I was discovering a beauty and diversity that I had never known existed. In spite of this, I found myself longing for something more. While my craving for new experiences and adventures was palpable, I couldn't shake the feeling that I wanted to connect with people on a deeper level.

This was quite a paradox. My head was full of cold, hard logic, telling me to keep moving forward, but my heart wanted to know something else. As the pen scratched the paper, it dawned on me: to forge meaningful connections with others, I would first need to reconnect with myself.

This realization was humbling—but at the same time hopeful. If I could get to know myself better and confront my fears and insecurities head-on, then perhaps I would be equipped at last to make the connections I craved. And with that in mind, I set out to explore not just the world around me, but also the world within—journaling my experiences, meditating my emotions, and seeking out conversations that challenged my perspectives.

When the bus came to a halt, I made sure to take advantage of the stopover to stretch my legs. Outside, the sprawling skyline of Cincinnati, Ohio, bathed in the soft glow of dusk. I had to immortalize this moment.

"Yeah, yeah, take your pictures now," a man's voice echoed from behind me, his tone laced with darkness. "So people know where you went when you disappear."

His words sent a chill down my spine. Maybe it was nothing more than a cruel joke or a twisted thought, but the way he said it made me quite uneasy. I turned around to see who was standing a few feet away. But before I could react the man had disappeared into the crowd. I stood bewildered, the darkness pressing in around me.

Slowly I retreated back inside the station, my eyes scanning the area for all possible means of escape. I knew I couldn't move fast with my bright red backpack strapped to my back. Leaning against a wall, I tried to blend in with the crowd around me, hoping the intercom would soon call for passengers traveling to Detroit.

Scrolling through the list of available Wi-Fi networks, I saw "BusWi-Fi_2804" and "CincinnatiLocal"—but also "FBI Surveillance Van." Was the FBI really parked nearby? My stomach churned as I recalled the man's comment. Maybe having federal agents around wouldn't be a bad thing. You never know.

One hour later, the Greyhound was ready to continue its journey north. After he had closed the luggage compartment and carried out his routine checks, walking through the aisle with piercing eyes, the driver suddenly halted before me.

"You—Miss, you sit in the front with me," he said with concern. "It's not safe for a young woman like you to be on the bus alone at night."

I was relieved to have a better seat, and grateful for the bus driver's thoughtfulness. I noticed the presence of a man, sitting all the way in the back. He had reeked of alcohol when he passed me earlier and couldn't keep his pants fully on. I felt uncomfortable... But I didn't want to judge him, especially since I didn't know his story. For I became increasingly aware that all people are different. And we all have our own coping mechanisms.

Oh Canada...

Crossing the border was like rolling into a different world, way more laid-back than the U.S.—the border patrol officer even failed to stamp the correct date in my passport. It was past midnight when the Greyhound drove through Windsor, its streets lined by terraces filled with people laughing and drinking. This was a pleasant surprise. I didn't expect the atmosphere to be so European. I didn't expect to feel so at ease.

Stopping in Toronto in the early hours was a different story. I was greeted by a biting cold while the city seemed asleep, with most establishments closed and hardly anybody outside. I walked around for some time, but that gloomy, ghost town atmosphere increasingly weighed me down. I saw every alley as a threat, every shadow as a black hole. The further I moved away from the bus station, the more insecure I felt; not physically, but psychologically, cornered by streets devoid of life. I hurried back to the bus and slumped into my seat, exhausted.

Whenever I feel vulnerable and alone, my mind will drift to memories of my mother. This time it took me back to her final moments, and tears threatened to spill down my cheeks. Images of her breath slowing flickered in my mind's eye. I recalled being in denial, refusing to believe that she was departing, clinging to the hope that she would recover, but deep down inside I knew it was time for her to go. I remember looking at my father, my hero, hoping he would fix everything, yet knowing he couldn't fix this. I felt the pain I could neither bear nor comprehend then.

But even in my grief, I hadn't forgotten the light that shone through the glass roof on that cold February day—a sign of hope, a reminder that life still held brightness and joy, even in the darkest of times. I wanted to honor her memory and make her proud. I took a moment to get myself back together, then wiped away my tears.

Hours later, I opened my eyes to an idyllic Canadian autumn scene flashing on the other side of the bus window: shades of brown, red, and orange painted the landscape, with pink-colored trees interspersed among them. My eye fell on one of them as I wondered why this particular tree was different. Although shorter than the others, it stood out beautifully and radiant, shining brightly among the warmer hues.

Did that tree feel different from the others or was it seen as an outcast? Was growing tall its ultimate achievement? Did size matter? Did it feel looked down upon? Are human beings any different? As humans, we constantly measure ourselves by certain standards. And then I realized I wouldn't mind being that little pink tree—different yet beautiful in its own way.

If anyone could help me make sense of these thoughts, it would be C, one of my closest friends back home.

> **I WOULD LIKE TO BE THE TREE**
> **THAT TURNS PINK IN AUTUMN.**

As I hit send, I couldn't help but chuckle at what I had texted. But C, who always seemed to understand me even when I was lost, would surely appreciate the deeper meaning behind my metaphor. Sure enough, a few moments later, my phone buzzed.

C:
> **YOU CAN GROW INTO ANY TREE YOU WANT**
> **TO BE, AS LONG AS YOU SETTLE YOUR ROOTS**
> **IN SOIL WHERE YOU CAN EXTRACT ENERGY.**

That's so beautiful, I thought, smiling. I read the message again, merging his metaphor with mine. Finding "fertile soil" was an essential part of my journey. But so was learning about myself, who I was and what I wanted. By envisioning myself in the future and setting ambitious goals, I could map out the path toward my dreams. Just like that little pink tree that blossoms in the right soil, I too could grow and flourish once I found my place in the world...

My phone buzzed again.

YOU ARE OK THOUGH, RIGHT?

TELL ME SOMETHING FUN, SO I WON'T WORRY ABOUT YOU.

Just then, Ottawa's skyline came into view, and I suddenly remembered that the place I had booked for the night was a former jail converted into a hostel.

TONIGHT I AM SLEEPING IN A JAILHOUSE.

MANON.

I SAID SOMETHING THAT WOULD *NOT* MAKE ME WORRY.

•

The building was both beautiful and intimidating: its thick limestone walls and fortress-like architecture with narrow, barred windows made me feel small in comparison. As I crossed the black spiked gate, I noticed vines growing along the walls, adding an eerie charm to the imposing structure. At check-in, the receptionist escorted me to my room, regaling me with tales of the building's history and also warning me about the ghosts of former inmates that supposedly haunted the halls at night. Just what I needed.

I had opted for one of the larger room-cells, a far cry from my previous preference for private rooms. Traveling solo had taught me that more company equals more fun, and that the chances of meeting interesting people are greater in a crowd.

When I sat down on my bed, I heard the door lock click loudly. I looked around, only to see that all the other beds were empty. Sitting there, alone, surrounded by a deafening silence, gave me the creeps. In spite of the unnerving setting, I was so exhausted from my twenty-two-hour bus trip that I immediately dozed off when I rested my head on the pillow. So much for contemplating my plans for Canada.

Suddenly, my eyes shot open at an unfamiliar sound, or maybe just leaves rustling in the wind. I had heard something. I walked over to the window and looked out—nothing there. A loud bang made me jump back onto my bunk bed. That's when I saw it: an enormous squirrel, clutching a tiny nut in its paws and staring into my eyes, outside my window. I shook my head. It was just a squirrel. I took my daypack, left the room and shut the door behind me.

It was a pleasant day for exploring, and Ottawa was incredibly pedestrian-friendly—a refreshing change from most American cities. I headed to Hotel Fairmont Château Laurier, which had an enchanting castle-like structure that added to the magical ambiance of the area. As I made my way toward Parliament Hill, I marveled at its Gothic building. With its pointed arches, green copper roofs and flying buttresses, it was an echo of medieval cathedrals.

From the south bank of the Ottawa River, my eyes fell on the Alexandra Bridge, its steel framework offering a striking contrast to the stone constructions I had just admired. As I strolled along the pedestrian walkway—which links Ottawa, Ontario, with Gatineau, Quebec—a light drizzle began, but it didn't dampen my curiosity to discover the opposite side of the river. Crossing into Quebec, a neighboring province, I noticed the signage gradually shifting from English to French —or *Québécois*—reflecting the region's bilingual nature.

Upon reaching the Canadian Museum of Civilization, I looked back to catch another glimpse of the bridge I had crossed—now *Pont Alexandra*—and scanned Ottawa's skyline across the water. Maple trees in bright yellow and orange fall colors lined the riverbank, their leaves reminding me of the vivid brushstrokes of an Impressionist painting. Drops of rain rippled the river's surface and wetted my hair. It didn't bother me; I didn't hide from it—in fact, I loved every minute of it, feeling grateful to be surrounded by such beauty.

As the night fell, I returned to the cell-like room. The uplifting energy from the walk was immediately overshadowed by the loneliness instilled by those cold stone walls. I reached for my phone and messaged the German-Croatian. He quickly responded.

The German-Croatian:
WELL, WELL, WELL. IF IT ISN'T MY
LITTLE SMARTY-PANTS RETURNING.

His snarky comments and genuine, attentive questions often brought a smile to my face. I felt grateful for his virtual presence, especially when the days seemed long and aimless. I knew he wanted more than just friendship. I didn't deserve his unwavering attention—but I also didn't want him to go away. I felt reassured with him in my orbit. I didn't feel alone.

I woke up the next morning mulling over the previous night. I felt like my emotions had clouded my judgment, and I realized that it wasn't fair to him. Clearly, I was uncertain of what I wanted. Yet, haunted by the shadows of my last relationship— I was certain of what I did *not* want, and clinging to the first nice guy who came along didn't seem like the best approach. I needed space to heal and understand my inner self.

Suddenly, the cell door rattled and three chatty girls entered the room—some company at last. Two of them were from Melbourne, Australia, which reminded me of an ongoing inside-joke I had heard from various travelers: "Wherever you go, in every hostel where you stay, you're guaranteed to find at least one Australian or one German. And if you don't, then you're probably Australian or German yourself!"

That evening we delved into Ottawa's roaring nightlife. The sound of live musicians echoed through the streets, beckoning us toward charming old bars with weathered brick facades and warm golden lights spilling out of their windows. The scent of fried snacks and craft beer mingled in the air, drawing us in.

As we stepped into a venue, we were greeted by the sight of an old rockstar, perched on a chair atop the bar, strumming his guitar with such fervor that he seemed oblivious to his surroundings. The music was a lively mix of classic rock and folk, energizing the crowd that swayed to the rhythm.

"Cheers!" we toasted to our adventures, savoring the variety of refreshing local brews.

The energy reminded me of Amsterdam on a weekday—locals having fun with everyone seeming to know each other. We danced, laughed and sang along loudly. The guitarist played like his life depended on it, his fingers dancing over the strings, his passion for music evident in every stroke. People were shouting, holding bottles in their hands, their faces lit up with joy.

As the night wore on, the crowd grew larger. A group of Canadian soldiers decided to join us, adding to our eclectic pack. They claimed we couldn't leave Ottawa without trying the poutine—a hearty plate of fries smothered in cheese curds and gravy. At first glance, it appeared messy and unappetizing, but to our delight, it was absolutely delicious.

"You're the most angelic person I've ever met," one of the soldiers said after watching me devour my plate.

"Angelic?" I exclaimed, laughing.

With the possibility of gravy still lingering on my cheeks, I had my doubts about whether it was actually a compliment. The soldiers, however, appeared to be true gentlemen and walked us back to our hostel.

As we said our goodbyes in front of the old jailhouse, I could see the confusion on their faces—especially on the face of the one who had lifted me up and carried me in his arms the last two streets. What can I say about that? It was a welcome break for my tired feet.

•

Gazing out the bus window and daydreaming about what awaited me in Montreal, I watched the clouds drift across the crystal blue sky. The Lake of Two Mountains shimmered in the sun, its warmth on my cheeks like a comforting blanket. *No matter what life throws our way*, I thought, *the sun shall always rise again*.

The bus dropped me off on one end of Montreal; my hostel was on the other. After taking the metro, I still had a twenty-minute walk ahead of me. So I trod on, heavily backpacked, observing buildings and people, absorbing the new city and its atmosphere. Suddenly I was struck by the delicious aroma of freshly baked bread, wafting from an artisanal bakery nearby. Peering through the window, I couldn't believe what I saw—a Dutch Stroopwafel?! This delicacy from my homeland is not easy to come by, but over the past few years, it has gained popularity internationally. Unable to resist I bought one, savoring every bite; the creamy texture, the crunch... Kudos to Canada for doing justice to this regal treat.

Coincidentally, the next day I woke up in a room full of Dutch girls. I hadn't been surrounded by so many of my compatriots since leaving the Netherlands, nor had I heard my mother tongue fill the air for four weeks, so hearing them talk was somewhat disconcerting. I felt like a foreigner at home, a stranger to myself. At the same time, I wanted to speak to them in my language. Or should I just say, "Hey, I'm Dutch, too?"

As it turned out we were all wearing red Nike sneakers, in different shapes and sizes, so I used that as an icebreaker. We immediately hit it off, diving into conversations about our international endeavors and plans for exploring the city. One of the girls studied in Boston and was visiting Montreal for the weekend, while most others were attending a Canadian university. I normally prefer to interact with people from other cultures, to learn and discover new things, but there was something reassuring about connecting with fellow Dutchies in a foreign country—familiarity in the unfamiliar.

We decided to stick together and hike to the viewpoint of Parc du Mont-Royal. A little bit of rain doesn't stop a group of Dutch girls. The gloom of cold and misty weather is nothing new for us. We started our exploration by taking the Rue Peel Steps, a steep timber staircase that transitions from the more mercifully flat downtown to the summit of Parc du Mont-Royal. Our breaths became puffs of mist in the chilly air as we continued upward.

Reaching the top, we were greeted by the imposing Mount Royal Cross, *La Croix,* a towering modern steel structure. We walked around the monument, feeling its presence as we took in the swirling autumn leaves, each step crunching beneath our feet. I looked at the other girls taking pictures and at the children running around, throwing leaves at each other. They made the forest foliage fall all over again, their laughter bouncing against the trees.

One leaf, in particular, caught my eye—a pink leaf that gracefully floated down and landed at my feet. It felt like an omen, a sign that I was not alone—a reassurance showering me with comfort. My thoughts turned to my mother. I wondered if she was somewhere above the clouds, making things happen, shaking trees.

●

A couple of days later, some of the Dutch girls invited me on a short trip to Quebec City by car. So I figured, why not? I didn't know much about Quebec—or Canada for that matter —but had enjoyed what I had seen so far. Part of the reason why I had decided to leave home was to say yes to life's opportunities. I was going to embrace things as they came.

Unfortunately, the rain never stopped. Still, we managed to visit Fairmont Le Château Frontenac, a French Renaissance-style, castle-like landmark rising above the city and renowned for being the most photographed hotel in the world. We then ambled through Quebec City's narrow streets, where the scent of fresh pastries wafted from cozy bakeries, just like in Montreal, and colorful storefronts lined the cobblestones. Once again, the chilly air contrasted with the warm lights glowing from the cafés.

A part of me wished the weather had been better so we could have roamed around much longer and gotten truly lost in the numerous winding streets, where each turn revealed as charming a sight as the last. But another part of me appreciated the rain and cold, for it reminded me of how unprepared I was for autumn. On the drive back to Montreal, we made a quick stop at the mall to buy me a warm winter coat before heading to Montmorency Falls.

Distinguishable from the autoroute, the falls dove into the depths at an impressive 272 feet. We parked the car close to the cascade where the water was forcefully thrust into a shallow reservoir feeding the St. Lawrence River. Walking around the site, we spotted a wooden staircase clinging to the flank of the cliff. We ascended the nearly five hundred steps, all the way to the top, where the barren mountainside turned into a dense forest trail. Next, we made our way to the suspension bridge that spanned the crest of the falls, the scent of trees and fresh water following as we walked.

At the crest, I came to a ledge where I looked down: the water plummeted into the basin, roaring as it smashed against the rocks below, throwing up a cloud of spray. The soft mist enveloping my body sent shivers down my spine.

As we descended the winding stairs back to the car, I noticed that some of the clouds were melting away. At the bottom of the steps, the falls glistened in the sunlight, and a low-hanging rainbow emerged overhead, as if one could almost touch it. In awe, I twirled around, gazing up at the sky, smiling at the kaleidoscope of colors arching overhead. I felt strong and humble at the same time. *Beautiful things will happen*, I thought as I left the spectacle behind.

•

By the time I got back to Montreal, the aura of that lovely morning had faded—all I could think about was how exhausted I was, again. I had accidentally booked the wrong hostel, and to top it off, my sense of direction was failing me miserably. I wandered around for what seemed like hours, taking wrong turns, going around in circles. The weight of my backpack—along with the constant movement of the past few weeks—was taking its toll. I craved a steaming hot shower, my pajamas, and a good movie.

"You can go put your backpack in the room, and when you return, I'll explain everything to everyone," a receptionist said after I had finally found the hostel, handing me a set of keys.

I nodded wearily. "Wait," I uttered, mid-nod. "What do you mean, everything to *everyone?*"

The receptionist's gaze fixed on something behind me. I turned around to see four guys standing a few feet away, and locked eyes with one of them—potentially the most beautiful creature I had ever seen.

"May I ask where you're from?" the tall, blond stranger inquired.

I should probably stop staring and start speaking, I heard my inner voice say. "The Netherlands, and you?"

Please don't say Germany, please don't say Germany, please don't say Ge—.

"I'm from Germany, but my family lived in Amsterdam for a while, and I absolutely loved it there!"

Decent answer.

I nodded, then started fidgeting with my backpack, unsure if we would just stand in the doorway staring at each other all day. He was smiling. Suddenly, my exhaustion and desire for a quiet night disappeared. I wanted to get to know him.

"Would you like to join me for a walk downtown and have dinner with us tonight?" he said after a brief moment of silence, as if reading my mind.

We exchanged numbers and agreed on a time to meet up. Then I headed straight to my room, frantically rummaging through my backpack in search of something that might make me look more sophisticated. As I stepped into the shower, I caught a glimpse of myself in the mirror—a very disheveled version of myself. Of course, I looked like *this* when I ran into *that.*

We met at reception—just the dashing German and I—and we went for a stroll. The city was aglow with colorful lights. Hues of purple and red tinted the trees lining the streets—a mesmerizing blend of concrete and nature, an urban forest.

One tree caught my eye again as we passed City Hall; it stood tall and proud, its leaves illuminated by vivid pink spotlights.

As we wandered around chatting, I reflected on how different this felt from my past relationships. If this was what instant chemistry felt like, I realized I had been settling for far less. Nothing else seemed to matter—not even the group of people joining us for dinner. It was just him and me, lost in the beauty of Montreal's enchanting nightscape.

This is becoming a problem, I thought as we entered the restaurant to meet the others. I left everything behind to travel the world and reinvent myself—not to get sidetracked by some guy on the first continent I visit. Didn't I make that clear to myself already? And why do they always have to be German?

Still, it was impossible not to catch his gaze across the dinner table. Every time our eyes locked, I tried to remain calm and collected, but I could see something in his eyes, something I interpreted as curiosity, that made my heart beat so loudly I was sure he could hear it.

His look—and the way it made me feel—stayed with me as I lay in bed that night. It had been a long day and my body called for sleep. My mind, however, raced like a wild horse. I imagined us strolling hand-in-hand through the city, getting lost in its romantic, cobblestone lanes. I wanted to share my visions for the future and listen to his thoughts on the meaning of life. Our conversations were deepening our connection with every word. I couldn't think of a place I would rather be.

I woke up the next morning haunted by the realization that my time in Canada was running out. As much as I didn't want to think about it, I was scheduled to hop on the Greyhound for Boston that night, leaving me just twelve hours to spend with the German. Even as the rain lashed against the windows, I didn't care. We needed to go for one last walk together.

As we wandered along the river in Old Town, the pink-tinged trees offered a soft escape from the downpour. Despite knowing each other for only one day, the conversation flowed so effortlessly that I felt like I had known him for years.

I opened up about why I left home, sharing both my excitement and uncertainty about starting anew. He listened with empathy as we dove into our dreams and fears, discussing what it meant to be truly pursuing our passions and how our deep love for our family shaped us. We joked and laughed, and for once, I felt I could be unapologetically myself. I couldn't believe how this momentary connection was making such a strong impact on me.

I talked about my love for the little things—the cozy glow of street lanterns, the smell of freshly baked bread—and laughed about my knack for getting distracted by shiny objects, both in life and when shopping. He laughed too, admitting he shared my appreciation for nice things, running his hand through his golden hair and gesturing to his designer clothing, almost as if to prove it.

Standing beneath the pink canopy of a tree, his arm wrapped around me, our bodies breathing in the same rhythm, I knew this brief encounter would stay with me forever. Yet the reality of our impending separation lingered in the back of my mind—I had months of travel ahead of me, and he was studying in Canada for the semester.

After a quick stop at the hostel, he accompanied me to the bus station. The rain had turned to drizzle, and as we stood near the platform, shivering in the evening air, he pulled me closer and held me tight. I felt warm and safe in his arms. Then, he leaned in and kissed me softly.

"What took you so long?" I asked, my gaze locking onto his, trying to find any clues within his expression.

"Maybe, because we both know that you're leaving," he answered with a hint of sorrow, holding me even tighter, then kissing me on the lips again.

Time seemed to have stopped as the sounds of the city faded against the soft patter of the rain. The thought of tearing up my bus ticket and staying with him forever was tempting, but deep down, I had a promise to keep. I had promised myself to learn how to love and accept myself before committing to someone else. I had to discover first where I belonged and what I was made of. I had no other choice but to leave.

"Well," he said as he broke the silence, "you say you connect with people sharing baggage. I may not have much emotional baggage"—he paused, glancing at my backpack—"but I sure can carry your baggage for you!"

He took my backpack and carried it toward the platform as I admired his smooth demeanor, wondering what might be going through his mind. Would we ever cross paths again?

The bus door opened before me, I gave him a final, tight hug, trying to imprint his sandalwood scent into my memory, feeling the weight of the moment before releasing him and turning away.

"So, white gold, huh?" I heard him say behind me as I stepped aboard.

I looked over my shoulder and smiled at him one last time. He had been listening to everything, every detail, and he remembered. But as I settled into my seat and searched the crowd for his smile, he was nowhere to be found. He had disappeared back into his own life, leaving me with nothing but a memory.

The border crossing into the United States felt different this time. A jolt of disappointment hit me instead of the usual excitement. But then I reminded myself of my plans for the days ahead: I had friends to meet in Boston and New York City, then a flight to Amsterdam in seven days.

After the Homeland Security and Border Patrol officers cleared the bus, I settled into my seat, reaching into my backpack for my phone, curious to see if there was any news from the German. Instead, I found a message from the other German, the one from Las Vegas.

The German-Croatian:
**GERMANY CAN'T KEEP UP WITH YOU
AND ALL YOU HAVE EXPERIENCED.**

**YOU SHOULD PROBABLY LEAVE IT OFF
YOUR ITINERARY.**

I had offered hope before where it wasn't mine to give, and it quickly made me feel like a terrible person. His undeniable energy showed cracks, fractures that deepened with each passing day—until they would inevitably break. Maybe this journey was just a chain reaction of unanswered feelings. Unanswered feelings circling the globe.

Despite hardly knowing either of these guys, the fact that I was having a "thing" with both of them made me feel like I was cheating. I scrolled through the messages. A series of nagging thoughts crossed my mind: Should I go for full transparency? Would either of them want to know? Am I overthinking all of this? Would they overthink it as much as I am? I closed my eyes, hoping tomorrow would bring some clarity.

The message I had been anxiously waiting for arrived while I was sleeping.

The German:
FIRST OF ALL, THANK YOU FOR ALLOWING ME TO SPEND AT LEAST TWO DAYS WITH YOU. I REALLY DIDN'T WANT TO MISS THEM.

Trying to predict human behavior can be challenging, and the chemistry between men and women easily misunderstood. However, this time, something told me he felt the same way as me. So I pushed the worst-case scenarios aside—thoughts like, *you'll never see me again, it was all a mirage, forget it ever happened*—and continued reading.

I NEVER HAD THE OPPORTUNITY TO TELL YOU THAT YOU ARE TRULY A WONDERFUL WOMAN IN MANY WAYS. WE SHARE SO MANY THOUGHTS AND OFTEN THE SAME TYPE OF HUMOR. I WISH WE MEET AGAIN SOMEDAY AND THAT YOU STAY EXACTLY AS YOU ARE —UNTIL THEN.

A wave of calm washed over me, his words both reassuring and soothing. They put my mind at ease.

•

It was an early morning when the bus pulled up to Boston South Station. Amidst the crowd, I spotted my Dutch bunk mate, L, whom I had met in Montreal just a few days earlier, waiting for me on the platform.

Seeing the exhaustion in my eyes, she offered to take me back to her place to rest for a while before catching up later. I appreciated the prospect of a comfortable bed, especially in a room with a door where I wouldn't feel like a spectacle for strangers to stare at.

I woke up a couple of hours later and looked through the window. The weather was nice for a fall day in Massachusetts. The private shower, laundered clothes, and cozy pillows had lifted my spirits. I was staying in Somerville, just northwest of Boston, and decided to take a walk to Cambridge so I could finally see Harvard University. It had been a dream of mine for years to visit this prestigious Ivy League institution.

I had recently started a virtual course on Justice, offered by the university, where I had the privilege of learning about moral and political philosophy from one of their highly recommended professors. But now, as I stood in front of Harvard's grand library, it felt as though I were a student here —if only for a brief moment.

I sat down on the steps, absorbing the surroundings. The ground was covered with brown and red leaves, but some of the trees still boasted green and yellow foliage, standing tall between these impressive buildings. And there it was again— the pink tree, in the middle of a small empty patch of grass. Though smaller than the others, its bright colors radiated with an unmistakable fierceness.

I leaned forward and rested my face in my hands, lost in thought. When I opened my eyes again, my gaze drifted down to my feet. My trusty red Nikes had carried me to this point, and the pink tree had guided me throughout my travels in the northeast. In a strange way, these familiar sights made me feel less alone, like pillars of comfort amidst a sea of new and unfamiliar experiences.

Seated on the steps of the grand library, I decided to check if this world-class institution offered free Wi-Fi access. With a few taps on my iPhone, I scrolled through my social media accounts, marveling at the fact that I could connect with friends and family from around the globe. It made me wonder if Mark Zuckerberg had envisioned this when he created Facebook in the very spot where I was sitting.

Suddenly, a notification caught my attention.

The German:
**WHAT ON EARTH ARE YOU DOING
WALKING AROUND HARVARD ALL DAY?**

It was clear that he had been following my social media updates closely. I pondered how to reply, and in the end, instead of trying to articulate my thoughts and emotions, I decided to challenge him with a question.

**WOULD YOU PREFER I WANDERED
AROUND NIAGARA FALLS?**

Niagara Falls was the nearest tourist spot I could come up with, given his university's location in Canada. I was hoping he would take the hint and make the effort to see me; after all, he had expressed a desire for us to spend more time together.

Besides, even though I was no longer in the vicinity of Niagara Falls, it wouldn't be *that* difficult to go back.

WE ARE IN THIS ADVERSE SITUATION.

**VISIT ME. VISIT ME HERE IN CANADA
OR IN BERLIN.**

Waiting months and months to potentially see each other in a completely different country didn't seem like the best use of our time. Adverse situations, as he called it, are never easy to navigate—and this one was no exception. There were some significant challenges in the short term, and potentially even more catastrophic ones in the long term. I didn't care. I just wanted to go back to Canada and see him again.

**I MIGHT BE ABLE TO CROSS THE
BORDER AGAIN.**

IF YOU HAVE TIME?

A younger version of myself might have deemed such a suggestion outlandish. Yet now, I couldn't have been more confident when I hit send.

I WILL MAKE IT POSSIBLE.

His response was almost immediate. It made my stomach flutter.

Later that day, I met my friend and host for a Bostonian evening. We stepped into a crowded market hall filled with merchants and started with maple-bacon donuts, their sweet and savory flavors melting in our mouths. Afterward, we ventured into an Irish pub for hearty nachos and a cold beer. The place buzzed with laughter and clinking glasses. We admired how indulgent this city felt, the atmosphere sweeping us along in its embrace.

As night fell, L and I wandered through the streets, now draped in the soft glow of streetlights and the inviting murmur of the many pubs. Despite having met her so briefly at a hostel, her enthusiasm made me feel welcome, and her love for the city was evident in every place she showed me.

We stopped in our tracks, drawn by the sound of an upbeat, jazzy blues saxophone rendition of *Rock Around the Clock*. Moving toward the music, we found a young boy performing in a square. He wore a fedora and a white shirt with a pinstripe vest under a black leather jacket, his fingers dancing effortlessly over the saxophone keys. After a few minutes, he exchanged his saxophone for a piano, seamlessly transitioning into an equally impressive performance. Each note he played was a cascade of brilliance, filling the air with energy and making the city come alive in a new way—quickly becoming a place I loved.

When I nestled into my comfortable bed that night, the text messages from the morning came back to mind. *I will make it possible.* Indeed, I had nothing to lose by crossing the border again. After all, it was only so many hours away...

My train of thought was interrupted by the buzzing of my phone on the nightstand.

The German:
**I WOULD REALLY LIKE TO SPEND SOME
ADDITIONAL TIME WITH YOU.**

**I HOPE YOU ARE ENJOYING BOSTON.
AND THAT LEAVING ME WAS WORTH IT.**

**IN MY DREAMS, I PICTURE YOU STROLLING
THROUGH HARVARD WITHOUT A CARE IN
THE WORLD, FILLED WITH WONDER.**

I have to go back. I could take a bus to Canada on Monday. While repeating the plan in my head, I realized it sounded a bit crazy. Nevertheless, this newfound adventurous version of myself was fueled by honesty and fearlessness.

Unfortunately, altering the plan meant sacrificing some time in New York, which was next on the agenda. So, with only Sunday, Monday and Tuesday left before flying back to Amsterdam on Wednesday, I decided to head to the Big Apple first and spend a night there before heading north again.

The German:
WHY ARE YOU ON A BUS TO NYC?

**ISN'T THAT FURTHER AWAY FROM
NIAGARA FALLS?**

YES, BUT IT'S MY FAVORITE CITY.

**I WOULD LIKE TO SPEND SOME
TIME THERE.**

**I WILL TAKE THE BUS BACK TO
CANADA TOMORROW.**

It might not have made much sense, but as long as I understood my reasons everything would be fine. He might not have understood my logic, but he understood my feelings.

**I KNOW IT IS NOT THE EASIEST WAY,
BUT THE ONLY WAY.**

**AS LONG AS WE SEE EACH OTHER,
IT IS WORTH IT.**

•

Well into the four-hour ride from Boston to New York City, the magnificent skyline of Manhattan suddenly emerged. A long row of clustered skyscrapers made the city seem endless, their towering presence nearly filling my entire field of vision, with glass and steel gleaming in the bright afternoon sun.

After reaching the Port Authority bus terminal, I consulted my Manhattan map to plan my route. Despite being familiar with the city's straightforward grid system, I wanted to gauge the distance I had to cover. To my delight, my hostel was located less than twenty blocks away. *I can do that!* I thought, and set out on foot toward the Upper West Side.

Upon entering my dorm room, I was surprised to find it unoccupied. It echoed a similar solitude I had experienced in Ottawa, but this time, the dynamic backdrop of the city that never sleeps made the isolation sting less. I gazed out of the window: the world outside was a blur of yellow taxis, distant sirens, and the fading sunlight. With no time to waste, I ventured out into the evening and headed to Times Square.

Despite the darkening sky, Times Square's bright lights and constant buzz made it seem like daylight never truly dimmed. I stopped in the center of the square, gazing up at the neon signs flashing overhead, their electric colors competing for attention like eager performers on stage.

As I moved through the crowd, the city's noise faded into the background. The asphalt gently vibrated beneath my feet, sending small quakes through my body and grounding me in the moment. The extra bus ride was worth every second. I was thrilled to be back in this magical place.

"Stop, right there!"

My dance with the city was interrupted by a voice. Startled, I scanned my surroundings. My eyes landed on a man with a bulky camera lying on the ground next to me. I was standing in the middle of a crosswalk, oblivious to the world around.

"Hold it right there, this is great!"

As I processed what was happening, I noticed the stranger aiming his camera at me. I hesitated for a moment, unsure of what to do. Ultimately, I decided to go with the flow and froze in the moment, allowing him to capture the scene.

"Look," the stranger showed me his camera screen. "Now let me take a few with your phone."

I was apprehensive as I handed him my phone; he could, after all, run away with it. But he could also be a kind-hearted soul looking to spread some joy in the world. Luckily for me, he was the latter.

"I am sorry, I couldn't resist capturing that moment," he said, handing me back my phone with a smile on his face.

Puzzled, I asked, "Capture what, exactly?"

"I have never seen anyone so in love with New York City."

The photographer turned out to be a genuinely kind person, equally inspired by the energy of Times Square. We walked around for a while, talking about everything under the sun—from the *Humans of New York* series to European culture and world history—and ended up having dinner at an Irish pub just off Broadway. It was astonishing to realize that just a few hours ago we were complete strangers, yet now, we shared experiences and a mutual thirst for knowledge. This forged an unexpected connection. The world is indeed full of surprises—all we need is a little faith in humanity to discover that.

After dinner, he kindly escorted me back to where he had first found me. We bade each other farewell. Despite the late hour, I couldn't bring myself to leave Times Square just yet, so I stayed behind to soak up more of the city's energy.

As the night wore on, the crowds grew louder and more frenzied—groups of revelers out to party, lonely figures nursing drinks, street performers in colorful suits trying to make a living... The atmosphere was electric, I felt as if I was part of something bigger than myself.

I settled on a large concrete block—the perfect vantage point to observe the world around me. As I sat there, a bunch of memories came rushing back to me, flashing before my eyes like scenes from a movie. The good times, the bad, my beloved family and friends, the betrayals and broken hearts, and all the struggles and setbacks along the way—there was so much to appreciate in the good and so much to learn from the bad.

Then, my thoughts drifted to the German-Croatian: I knew I had to be honest with him about meeting the other German at Niagara Falls, even though I owed no explanations. Being truthful, however difficult, was the only way. I didn't want anyone else to feel blindsided like I had been before.

> **I NEED TO BE HONEST WITH YOU**
> **AND I DON'T WANT TO HURT YOU.**

Original start, really original, I thought to myself, rolling my eyes. But before I could even consider elaborating, a flurry of messages kept coming in non-stop.

The German-Croatian:
> **I JUST HAVEN'T HAD THAT FEELING...**

YOU KNOW, A GIRL MESSAGING ME AND
MY HEART JUST BEATING FASTER.

AND I DON'T WANT YOU TO COMMIT.

I AM NOT A DISTANCE RELATIONSHIP
KIND OF GUY.

WHO AM I, TO ASK THAT FROM YOU?

I NEVER WANTED TO MAKE YOU FEEL
UNCOMFORTABLE. I'M SO SORRY.

YOU ARE PROBABLY THINKING: WHAT
THE HECK IS THIS GUY TALKING ABOUT?

I GOT HIM FIGURED OUT ALL WRONG.

My ears were ringing. *Please bear with me for a moment*, I thought while trying hard to articulate what I needed to say.

I DON'T KNOW HOW TO RESPOND
TO THIS RIGHT NOW.

I JUST WANT TO BE HONEST.

I HAVE COMMITTED TO GO ON A
DATE. I AM SORRY...

The chat window showed those ominous three dots, signaling that he was typing. Part of me didn't want to read what was coming; I felt ashamed of the disappointment and hurt I was causing.

WOW... I AM NOT GOING TO LIE, IT HURTS.

SOMETIMES I LIVE IN MY LITTLE FAIRYTALE
WORLD.

BUT IT IS YOUR LIFE. SO, IF YOU LIKE HIM,
GO AHEAD.

HE IS A REALLY LUCKY MAN.

DON'T BE SORRY FOR HONESTY.

**I GUESS THERE WON'T BE A BERLIN
TRIP THEN, HUH?**

ENJOY YOUR DATE.

My stomach knotted, guilt weighed me down. Struggling to deal with the chat, I looked away from my phone, toward the bright, neon colors of the city.

Ouch—a sudden jolt of pain shot through my scalp. I looked around, confused. That's when I noticed an elderly man standing nearby, holding a handful of my long, blonde hair. I watched in astonishment as he brought the tuft to his nose, smiling. *Alright, that's my cue to leave. Times Square just got a little too strange for my liking.*

I opened my eyes the next morning to see my phone screen flooded with a fresh set of messages.

The German-Croatian:
IF YOU WANT TO GO...

IT'S LIKE YOU SAID, I DON'T OWN YOU.

I DO LIKE YOU AND YOU KNOW THAT.

**I AM NOT GOING TO REPEAT MYSELF
EVERY DAY.**

**DON'T THINK I CAN TOP YOUR DATE BY
INVITING YOU TO BERLIN.**

BUT YOU ARE ALWAYS WELCOME.

I lay in my bunk bed, heart aching, and gazed up at the ceiling. The sounds of the bustling city outside filled my ears. *There was a whole wide world out there*, I told myself. I had to keep moving.

I went out for a walk, planning to explore Manhattan from top, or middle, to bottom—from Central Park to the Empire State Building, through Greenwich Village and Battery Park. There's something about New York that calms my nerves, something that makes me feel like I'm exactly where I'm meant to be. Walking its streets is the best way to access this state of being.

After some hours, I paused before the new World Trade Center that filled Ground Zero, my gaze drawn upward to the towering structure. I had watched it take shape over the years, during my trips across the Atlantic Ocean. I still remember the first time I saw it in 2009, when it was just a foundation, ground work of steel and concrete. Each time I stood in its shadow, I thought of the original Twin Towers that once defined New York's skyline. I also thought of the thousands of people inside those magnificent buildings, victims of terror on that fateful day in September 2001.

Even though I was only nine years old at the time and living on a different continent, I remember the events as if they were yesterday. The news of the first plane spread like wildfire, even with a six-hour time difference from the East Coast. I had just been picked up from school by my mother when my brother A called to tell us about it. And when the second plane hit, the phone rang again, shattering our sense of security and marking a moment that would change the world forever.

"Turn on the TV right now. It's not an accident—it's an attack," A's urgent, panicked voice echoed in my ears, sending a prickling sensation creeping up my arms.

Before that day, my world had been a blissful place of unicorns and Barbies. But as I watched the terror unfold on the TV screen that day, I felt a cold hand grip my heart. How could this be happening? How could humans inflict such pain and destruction on their fellow beings? It was the moment that shattered my innocence and awakened me to the harsh realities of the world. For the first time, I realized that evil existed, and not just as a fictional concept in books or movies. It was real. And it was happening now, right before my eyes.

That night also sparked a deep curiosity to understand the complexities of the world and its people, to seek out different perspectives and viewpoints. I may have been just a child then, but the seed of my desire to learn and grow had been planted.

As I was standing where this tragedy had happened, I felt a strong connection to the city. It had endured so much pain yet had risen from the ashes. New York wasn't a victim of its circumstance; it was a beacon of hope that could overcome anything. And looking at that magnificent new tower, I felt inspired to embody that same message and become an inspiration for others. I realized that no matter how lost or broken you feel, no matter how much pain you have suffered, you can rise again.

Later that night, I found myself alone once more, this time in a desolate, bleak station, waiting for a bus at 12:35 a.m. As I was sitting on a cold, steel bench under a flickering lantern, I pondered what I knew about the man I was going to meet again in Canada.

I knew he grew up in privilege, shielded from hardship. His father was a prominent figure in the luxury car industry in Europe, and he had recounted stories of his parents attending grand banquets with German leaders. His family was close-knit and it seemed that he had imbibed all the right values from them. In contrast, I had had a difficult childhood after my mother passed, having been labeled a half-orphan at the age of twelve. While his glass seemed to be overflowing, mine was perpetually half-empty.

But even with our differences, I also felt that we were not so different after all. Two human beings, trying to make our way in the world the best way we could. Besides, I acknowledged how privileged I had been being able to embark on this journey. If my mother was still alive, our worlds wouldn't have been so far apart.

**WHAT IS CANADIAN CUSTOMS
GOING TO SAY?**

I asked him as I sat there, wondering.

The German:
TELL THEM THE TRUTH!

**OBVIOUSLY, YOU HAVE A STRONG DESIRE
TO GO SEE THE NIAGARA FALLS.**

**AND CANADA IS FAMOUS FOR BEING
MORE BEAUTIFUL.**

He appeared to be in good spirits, and his optimism was well-founded. I responded hesitantly, knowing that I wanted to see him, yet still unsure if it was the right move to go back to Canada. In contrast, his confidence only increased with each subsequent answer.

**AND OF COURSE, IT IS ME WHO IS
WAITING FOR YOU.**

Canada

The Canadian customs officer raised an eyebrow as he inspected my bus ticket; it showed a twenty-three-hour stay before my return to the United States.

"You must really want to see the Falls," he said with a grin that made me wonder if he knew the real reason why I was visiting. "It's true what they say," he continued. "It's more beautiful from the Canadian side."

We arrived at Niagara Falls Bus Terminal in the morning, and I went straight to the Hilton to check in. Even though I knew I shouldn't be spending so much money on accommodations, I wanted to impress him. And impress him I would!

I gasped when I opened the door to my twenty-ninth-floor room, a panoramic view of Niagara Falls stretching outside the floor-to-ceiling window. For several minutes, I stood there, frozen, taking it all in, before filling the bathtub. Despite my no-boys-in-my-room policy, I had to share this with him. Today was all we had after all.

As I settled into the warm embrace of the bathwater, I realized that it was exactly six months to the day that I had broken free from the relationship with someone who never truly appreciated me. *How ironic*, I thought. *Here I am, on this very day, making a move to* get *to know someone new*.

After the bath, I texted the German saying I had arrived and was waiting for him. I paced around the room, checked myself in the mirror countless times, scrutinized every inch of my face, and tried to determine the most flattering angle from which to greet him.

The German:
I AM AT THE HILTON.

TAKE THE SOUTH TOWER ELEVATOR TO THE 29TH FLOOR.

My hands were shaking, my heart racing. I held my breath, straining to hear the elevator ping. The anticipation was suffocating. I closed my eyes, steadying my breathing. Then, I heard the knock on the door.

He walked in with a wide grin on his face—calm and collected. On the inside, I was still freaking out. Yet in some kind of defense mechanism, I automatically slipped into nonchalant mode, brushing him off, acting as if I didn't have a care in the world. He wasn't fooled. It only took about ten minutes before he pulled me into a warm hold, clutching me tight with both arms.

"Breathe," he said softly. "Let's go for a walk."

Once more, his kind and reassuring words put me at ease. Taking a leisurely walk along the river was an excellent idea.

The falls roared in front of us, the water plunging down with a force that seemed to shake the earth. We stood shoulder to shoulder on the promenade, the mist hanging in the air like a fine veil. When his hand gently brushed against mine, he took hold of it. I squirmed nonchalantly, the gesture too intimate for my guarded heart, but I didn't pull away. I felt his eyes on me, and for the first time that day, I managed to meet his gaze.

Cold and ready for food, we decided to wander into a nearby neighborhood for some authentic Italian cuisine. A cozy bistro with flickering candles caught our attention. We decided to pop in and indulge in a bottle of Prosecco and two orders of mouth-watering Fettuccine Alfredo. Before we knew it, we had lost track of time.

After dinner, we walked back to the hotel along the river's promenade. The streets were dark, but the falls were aglow with an array of colors, transforming them into a living, watery rainbow—as if a Kandinsky painting had come to life.

The colors stretched across in long, sweeping strokes, each hue blending into the next.

As we stopped at a quiet viewpoint, my pulse quickened. I turned to him, the colors of the falls dancing in his eyes. He reached out, sweeping a strand of hair from my face, the droplets leaving it slightly damp. With a look that made my breath catch, he pulled me close, his hands firm yet tender, the warmth of his touch chasing away the cool night air. With unrestrained passion, he kissed me, surrendering to a moment so perfect, it felt as if the entire scene had been crafted just for us. When I turned away, facing the falls, I closed my eyes, holding on to the moment.

Standing behind me, he wrapped his arms gently around my waist and rested his head on my shoulder.

"Life with you could never be boring," he whispered.

For the first time in a long while, my heart was set ablaze.

Back in Times Square, I took a seat on the same concrete slab from three nights prior, the energy of New York City pulsing through and around me again. Once more, a whirlwind of emotions surfaced, slowing time and prompting me to reflect on what had happened and what lay ahead.

The German and I acknowledged that nothing could break the connection we both felt; we couldn't let that happen. Yet he also knew I had to keep going. The eager anticipation to see each other again became more reserved. What had been a plan for a quick reunion now stretched into months of uncertainty, unless we could bridge the distance. It scared me to walk away, knowing I might be turning my back on the only chance we would ever have—the only chance to be together.

Was I really willing to give up my journey for a man who had swept me off my feet? Was it love—not belonging—that I had been searching for since my family fell apart? Was their a difference? Or was I simply romanticizing this connection to escape the challenges of traveling the world alone?

As I dug for answers, a gray-bearded man sat down beside me, holding up a sign that read, "I need money for everything our government doesn't want me to have." *Charming*. Here I was, torn between self-discovery and romance, while he had distilled life's complexities into one question: What do I want?

His bluntness pierced through my confusion, reminding me that sometimes the most profound truths are deceptively simple. I realized that clarity amid chaos was what I needed, which meant addressing more than just love and belonging. I had to chart my own course, not the German's. Yet even as reason triumphed over emotion, a yearning remained—I wanted his commitment. I wanted him to *love* me.

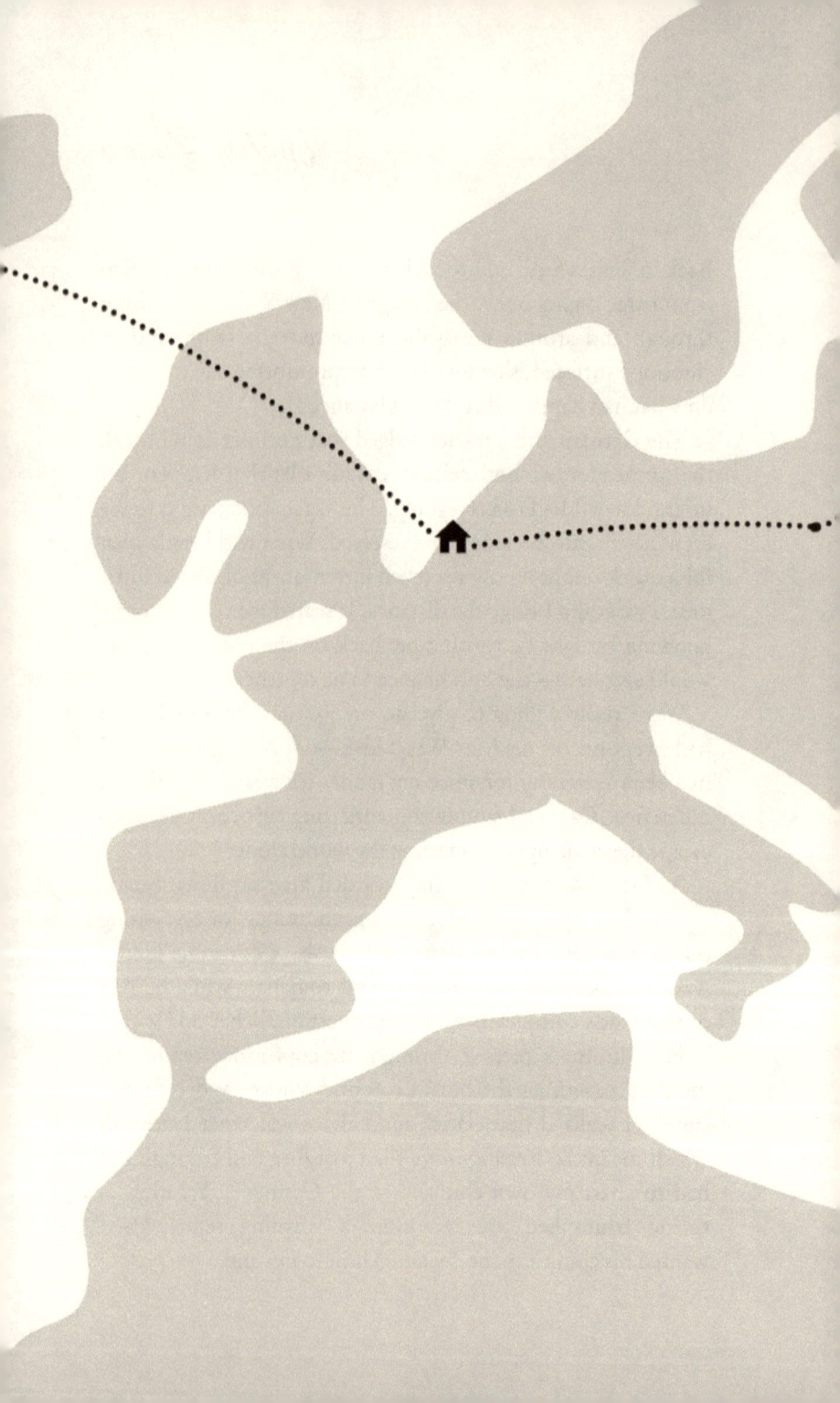

Back home, I soon felt the weight of the trip catch up with me —or rather, I realized what I had left behind. My insecurities slowly overpowered me, making me afraid; afraid of making the wrong decisions, of losing my direction.

During the first week, the German and I video called for hours. I couldn't stop thinking about him, but at the same time continued to be haunted by the specter I had conceived on my last night at Times Square: What if I'm using him as an escape, a way to take the easier path and run back into the arms of someone who can hold me and make me feel safe?

"I see you as a strong and joyful woman, and I know you have a big journey ahead of you," he told me during one of our calls, reassuring me while encouraging me at the same time. "There will be plenty of exciting moments and people to meet along the way. So don't feel sad about us. We have a strong connection, and I believe that won't change anytime soon. Keep that beautiful smile on your face, like you always do, because that's how I hold you in my mind—more often than you might think." After a pause, he added, "Go and collect your Master of Science degree!"

Clad in a stunning new dress that my godmother had gifted me, my family and I drove to Amsterdam to attend the graduation ceremony. As I walked around the beautiful campus of VU University, saluting friends and colleagues, receiving hugs and congratulations from loved ones, I could feel my body tingle with pride and joy.

The professor who had guided me through writing my thesis and conducting the research handed me my degree alongside a personal note.

"You went through a difficult episode, which made it tough to focus. Nevertheless, you made it—very impressive!"

His words meant a lot; for they recognized the obstacles I had overcome and sacrifices I had made to achieve this goal.

I stood on the podium with four amazing guys from my class who had become close friends. These compassionate, brilliant people had been by my side through thick and thin. Without their unwavering support, I would not have been able to make it through my studies.

We held each other tight, beaming—basking in our shared achievement. I felt like Reese Witherspoon's Elle in *Legally Blonde:* elated, triumphant, loved.

"We did it, boys!" I exclaimed as I shifted the tassel on my graduation cap to the other side.

A few days later, I drove back to Amsterdam to meet up with one of my American friends I had met in Las Vegas. Before joining her, I parked just south of the city center and hurried up the stairs to catch the subway. As I made my way to the platform, I felt an electric energy coursing through my veins. There was something magical about being in Amsterdam: the candid culture, the canals, the rich heritage, the gatherings and celebrations with friends.

"Manon?!" a voice called from behind.

I stopped short, and when I turned around, I saw my exboyfriend standing there, his new girlfriend clinging to his arm.

"Hi," I said, chuckling despite being flabbergasted. "Funny seeing you here!"

What are the odds?! Throughout the years we had been together, we had never run into each other anywhere—yet now we crossed paths at an obscure station in the country's largest and most populated city. If someone had warned me about the encounter, I would have assumed it would hurt me, or at least stir up some emotions. But to my surprise, I felt nothing. Nothing but confidence in my new path.

With purposeful strides, I boarded the subway, heading to Museumplein for a picnic. This was my new reality—meeting people from far away places, sharing a glimpse of my backyard just as they had shared a glimpse of theirs.

•

My alarm clock blared at 3 a.m. on the final morning in my childhood home in Oud-Beijerland, jolting me awake. I gazed out my bedroom window, at the view I had admired so many times before: the Rotterdam skyline twinkling in the distance beyond the dark fields of farmland. The last few days had been full of tough conversations, joyful celebrations and emotional goodbyes, but now it was time to get myself together and prepare to leave again.

I wandered through the house I had called home for twenty-three years, trying to imprint every detail in my memory. This was where I had grown up, where I had shared countless happy moments with my family. But it was also the place where my mother had taken her last breath—right there, on a bed in that corner—leaving a void that would never be filled. After her passing, the house had lost its warmth; it had become a cold, lifeless shell. Things would never be the same. Still, I cherished this place with all my heart. It was hard to imagine a life without it—without a place to call home.

I slipped into my shoes and grasped the doorknob of the heavy front door, feeling the icy November air sting my lungs. This was it, the last time I would step over that threshold, as my father prepared to sell the house. I closed the door behind me and took a deep breath. It was time for me to go.

Ellen Johnson Sirleaf once wrote, *If your dreams don't scare you, they aren't big enough.*

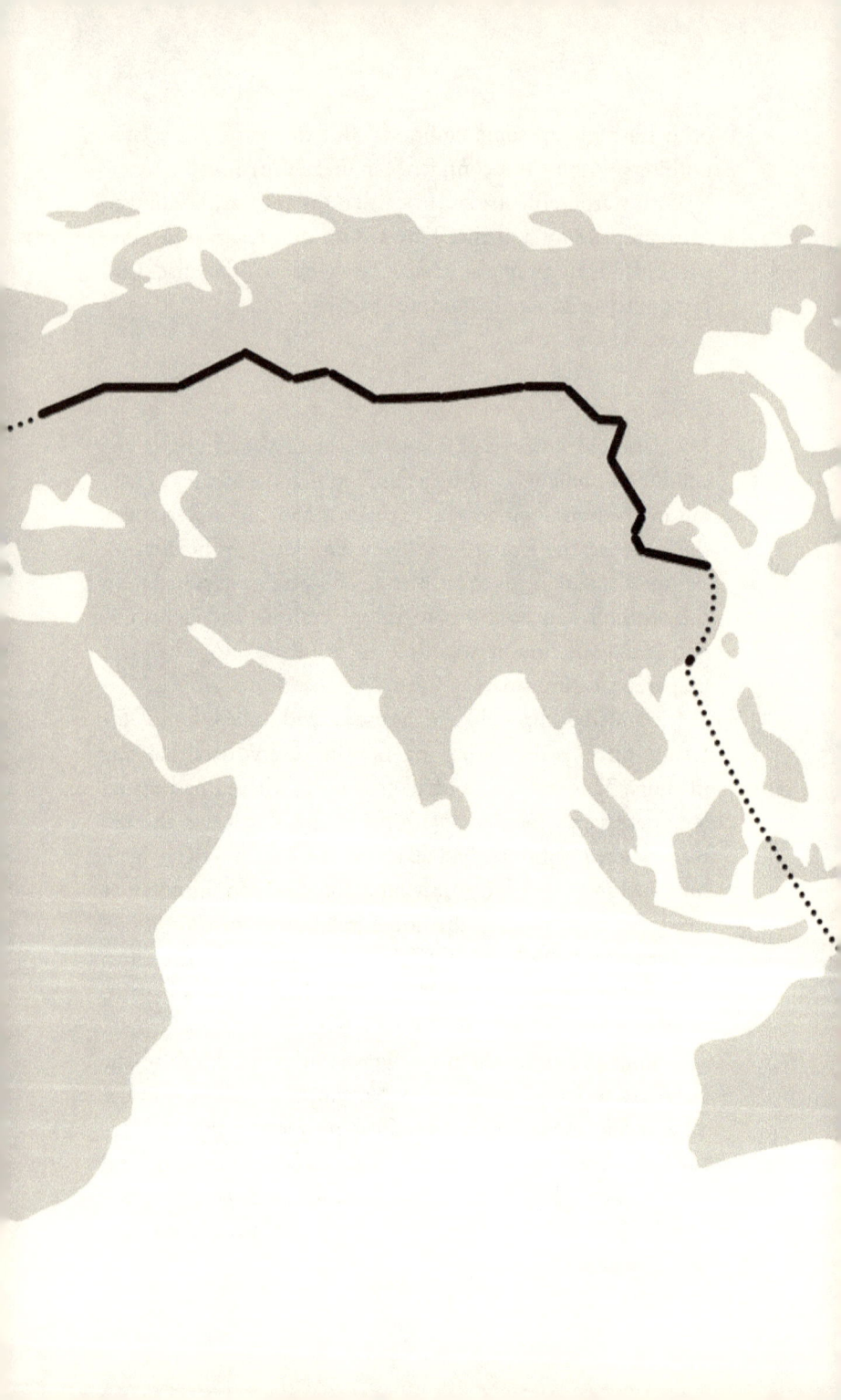

PART TWO

A COLD TRAIN OF WANDERING THOUGHTS

Poland

Chatting with a friend at a birthday party after my break-up, I mentioned my plan to go backpacking. She expressed her own desire to return to China and learn more Chinese, recounting how she had traveled there before via the Trans-Siberian and Trans-Mongolian Express.

"I would love to experience that train ride!" I exclaimed.

"Then why don't you take me to China?" Z responded just as enthusiastically.

Everyone at the table, ourselves included, laughed. But then I stopped and watched her closely.

"Let's do this," I said, the sudden conviction in my own voice taking me aback.

"I'm in," she replied with a grin.

Over the following weeks, we began to make arrangements and applied for both the Russian and Chinese visas. Our original plan was to fly to Kiev, Ukraine, and then to Moscow,

Russia, where we would board the train eastbound. However, due to the Russian-Ukrainian conflict, our flight was canceled, so we decided to fly to Warsaw, Poland, and proceed to Russia from there.

Five months later, we hugged our families goodbye at Amsterdam Schiphol Airport. Unlike my trip to the United States, this departure felt like a major turning point: my journey had transformed into an ongoing quest, with no clear destination in sight. At the same time, it reminded me that I wasn't leaving home because of a lack of love. I had to go further in order to repair what was broken deep inside.

During our layover at Warsaw Chopin Airport a few hours later, memories of my mother playing Chopin's *Nocturne Op. 9 No. 2* on her grand piano flooded my mind. I reached into the front pocket of my hand luggage and retrieved my small travel diary. Inside were two handwritten notes; one from my father, and the other from my brother, A—the one living in Amsterdam, the younger of my two older siblings.

My daughter Manon,
From the moment you were born, I have loved you.
Now, you are standing confidently in this grown-up world.
I have to let you go, because you are spreading your wings.
Know however, that I always carry you with me in my heart.
Good luck and enjoy your trip around the globe.
Your dreams are coming true.
Dad

My dearest sister,
No matter how far away you are,
you are always close by in your brother's heart.
I love you so much. Enjoy this time to the fullest.
Love,
Your brother

Russia

Having done some research and taken extra precautions—noting down the names of the metro stations, transfer points, and streets that would lead us to our hostel—we felt prepared and confident about navigating Moscow. Yet upon arriving at Sheremetyevo Airport's metro station and seeing numerous signs we couldn't read, we were reminded that the Russian alphabet was very different from ours.

"Excuse me, ma'am. Could we please have two tickets to this station?" we asked the lady in one of the ticket booths, handing her a piece of paper with the name of the station we wanted to get to. "And could you tell us how to get there?"

Unfortunately, it didn't seem like we would receive any help from her regarding the route: she simply mumbled something in Russian and flashed a price on her calculator, then returned her attention to the computer screen.

Tickets in hand, we headed back to the platform. There were multiple trains departing, and it was now up to Z and me to determine not only which train to board but also which direction to head. Our cheat sheets in the Latin alphabet were rendered useless, and we couldn't resort to Google for quick answers. We needed a new plan.

"Is there anything on us that has the Russian alphabet?" Z said suddenly.

In a eureka moment, I exclaimed, "Our passports! Check our passports!"

When we received our visas from the Russian Embassy, we were surprised to find that our names had been transliterated into Cyrillic. By comparing the Cyrillic and Latin letters, we were able to decipher some of the signage and find the correct train to take us into the city. As for the direction, we assumed there would be a station map onboard that we could use to figure it out. And sure enough, we did.

Night was falling and the temperatures had dropped by the time we finally arrived at the hostel. Our two-person bedroom was compact but cozy, and, perhaps more importantly, provided us with some privacy before we embarked on a series of overnight trains the following evening. After freshening up, we set out on a mission to find a restaurant. Being such a bustling metropolis, Moscow should have plenty of culinary options to offer.

We were strolling down the street when we stumbled upon a charming building with a sign that read, "Beverly Hills Diner." It was the most American-looking diner I had ever seen, even more so than many diners in America: a neon sign flashed at the entrance; inside, colorful leather stools surrounded a cobalt chrome bar and posters of stars like Elvis Presley, Marilyn Monroe, and Audrey Hepburn covered the walls. The menu wasn't Russian, but what did we expect. Still, we were intrigued. Funny how we often gravitate to familiar things for comfort and safety.

Ready to indulge, we ordered an appetizer of egg rolls, loaded potato skins, onion rings, and fries—not quite Russian cuisine. As we ate, Z noticed Justin Bieber's album, *Purpose*, playing from the ceiling speakers.

"Ah, there's your song," she said.

I smiled. This album was a frequent topic of conversation between the German and I; hearing it made me think of him, and I knew he felt the same.

"He's like a unicorn, isn't he?" Z added. "A rare creature that just makes you happy."

I smiled and nodded, then pulled out my phone and snapped a picture of our fine dining experience and sent it to him. A few seconds later, my phone pinged.

The German:

YOU'RE SMILING ALL OVER YOUR FACE.

IT SEEMS LIKE YOU ARE HAPPY.

Smile—that's something people didn't seem to do around here a lot: not when walking in the park, not in restaurants, and certainly not when purchasing a ticket or asking for directions on public transportation. We had just started to doubt their ability to raise the corner of their mouths when someone suddenly smiled back at us as we were strolling around the Red Square. I looked at Z in near-shock.

"They do smile!" she exclaimed.

Immediately after that, the Russian man started moving toward us, his gaze locked on mine.

"Can I kiss you?" he asked bluntly, still smiling.

Dumbfounded, all I could muster was, "No, thank you."

Before he had a chance to react, Z grabbed me by the arm and pulled me away.

"Let's keep walking, blondie," she whispered, giggling at the same time. "Maybe no more smiles for you tonight?"

The following day, with a few hours to spare before our Trans-Siberian train ride, we set out on another walk. The city's unique charm had begun to grow on me as my eyes were drawn to golden peaks mingling with intricate baroque details, while grand facades seemed to tell stories of the past with every glance. Each street we crossed revealed something new— buildings that weren't just historic but demanded attention, daring me to look closer, to uncover their secrets.

We paused to watch a group of locals gathered in a spacious park, intensely focused on a game of chess. Their quiet concentration contrasted strikingly with the winter holiday décor. The small enchanting lights brought the city to life, making it feel dynamic and beautiful.

Continuing our stroll, Saint Basil's Cathedral rose before us like a whimsical dream against the crisp November sky, its onion-shaped domes painted in a riot of colors and patterns. Standing tall for centuries, it had become a symbol of the country—audacious and mysterious. Likely created as a show of force, rumors claimed it was built without any blueprints, and whispers suggested that the man who became the first tsar of Russia had blinded its architects so they could never build something this beautiful again. Walking away toward the train station, I turned back one last time, wondering what secrets those towers might reveal if only they could speak.

Sitting on a platform bench, I eagerly awaited the sound of our approaching train—there's something soothing about the rhythmic thrum of those massive machines, perhaps even more so than buses. Trains also offer a unique perspective.

Unlike planes, which cover great distances in mere hours, or buses, which often stick to well-traveled roads, trains chug along at a steady pace, allowing you to soak up the landscape and to stop regularly, giving you the chance to experience places you otherwise wouldn't see. In that sense, trains are an ideal embodiment of the spirit of adventure. And that's exactly what I was after.

•

Frost formed star-shaped crystals on the windowpane. Our open-plan rail car was crammed with at least thirty other passengers, mostly locals traveling long distances to see family or to relocate, we assumed. I couldn't spot a single foreigner.

It was a third class train ticket, meaning we each had a bunk —no doors, or even mattresses for that matter. At the end of the wagon was a small restroom, equipped with a steel sink and a toilet that offered a clear view of the snowy train tracks below when flushed. As uncomfortable as our quarters would seem to most people, I felt so lucky to be here.

Beside her bunk, an older lady unpacked her breakfast—a small basket filled with apples and hard-boiled eggs.

"Babushka," she introduced herself with a smile.

Using words from various languages—as well as plenty of gesturing—we managed to communicate with her to some extent. *Babushka,* which means grandmother in Russian, told us she was used to traveling for days just to see her family. My first thought was: *what kind of family would let such a lovely elderly lady undertake such an arduous journey alone?* But I soon realized that, probably due to her circumstances, this was the only way for her to visit her loved ones. Later, we found out that this was normal practice—given the size of the country.

Besides, despite looking vulnerable and frail, *Babushka* was anything but. Even surrounded by strangers in an unfamiliar place, she commanded respect from the young men sitting on their bunk beds next to ours. Whenever they tried to approach us, she would say something in Russian and they would retreat. We were grateful she was watching over us.

During our first two nights and full day on the train, we passed by several cities—Vladimir, Nizhny Novgorod, Vyatka and Perm—as an endless train track stretched out before us, cutting through leafless forests, branches snow-covered.

The peaceful landscape outside the window contradicted the chaos inside the train, where people were moving or talking without pause during the day, while pillows and sheets littered the floor. Still, Z and I managed to find some pockets of quiet, particularly when we went to the "kitchen"—a corner at the beginning of each wagon with a table, an outlet and a metal boiler, which we used to make instant noodles or oatmeal.

To our surprise, the train car would sometimes suddenly fall into an eerie, deafening silence. When this happened, it was a welcome change from the hubbub. Yet it was also a moment of tension, at least for us. Traversing long distances, nothing but wilderness around, made us feel isolated, disconnected, vulnerable. Maybe nothing would happen. Nevertheless, we didn't want to draw any attention. We would whisper to each other, or sit in silence, lost in our own thoughts.

We also delved into books. Z was busy studying French, whereas I undertook an in-depth analysis of Immanuel Kant's theories on morality and ethics—not the most uplifting read, but certainly a fascinating one. Kant's philosophies had a lasting influence on contemporary debates surrounding social justice and human rights, so much so that his ethical framework remains a vital and thought-provoking part of modern philosophical discourse. As I said, not particularly uplifting, but given the fact that a big part of this journey was to question my views on life, why not immerse myself in works that challenge my thinking and push me to grapple with more complex issues?

·

The sun began to lighten up the dark sky when we arrived in Yekaterinburg, one of Russia's largest cities, situated just north of Kazakhstan, eleven hundred miles from Moscow. Our plan was to spend just one night here, a quick pitstop to break up the long train rides. Tired, we went straight to our hostel in the city center. But before catching up on some much-needed sleep, we wanted to let our loved ones know we were safe.

After connecting to the internet, our phones started to buzz. To my surprise, there were no new messages from my German. It felt strange not to hear from him. I therefore opened our conversation and sent him a little heart emoticon.

Almost immediately, he answered, and a flurry of messages ensued.

The German:
YOU HAVE INTERNET?!

I WAS ABOUT TO WRITE YOU TONIGHT!

GO ON THE NEWS STRAIGHT AWAY.

DO IT.

NEWS.

NOW.

"We have to turn on the television," I said urgently to Z, wondering what was so pressing. "I think something has happened."

We went into the hostel dining room, where there was a television mounted on the wall. As we looked for news, my phone pinged again.

IT'S PARIS.

Paris, what? I thought. And then we saw it on the screen: The City of Lights had been shaken by terrorist attacks, with suicide bombers and mass shooters leaving devastation and pain in their wake. Paris was bleeding.

WHEN DID THIS HAPPEN?!

YESTERDAY.

We sat in silence for a while, stunned, staring at the footage. Another heartless, incomprehensible act.

As I made my way to our bedroom, all I could think of was the people in and of Paris, going about their lives, unaware of the fate that awaited them. I felt my hope in humanity, my desire to see good in the world, waver. But then I remembered that hopelessness is not an option. If anything, episodes like these should reinforce my resolve to work for a better world. Even if it feels like an impossible task. Even if I can only make the smallest of impacts.

Later that day, still processing the morning news, Z and I agreed we shouldn't shy away from the world; we had to get out there and live. I told her about how, in times of adversity, I had always found solace within the walls of large cathedrals. We set out on a walk to the Church on Blood or the "Church on Blood in Honor of All Saints Resplendent in the Russian Land," a blinding white Orthodox church with glistening golden domes.

This architectural masterpiece stood as a solemn tribute to the tragic end of the Romanovs, the imperial dynasty that reigned for over three hundred years, culminating in the bloody assassination of the Tsar and his family.

Such was its historical significance that I felt compelled to remove my warm faux-fur hat upon entering. All of a sudden, a security guard jumped in front of me yelling in Russian.

"I'm sorry, I don't understand Russian," I responded softly.

Yet the man continued yelling, staring at me angrily and pointing upward.

"Nyet Russkiy," I tried again.

He stopped speaking and stared me down, unblinking; I remained frozen, awaiting his next action.

"Hat," he said in a strong Russian accent.

In a swift motion, he snatched my hat and placed it back on my head, covering both my ears, then walked away.

I moved into the nave, disappointed for unintentionally causing offense, suddenly aware of how small and singular I am in a vast world of diverse ideas, perspectives, and practices.

Back at the train station the following day, we had our first significant scare: none of the information boards displayed our train's departure time. Though we were seasoned interpreters of Russian signs by now, this puzzle stumped us.

After asking around and locating a fellow passenger who spoke English, we discovered that long-distance trains operate on Moscow Time, apparently to ensure consistency for travelers. That's great if you know about it. But in our case, the 15:31 on the ticket was actually 17:31 local time in Yekaterinburg. Thankfully, traveling eastward meant only an extra two-hour wait—nothing compared to the two-night journey that lay ahead.

•

After leaving Yekaterinburg, we passed Tyumen, Omsk, and Novosibirsk, with nothing but barren, frosty landscapes in sight. Thirty-six hours later, we finally spotted Krasnoyarsk in the distance, where we stopped for a few hours.

As soon as my red Nikes touched the platform, I realized I was completely unprepared. At -9 degrees Fahrenheit, my toes began to numb. Z and I braved the cold in search of a hot meal. We strolled around, smiling and singing loudly. But upon arriving at one of the main streets, our excitement vanished: there wasn't a soul around, and the storefronts of renowned global brands, usually glowing and bright, now stood dark and still, as though sheltering from the frigid air.

The more we walked, the harder it became to breathe—and to stay calm. Trembling and hungry, I glanced at Z. It was incredible to think that we once disliked each other—both of us too ambitious and outspoken to share oxygen. Yet mutual friends and events forced our big personalities together. The more time we spent in the same space, the more we learned, leading to a mutual appreciation for our straightforwardness and tenacity; there was no nonsense between us. These shared values forged our connection. I was so grateful to have her by my side.

•

Unlike in Krasnoyarsk, we had a fourteen-hour layover at our next stop, Irkutsk, giving us ample time to explore the surroundings. At the train station, we were advised to visit Lake Baikal—the world's deepest freshwater lake by volume and, as we were told, the largest inland lake in Europe. It felt somewhat strange to associate the latter description with this natural wonder, considering we had journeyed days away from Europe. We were in Siberia, near the Mongolian border, I was certain we had reached Asia. Either way, after learning more about the lake in Z's *Lonely Planet,* and knowing how close we were, we had to go see it.

Small buses regularly shuttled to the lake, so we hopped on one. As we observed the traffic, we shook our heads. It was a frenzy, with drivers weaving in and out, unsure of which side of the road they were on, as vehicles darted in every direction.

After an hour, the bus halted by the lakeshore in the village of Listvyanka. Stepping out to take some photos, we were hit by biting cold air that stung every inch of exposed skin within seconds. A digital thermometer hanging by a closed storefront read a staggering -11 degrees Fahrenheit. This was the coldest temperature I had ever been in. It was also a tangible reminder of the unforgiving nature of Siberia, where the elements reign supreme and mere survival tests one's resilience.

Watching the scenery—the pristine white snow blanketing the ground, cold steam rising from the surface of the vast lake, the sun beaming brightly against the ice—it felt like we were at the edge of the world. I longed to stay there, contemplating. But by now, the cold had already penetrated my body, making my skin tingle. My toes had lost all sensibility, and my vision blurred as the icy air frosted my eyes. The beauty begged me to stay, even through the haze. My legs not moving—frozen by both wonder and the chill of the world around me.

After twenty-five minutes, the cold became unbearable. We spotted a small building with floor-to-ceiling windows near the bus stop, thinking we could wait there for the next bus to take us back. The place appeared empty, but the door was unlocked, likely a ticket office or a spot to withdraw cash.

Grateful to find some shelter, we hurried inside, the glass walls offering a clear view of the lake as we escaped the biting cold. My eyes, though bloodshot, slowly began to restore, and I huffed breath onto my hands, attempting to generate heat. This unique place was worth every bit of sacrifice.

Back in Irkutsk, sitting in a café and finally feeling warmer, I went through the photographs I had just taken. One shot captured the expansive lake under a baby-blue sky, with a few birds soaring gracefully above its surface and that single fishing boat, lying idle, unlikely to sail anytime soon. In another, I tried to capture myself witnessing it, the lake reflecting in the ice in my irises, my Siberian hat pulled snugly over my ears.

I marveled at the power of photography, its potential to encapsulate the essence of a moment, preserving it forever. Ed Sheeran's song came to mind:

"We keep this love in a photograph
We made these memories for ourselves
Where our eyes are never closing
Hearts are never broken
And time's forever frozen, still"

Thinking of those lyrics I was taken back to my bus journey from New York City to Niagara Falls, where this tune played on repeat, creating a soundtrack to that chapter in my story.

Similarly, the photographs I was reviewing formed a sort of structure, a backbone, for the things I had experienced. They weren't just visual representations. These were fragments of emotions and thoughts. And while I had the sensation of standing still when I looked at them, it was hard to forget that I was, in fact, moving away from that very moment.

As for memories and love, were they truly forever frozen and immune to the passage of time as Sheeran suggested? Or were they ever-changing, elusive forces that require constant effort and adaptation to keep alive?

"Hello." A voice interrupted my musing, also startling Z who sat across the table sipping her tea. We looked up and saw a group of men forming a half-circle around our booth; they talked among themselves in a language that seemed vaguely familiar, yet perhaps not Russian. While I usually welcomed spontaneous conversations, the way they had approached us— abruptly, collectively, domineering—felt suffocating.

"Thank you for stopping by, but I would really like to finish my tea now," I calmly asserted, hoping that a polite request would suffice.

The men snarled at us in their language, laughing raucously.

"Please, go," I pleaded.

Suddenly, there was a resounding clap. I flinched. One of them, presumably the leader, stepped forward. The laughter ceased, a palpable sense of unease hung in the air.

"You come to my country and disrespect me," he snapped leaning in, his hefty body looming over us. "I should shoot you in the face."

Perplexed and at a loss, I lowered my gaze, staying silent. After a brief, heavy pause, he turned and walked away. Then one by one, the group began to disband.

"That was...eh...unusual," Z remarked, half-ironically, half-astonished herself.

Hands trembling, I was unable to shake off the adrenaline coursing through my veins. Both the elements and the unsettling encounter left me feeling exposed and vulnerable. I yearned to retreat to the Trans-Mongolian train carrying us away from Siberia, to close the door of our private cabin for the next leg of the journey, hiding away from it all—lock the door and shut out the world.

Crossing borders is hardly a fun process, yet it's not usually unsettling or nerve-wracking either. On the Russian side of the Russia-Mongolia divide, however, it was.

We sat on the train for a grueling four hours while military guards searched every inch of it, climbing up bunk beds, opening compartments, and taking our passports to be checked, somewhere. The train remained motionless; no one was allowed to step outside. While annoying, these measures were understandable—except that they locked the bathrooms, and having just woken up, Z and I really needed to go.

The thought of being in this no-man's land while some grim-faced soldier walked away with my only valid form of identification made my stomach tighten. But what troubled me even more was the urgent need to use the restroom. So, I waited outside our cabin, keeping the restroom in my line of sight. When the woman guarding the door momentarily stepped away, I seized the opportunity and made a dash for it. Such was the urge that when the floodgates finally opened, I let out a big sigh.

As I sprinted back to our cabin, I heard someone yelling behind me. Glancing over my shoulder, I saw that the female guard had returned; she glared at me, locking the door shut.

Z looked at me, goggle-eyed, her gaze translating her own urgency to use the toilet.

"I am so sorry," I mumbled, then closed our cabin door.

Mongolia

Only fifteen minutes after crossing the border, the train came to a halt again. We had reached the Mongolian side of the divide and the meticulous process of border control started anew. We handed over our passports, and as we were waiting for their return, watched the Mongolian soldiers combing every nook and cranny of the wagons. Thankfully, this time the procedure took only half as long—two hours instead of four. But again, the bathroom doors were kept locked.

Continuing onwards, the landscape gradually transformed. Snow-covered pine forests gave way to fields stretching as far as the eye could see. The vast, desolate expanse, coupled with the hypnotic whoosh of the train sliding on the tracks, plunged me into contemplation. *What am I meant to discover from all this?* I wondered. *How will these experiences shape my story?*

As the train sped along and the questions sank in, a familiar idea came to mind which slowly gained momentum. *I should write a book*, I whispered to myself. This was something I had wanted to do for a long time—something that both intrigued and intimidated me: revisiting that fateful day in February 2005 when my mother passed away. The day that everything changed. Staring at the winter scenery, my mind drifted back to that morning ten years ago.

On that day too, even though I was only twelve years old, I was overcome by a sudden desire to write. To do so, I wanted to see more books, read more, and learn from them. Sensing my eagerness, one of my brothers proposed to take me to the bookstore. I was brimming with excitement when we returned home, clutching my new purchase. But as I bounded up the stairs, I caught a glimpse of my mother in the orangery. The soft daylight streamed through the glass roof and the many glazed windows and doors, illuminating her face. She was lying in a hospital bed, still and serene. Aching yet helpless, I ran into the sanctuary of my room upstairs.

Inspired by the new book, I powered on my computer and opened a blank document, thinking I could just start, go for it —write a book myself. As the cursor blinked, I pondered what life without my mother would be like. In Dutch, I typed, *A life without a mother—how would that be?*

Suddenly, my oldest brother's voice resonated through the house, calling for my father to come downstairs. Uncertainty gripped me as I contemplated whether I should follow him.

But a few moments later, some invisible force compelled me to abandon my seat and join them, as if I were being pulled up and my legs moved on their own. Descending with measured steps, I felt my body cool as I saw my brother and father gathered next to my mother's bed, their eyes fixed intently on her face.

A heavy weight settled upon me, casting a shadow over the room. My mother lay there, her breathing still audible, a fragile rhythm amidst the backdrop of silence. A storm of questions raged within me, a tempest of confusion and doubt. I turned to my father, seeking answers in his gaze.

"What's going on?" I asked.

With a deep breath, he uttered the words that shattered the fragile illusion I had clung to. "Mommy is dying."

It felt surreal, incomprehensible. My mother's light, usually full of vitality and verve, was dimmed by the suffocating grip of cancer. Her appearance now barely resembled the radiating woman she had always been.

As I took in every inch of her, my other brother burst into the room, his facial expression translating the seriousness of the situation. Together we stood quietly, tears forming in our eyes as we intensely gazed at her chest, searching for any sign of breath, transmitting to her the love and connection we shared.

The room grew more and more silent as we bore witness to the final chapter of my mother's journey. Each passing breath faded into a slower rhythm, carrying profound significance, like a fragile melody bidding farewell to a beloved symphony.

In the stillness of that poignant moment, I grappled with the weight of the inevitable, the irreversible. The breaths grew fainter... And then, in the gentle release of her final exhale, my mother surrendered to the embrace of the infinite.

On that somber February 1st, in that precise moment, the heavy clouds above us seemed to break apart, allowing a radiant beam of sunlight to pierce through the veil of darkness —It was as if the heavens had paused and nature itself was acknowledging the departure of my mother, as she embarked upon her journey beyond this earthly existence. This ethereal glow illuminated the glass roof above us, casting a gentle warmth over the room as we stood beside her cooling body.

The interplay of light and shadow mirrored the emotions that coursed through our hearts. She was no longer with us, but she was no longer in pain.

When I returned to my bedroom hours later, the document I was creating—the book I had started—was still open, its blank pages waiting patiently. I stared at the screen for a while, then shut it off. Something told me that one day, when the time was right, I would reopen that document. But first, there were wounds that needed time to heal, scars that needed space to fade. I couldn't go there now—not yet.

Fast-forward ten years, to a train in a faraway land—was now the time? I could hear the whispering echoes of a past waiting patiently to be told, but also the conflicting voices wrestling within me. *No,* one of them protested, *it is too painful, too exposing.* But another, filled with determination and longing, countered with an emphatic *Yes*! *No better time than now to finally give it a place!* The internal debate raged on, the pendulum swinging back and forth between doubt and conviction.

The train continued to hum, the vast landscape continued to pass by. *It's in my hands*, I thought as I gazed out the window. It would take courage, heart-wrenching vulnerability, and an unwavering belief in the power of storytelling... Ultimately, it was up to me.

Feeling refreshed, I closed my eyes and I made a silent promise to myself: one day soon, I will put pen to paper.

•

As the new day was dawning, we disembarked the train after another long stretch, having spent a surprisingly comfortable night aboard the Trans-Mongolian Express.

"Where do we go now?" I asked Z, who had arranged a car service in Ulaanbaatar.

"I'm sure someone will be waiting for us," she said.

Uncertain, nonetheless, about who would be sane enough to pick us up at such an early hour, we sought refuge from the cold inside the main hall of the train station.

"Do you think someone will be holding up a sign with our names on it?" I pressed.

"Not sure," Z replied.

Two and a half hours later, we were still standing inside the station. We had momentarily ventured outside to look for our transportation, but our search had been in vain. Restlessness and distress began to set in as I observed the sleepy crowd: families huddled together, some children wrapped in blankets, elderly couples leaning on each other, and lone travelers standing in dark corners, clutching their backpacks.

"The car! It's here!" Z suddenly squealed.

Whether we had miscalculated the time zones once again or they had forgotten about us, we finally found ourselves in the SUV, heading toward Hustai National Park.

Despite my desire to rest my eyes, I wanted to witness the transition from the city to the vast Mongolian steppe. Initially, the landscape was a haphazard sprawl of concrete buildings and tangled wires.

"This time of year, people burn everything they can find," our driver observed as we navigated a particularly cluttered neighborhood.

"They burn...their belongings?" I asked hesitantly.

"Yes," he replied. "Tables, chairs, books—even the shelves the books are on. Anything to stay warm."

Shocked, I peered out the window. The need to burn all your possessions for the basic necessity of heat underscored the harshness of winters in these lands. I was barely beginning to comprehend what it took to survive here.

Three hours later, we reached Hustai National Park. The rolling steppe, usually dotted with green in warmer months, was now covered in a blanket of snow, turning the vast expanse into a quiet, white wilderness that stretched as far as the eye could see. We hopped out of the car near an arching welcome sign. The only sound we could hear was the soft crunch of our footsteps as we walked up to the campsite, where a cluster of roughly fifteen yurts and a small concrete building stood grouped together, flanked by mounds of snow.

The guide took us to our yurt—a white tent with a circular structure and a wooden frame, traditionally called a *ger* and used by nomads for many centuries. As we stepped inside, the faint metallic smell of the electric heater greeted us, the small machine working overtime to generate warmth.

We walked around the circular room, each of us choosing a bed after admiring the red wooden frames with colorful carvings and running our hands over the soft fleece blankets. The space felt cozy and inviting—a perfect refuge.

After settling in, we headed to the small building on the

edge of the camp for breakfast. There we were welcomed by a man who led us to our table and brought us a plate with a cookie, an egg, two slices of cheese, an apple, and some slices of cucumber and tomato. It might not have been a lavish feast, but this was probably the best meal I had enjoyed in days.

Just as we were appreciating our after-meal tea, a rickety van arrived to take us on a sightseeing tour of the national park. Z and I jumped in the back, and as the driver sped along the snow-covered dirt road—up and down hills, around sharp bends—we were bouncing in our seats and bumping against the doors, laughing until we cried. Every few minutes, we hopped off to take pictures and contemplate the landscape—fields of frosted snow dotted by boulders that cast chilling yet magical shadows in the setting sun.

Back at the campsite, we could have used a shower, but our yurt lacked one, so we went without. The idea of venturing out for just five minutes to reach the communal bathroom, only to return with wet hair that would freeze into icicles in seconds, sent shivers down my spine. The temperature had plunged to a bone-chilling -24 degrees Fahrenheit—a new personal record.

Yet the arrival of the cold, silent night revealed a surprising beauty: in the absence of lights, millions of stars burst forth in a dazzling explosion of celestial particles. I had engaged in stargazing in various locations—from the mountains of the French Languedoc-Roussillon to the deserts of Morocco and Egypt—but this night sky exceeded all my expectations. There was something about its intensity and brilliance—the way the Milky Way stretched across the heavens like a river of light, so densely packed with stars that the blackness seemed nearly vanquished. It left me feeling both humbled and inspired. If only I possessed the artistic talent of Vincent van Gogh, I would have seized a brush and canvas to immortalize this view of a starry night.

In the morning, we set out on horseback with a ranger. Three small ponies, covered in thick fur, were saddled up with makeshift rope reins. Despite my lifelong experience with horses, this ride required a significant shift in perspective. Instead of guiding horses through the precise movements of dressage, I had to place my complete trust in these ponies, the true experts at navigating this rugged terrain.

The cold was another struggle, but fortunately, Z lent me an extra pair of pants and some knitted leg warmers; from her seemingly bottomless backpack, she even produced an extra pair of Timberland boots. Fully layered up, I mounted my furry companion, ready to seek out the mythical Przewalski horses in the vast white wilderness.

In a gentle trot, we waded through half a foot of snow, traversing up and down rolling hills as gazelles darted in the distance and snowscapes stretched endlessly ahead. Whenever I glanced directly at the snow, its reflection blinded me. So I closed my eyes, listening to my breath, the horse's breath, and the squish of the snow; feeling the sun warm my cheeks, and the wind, ever-present, turning my eyelashes into frosty sticks. I was gliding. Such a profound peace.

But the peace didn't last long. As we descended a slope, the ground beneath us shifted suddenly, prompting me to open my eyes to support my horse. For a brief moment, I hesitated to follow the steep straight path, but my horse clearly wanted to take it. In our indecision, we slipped and started sliding downward.

In moments like these, you simply have to commit—it's in the midst of uncertainty that mistakes are made. My horse and I quickly regathered ourselves, regaining control.

"You good?" Z asked as she slowly zigzagged down to lower ground.

"All good!" I shouted back, lovingly patting my little horse on the neck.

He was a spirited creature—fearless, strong; neither snow, steep hills, nor wild animals could faze him. He misstepped, he recovered. I wanted to be more like that horse, getting back up so easily every time I fell.

A few minutes later, as we were riding over a gentle rise, we finally spotted them. A small herd of no more than ten Przewalski horses—locally known as *Takhi*—stood peacefully in a valley, grazing on the dry grass that poked through the snowpack as they sought out patches of edible ground.

We halted roughly three hundred feet away from them and simply watched. About twelve hands tall at the shoulder, with a reddish-brown coat and a white muzzle—these nearly extinct animals were moving their hooves and brushing the snow with their mouths in such a collected, gentle way, as though the dry grass was their friend, not their fodder. *Such a privilege*, I thought, *to see them with my own eyes*.

A wave of nostalgia hit me. Old memories and doubts threatened to pull me away from the present. I strained to hold onto the fleeting serenity. *Stay here, Manon. Stay here.*

During lunch back at the campsite, we noticed a convoy of SUVs pulling in. Until then, we had been the only guests at the establishment, so our host approached us to explain what was going on and ask us a question.

"May I introduce you to our minister of environment and tourism? He is visiting and would love to meet you."

"Of course!" Z and I replied, excited to find out the reason for the minister's visit.

The delegation walked into the small communal building where we were eating, shaking the host's hand and greeting us with soft nods.

"You're traveling here from the Netherlands?" the minister asked.

"Yes, Sir," we confirmed, smiling.

"Our Ministry of Environment and Tourism would like to extend a warm welcome and express our deepest gratitude for the significant contribution the Netherlands has made to our nation," he declared.

Z and I looked at each other.

"Without your government's efforts," he continued after a brief pause, "the *Takhi* population would be extinct. We are forever indebted to you."

Unaware of the specifics, but thrilled nonetheless, Z and I nodded respectfully. It turned out that our country had recognized the significance of the Przewalski horse—the only breed never successfully domesticated—and the threats it was facing. In response to that, the Netherlands had launched a remarkable reintroduction program, gathering Przewalski from zoos around the world and, once the herds were "nature-ready," flying them back to Mongolia to be released into the wilderness. Who would have known?

After a one-night stay in Ulaanbaatar, we were back at the train station, waiting to embark on the last leg of our Trans-Mongolian journey. The city felt strangely foreign after our brief escape into the far-reaching, silent wilderness. It was as if time had shifted while we were away—or maybe my mind had. Out there, in the openness, with only the wind and the sound of our footsteps breaking the silence, life felt simpler, more deliberate. I could have stayed there much longer, letting nature cleanse my soul, unhurried. The idea of such isolation, yet profound connection to the land, tugged at me, offering a glimpse of a life far removed from the relentless pace of the city. Time—the thing I always felt there was never enough of—belonged to me again, unbound by schedules or obligations; just the endless sky, the rolling steppe, and air so fresh I could breathe again.

As I stood on the platform, I pulled my journal out of my pocket and quickly jotted down my reflections, my mind drifting to my dear friend Lazlo back in Holland. The concept of time—and my struggle to grasp it—wasn't quite the same for him. Every day was a gift, a reminder that it had to be lived. I looked at the empty track in front of me, feeling guilty for not being able to just enjoy every moment I was given. Despite his rare and terrible disease, Lazlo remained steadfast a beacon of optimism. In the whispers of the wind grazing my cheeks, I could almost hear his voice, full of wonder and excitement, urging me to keep pushing forward.

"I told you that I would be living vicariously through you on this adventure. So you simply have to tell me everything all the time. Otherwise, I won't know what I don't know!" he had exclaimed before I left.

I closed my journal and put it back in my pocket, his words echoing in my mind as the sun began to lighten the station, melting some of the ice that had formed on the platform overnight. I smiled, knowing I would update him as soon as I could.

At 7:15 a.m., right on time, our train—a deep-green metal snake, reminiscent of a Märklin model train—rolled into the station. *Here we go again*, I thought as the train hissed to a stop.

"China, here we come," Z said with a grin, nudging me toward the door.

"Lead the way," I laughed, gallantly extending my arm to let her board the train first.

She was eager to show me her China—the country she had fallen in love with. It was her passion that had brought us here.

When I thought about it, picturing myself as a dot on the world map, it was hard to believe I had come this far. I *was* in Mongolia. I *was* on my way to China.

China

After another thirteen hours on the train, it finally came to a halt. Outside, my eyes caught sight of yet another station, another platform, and another group of uniformed officials, blurred by the flakes of snow falling slowly from the sky. The Mongolia-China border checks were as fastidious as the Russia-Mongolia ones. For someone who grew up in border-free Europe, the endless procedures were wearing thin—not because they happened, but because of how long they dragged on. However, there was a small silver lining: we were granted permission to step off the train. It wasn't much, but the chance to breathe fresh air felt like a gift.

Sharing our four-bed cabin with a friendly backpacking couple—one was Australian, the other American, also made the passport control ordeal less tedious this time. Like us, they had started in Moscow, but they had taken more time for the journey, which meant there was plenty to talk about while waiting to be cleared by immigration.

The more they recounted what they had been through together, the more their journey fascinated me. I had never witnessed such companionship and respect between a young couple. Watching them reminded me that when you find your person, you grow strong together and become capable of running through walls. But it also triggered memories of my ex-boyfriend—or rather, of how he dismissed some of my dreams as crazy and unrealistic. He would never have gone on a trip like this, and neither would I, were he still in my life. Had we still been together, chances are I would have remained stagnant, never reaching for more.

Eighteen hours after the border crossing, the train screeched to a halt again, signaling our arrival in Beijing, the buzzing capital of China. We said our goodbyes to the young couple, grabbed our backpacks, and stepped out into the hazy air of the metropolis.

Out of the blue, while standing on the platform, I was overpowered by a wave of relief, so much so that I considered dropping to my knees and kissing the ground in gratitude that this part of my journey was over. This leg of the trip was a significant milestone, and although there was still much ground to cover, I felt proud of myself for having made it this far—and for keeping a positive attitude and stay open-minded along the way. I found a bench, sat down, pulled my journal out of my backpack and wrote: *Veni, vidi, vici—I came, I saw, I conquered. After twelve days, 143 hours on the train, and six different time zones, we finally made it to Beijing!*

From Beijing Railway Station, we walked to our hostel. Tucked away on a quaint side street adorned with Chinese paper lanterns, the building stood out as a hotspot for travelers. With double red doors and bicycles parked out front, lined with many small international flags, it had a welcoming, lived-in feel. My body warmed at the prospect of laying on a proper mattress and dozing off. But that would have to wait, because Z, eager to show me her China, the country she had spoken about so passionately for so long, insisted on taking me out for dinner.

Our first destination was the renowned restaurant chain, Din Tai Fung. Nestled within a sprawling mall, the place boasted sleek, modern décor and an open kitchen where skilled chefs meticulously prepared their famous dumplings. The sight of neatly set tables and the soft, ambient lighting sent a flutter through my heart; it was comfortable, warm, inviting. As soon as we sat down, the waiter brought us a basket on a floor stand to keep our handbags elevated—a practice, we were told, rooted in the belief that placing bags on the floor invites bad luck and financial misfortune. He then brought a teapot of lukewarm water, adhering to Chinese medicinal traditions aimed at detoxifying the body and enhancing circulation.

Z took charge of ordering, and before long, our table was filled with an array of steamed dumplings, garlicky spinach and other delectable dishes presented in charming bamboo serving baskets. And, of course, a refreshing cold beer. As my taste buds savored each morsel, I recalled my mother's joking words: "It's like angels peeing on my tongue." Indeed, this meal had transcended the mundane—especially after so many instant noodles and oatmeal.

Unfortunately, the pleasant memories of our delightful meal at Din Tai Fung were sullied on the walk back to the hostel. In the dimly lit street, a man squatted down on the sidewalk, mere feet from where we were walking, casually defecating as if it were the most normal thing in the world. He sat in plain view, unfazed by passersby, facing the street. We wondered if such behavior was common—despite plenty of public restrooms around. Granted, these often consisted of nothing more than a hole in the ground concealed behind a door, so perhaps it wasn't all that surprising that some people chose the sidewalk instead.

The following day, S, a dear cousin of mine, landed in Beijing. As she had recently gone through a breakup as well, I thought it would be a good idea for her to shake things up, so I had encouraged her to join me on my journey for a while. Initially, she had protested. "Cuz-y, all your plans—that's not for me," she would say. Yet eventually, curiosity had gotten the better of her and so she decided to give it a try. If anything, it would be a trial run for her dream of packing up everything and moving to Ibiza, a place she had talked about for years.

I remember how we went to the Chinese Embassy in The Hague to apply for her travel visa. I was excited about her joining me, especially since we had always been very close. She was like a sister and my love for her was boundless. I couldn't bear to see her sad or unsure of where life was taking her. I knew in my heart that she had the courage to accomplish anything she set her mind to, if only she would take the leap and embrace the powerful force she truly is.

As Z and I stood in the Beijing Airport arrivals hall waiting for her, I watched the flight information display closely, counting down the minutes. Then we spotted an enormous backpack with long, slender legs approaching us.

"She's here!" I exclaimed.

S quickened her pace, her face beaming with joy. I held her —and her oversized backpack—in my arms for quite some time, feeling proud she had taken this leap of faith. And just like that, our formidable trio was formed—three Dutch girls in their twenties ready to take on the world.

Our first mission? Keeping my cousin awake long enough to adjust to the local time and prevent her from succumbing to jet lag. After some brainstorming, we decided to visit the Summer Palace—the historic retreat of the Chinese emperors. Known for its serene lakes and imperial gardens, this palace complex is located just ten miles northwest of central Beijing.

After entering, we weren't sure where to start. It wasn't just a palace; it was a collection of reds, yellows and greens, with pavilions, halls and temples decorated with delicate floral motifs and swirling dragons, all surrounded by lakes, bridges and gardens. As curious as I was about what might be inside the structures, I kept walking through the enchanting forest-like landscape—a garden from a different time. A thin layer of snow pressed under my feet and the gray sky reflected off the water. I tried to imagine what this place would look like in spring, with blossoms in pinks and whites and the lotus pond coming to life. But even on this winter day, I could see why emperors sought refuge here, escaping their residence at the heart of Beijing—the Forbidden City.

As the day transitioned into night, we sought an authentic culinary experience to complement the rich history we had absorbed. We decided to treat ourselves at a traditional Hot Pot restaurant. The concept sounded intriguing—a fondue but with the twist of cooking meats, fish, and vegetables in a flavorful broth right at our table. As someone who doesn't eat fish, I insisted on having my own pot filled with vegetable broth to experiment with. Across the table from me, S and Z were feeling more adventurous, willing to try anything they encountered. However, in a country like China, known for its diverse culinary offerings, I questioned whether this was the right place to push boundaries.

Sitting there, peacefully simmering my mushrooms and bok choy in the vegetable broth, I watched their plate of shrimp on sticks being placed on the table. *Gross.* I tried to mind my own business at first, but then I glanced over and swore I could see one of the shrimp's tiny legs move. S and Z seemed oblivious.

"Um... I think those shrimp might still be alive," I casually pointed out, gesturing toward the plate.

"No way!" S called out, picking up a stick.

In an instant, the shrimp began to frantically swim through the air, flailing its legs wildly. Z jumped up and nearly dove under the table. I couldn't stop laughing, but even with tears rolling down my cheeks, I was disgusted at the scene.

Excusing herself, Z waved at the waiter. "Are these shrimp still alive?"

"Yes," the waiter responded matter-of-factly.

"Well, we would prefer them not to be."

"Yes," the waiter repeated, perhaps not fully understanding her request.

"Yes?" Z questioned.

"Cook in pot," the waiter clarified, again, matter-of-factly.

"I have to cook them alive?!" S jumped in.

"Yes."

"I can't bring myself to kill a shrimp!" S exclaimed, looking at the still-moving shrimp on her stick.

Slightly sliding my vegetable broth closer to me, shielding it from any additional surprises, I watched as the live shrimp were swiftly taken away from our table, never to return. *Poor little creatures.*

The following morning I woke up feeling refreshed and eager for what I anticipated to be the highlight of our trip to China: the Great Wall. A bus picked us up at the hostel and took us to Mutianyu, forty-two miles from Beijing, where we would explore a specific section of the Wall. The sky was vibrant blue, and the sun greeted us warmly. But it was still November, and the temperatures were still glacial, so I made sure to wear my Siberian faux-fur hat.

Arriving at a small tourist information center, we stepped off the bus to find the Wall obscured, perched high on the ridge above the village. Consulting a map, I was surprised that, despite its size, it remained hidden from view at this angle.

When we began our ascent from the village, taking a much newer, tree-covered staircase, I imagined the countless historical events the Wall had witnessed. We were told this section was one of the best-preserved and most carefully restored. According to the map, we started in the middle and could choose to walk either toward Tower One or Tower Twenty, covering a distance of approximately one mile in each direction—a mere fraction of the 13,000 miles of Wall sections still in existence.

Then I saw it. The sheer height and length of its ancient stones stretched out in both directions, undulating over ridges and valleys like a great, winding dragon, disappearing into the horizon. Overnight snowfall had transformed the top of the Wall, with rolling hills and layers of mountain peaks forming a glistening white blanket in the sun. The air was crisp and pure, and as I looked at S and Z, I could see they were just as struck by the view as I was.

Walking and hiking, we navigated up and down, dancing with the hills, the path ultimately leading us higher toward Watchtower Twenty. Gaining altitude, the snow-covered rock turned to ice, transforming the smooth ramps and uneven steps into a skating rink. Equipped with sturdy hiking shoes, Z dashed ahead, relishing the adventure. S and I hesitated for a moment, eyeing our footwear—my trusty red Nikes among them. But then we thought, *When will we ever be here again?!* We pressed on, clinging to the side of the Wall, slipping and sliding, but feeling magnetized—and motivated—by the panoramic views.

The final watchtower accessible to the public came into sight, each step increasingly heavy as we strained not to slip back down. Our progress halted at a near-vertical staircase—small steps, little to hold on to. Determination battled fear as I imagined breaking my neck if I attempted to reach the top. I crawled, digging my nails into the icy steps, occasionally grabbing a hand—or a leg—for support. Trembling, I finally reached the top and picked my knees up from the ground.

A handful of people waved their national flags, standing with a glimmer in their eyes. The many layers of mountains all around brought different shades of blue and white, adding depth to the scene. I turned around and traced the path I had just taken with my eyes, from tower to tower, unable to fathom how this was ever built. And where I stood, it wasn't the end—just the end of where I was going to go, the end of recent restorations, to make it less dangerous. But it wasn't safe either, especially in winter. I glanced back at the steep staircase I had crawled up, its icy steps mocking me like a fiend laughing at my struggle. I sat down, not trusting my feet, and began scooting down, step by step. I thought the cold would calm me, but adrenaline lit my skin on fire. I didn't stop until I reached the bottom, gripping it with both hands and feet.

It was a little over a mile back on top of the Wall, retracing our steps. What had been mostly up was now mostly down. A few fellow adventurers clung to the brick edges, trying to steady themselves. It wasn't a busy day and the vibe among those braving the icy conditions was amicable.

"This is going to take me all day at this rate," I muttered, pausing, legs shaking.

"What are you going to do now, cuz-y?" S asked, curiosity piqued.

I sat back down in the snow, suddenly seeing a clear path ahead. Taking a plunge, I chose an unconventional approach and decided to slide down. It wouldn't get me off the Wall, but it would definitely get me closer to the village staircase, even if just a few inch.

"Oh no, you're not!" I heard Z yell from further ahead.

"Oh, yes, she is!" S giggled and pulled out her phone camera to capture it.

"Off I go!" I shouted, feeling the bumps as I slid down, wheezing past fellow tourists who were carefully descending step by step.

After safely reaching the village below via the much less treacherous modern staircase, we had a bit of time before the bus took us back to our hostel. We found a quaint little restaurant for tourists, nestled by the bus stop: round tables with rotating serving plates presented us with delicious treats, accompanied by glasses of warm water. To our surprise, there was even Wi-Fi available.

I hoped my phone would ping as soon as I connected—and it did. I messaged *him* straightaway, recounting how the day had been so far.

The German:

**AM I THE ONLY ONE WHO THINKS YOU
ARE A LITTLE BIT CRAZY?**

RUNNING AROUND ON YOUR RED SHOES?

IN THOSE CONDITIONS?!

**I AM GLAD YOU MADE IT BACK WITHOUT
BREAKING ANY BONES.**

You and I both.

•

We sped forward as we bid farewell to Beijing aboard the famous high-speed bullet train—covering the eight hundred miles to Shanghai in just five hours. I was excited about the trip but also sad, knowing Z and I would soon part ways.

Having traveled together for the past two weeks and undergone joyful—as well as challenging—moments, it was fair to say our bond had strengthened. Shivering side by side in Siberia had reinforced our resilience; daydreaming on long train rides had deepened our conversations; sharing rooms had cultivated our intimacy. No doubt I was going to miss her. But by now, I was also aware of the inevitability of goodbyes when traveling. I was beginning to learn to hold on tight to what you have got while you have it, and then release it, gracefully and gratefully, when the shared time is no more.

But we still had time together. And time together, however little, was yet another thing that travel was making me even more conscious of. So when we stepped out of Shanghai Hongqiao Station that evening, I tried to stay in the present moment. I looked at my friend, calm and smiley, then I looked at my cousin, deep in thought. And then I looked at the city: a seamless blend of past and future, where ancient dynastic architecture stood side by side with futuristic skyscrapers and avant-garde art installations. Glancing at a side street could transport me hundreds of years back in time, while stepping into one of the city's many modern buildings could send me a thousand years into the future. The juxtaposition of elements created a surreal fusion that was both inspiring and mind-boggling.

At the hostel, red and yellow lanterns swayed gently from the ceiling, while plants spilled over shelves and windowsills. We took in the messy yet charming atmosphere, where wallpapered walls mixed traditional and modern art, creating a lively contrast.

Settling into our room, S immediately disappeared into the shower while Z and I unpacked.

"This is where we part ways in a few days," I said, glancing over at her.

She smiled. "I'm excited to be back here, but it's going to be quiet without you."

I nodded. "We've had a good run."

She looked at me, her voice softening. "I'm really going to miss this."

"It's been something special, hasn't it?" I sighed. "But it isn't over yet."

The next day, a hostel guest mentioned a Masquerade event at an exclusive nightclub. Through social media we secured an invitation and were added to the guest list. Knowing our trusty Nikes and Timberlands wouldn't cut it for the fancy dress code, we rushed to a nearby shopping center to snag a new outfit. We ended up at H&M, where the prices and selection were exactly the same as any other H&M I had ever stepped into—a safe, affordable choice.

Back at the hostel, giggling with excitement, we prepared for our glamorous night out. I slipped into a silver skirt, paired with a black lace top and black heels, while S and Z opted for elegant little black dresses. Looking into a tall mirror, we stood together—a trio of confident, stylish women.

As I took in our reflection, something stirred within me—a flicker of femininity I hadn't realized I had been missing. The elegance and grace that had taken a backseat to the demands of the road felt suddenly restored, as if I had reclaimed a piece of myself.

We hopped in a cab and gave the driver the address. He drove us to the Huangpu District and parked in front of a twenty-four-floor skyscraper near the river. Entering the building at street-level, we were momentarily disoriented by the large hollow lobby. Then we noticed a long table filled with an array of masks and accessories near the elevators, staffed by only a hostess and security personnel.

"You can pick out your masks and accessories here, and then we'll escort you upstairs," the hostess explained with a gentle smile.

Z opted for a shimmering silver mask, elbow-length, sexy red satin gloves, and a feathered hand fan in a vibrant shade of red. S held a black feathered fan and a striking silver and black mask. I gravitated toward a delicate black lace mask that matched my lace top. It was like stepping into a scene from Audrey Hepburn's *Breakfast at Tiffany's*.

The elevator ascended, the distant sound of music growing louder, and a deep bass rhythm permeated the air. The doors opened, revealing a dazzling entrance illuminated by a blue-hued tunnel, with a huge aquarium on one side filled with real sharks swimming gracefully within. The atmosphere was electric; the pulsating music prompted us to hit the dance floor immediately and embrace the magic of the moment.

A heterogeneous crowd, masked faces dressed in sharp suits and cocktail dresses, converged on the dance floor, moving in synchrony through the haze of a dim, seductive glow to popular tunes. Tall shot glasses with a mysterious gold liquid seemed to materialize out of thin air, while bottles of Dom Pérignon champagne flowed generously.

The place now resembled a Fitzgeraldian *Great Gatsby* extravaganza: opulent, passionate, intense. Female dancers in sparkling outfits, sequins catching every flicker of light, made the bartop their catwalk, spinning their feather shawls. Beyond the expansive glass windows, the city's skyline unfurled like a diamond necklace draped across the throat of night. It was a world of abundance, where anything we desired was readily available. The air was thick with the scent of money, lust, and the faintest trace of something sweeter—like a dream on the verge of coming true, or perhaps on the verge of shattering. It felt good; I felt alive. But it was also disorienting. Even the most gilded dreams must eventually give way to the light of day. I made my way back to the entrance to catch my breath.

Leaning against the aquarium, watching the tranquil blue light envelope the tunnel-like hallway, I noticed how isolated I felt—despite being surrounded by all these people. Seeking a sense of connection, I reached for my phone and messaged the German. Just then, a man with a striking Venetian mask and a dark suit approached me from behind.

"May I have the pleasure of a dance?" he asked in a deep, baritone voice.

"Thank you kindly, but no," I replied confidently.

"A woman as captivating as yourself shouldn't be standing alone, gazing at the sharks," he continued.

"I quite like the sharks," I retorted.

"I'm sure you do, but they won't sweep you off your feet, as you truly deserve," he tried again.

"I think I am involved with someone," I replied, this time not that confidently.

"You think? I suggest that the man who holds your heart figures it out, knowingly."

There was an air of mystery about him, reminiscent of the *Phantom of the Opera*. His calm presence was oddly soothing, yet my loyal heart wouldn't allow me to entertain any further interactions. Noticing that his attempts were pointless, the kind stranger bowed gracefully before disappearing into the darkness. I stood alone once more, captivated by the sharks.

The following morning, while I sat in the hostel lobby waiting for Z and S, a roommate we had briefly met came stumbling through the door with a girl on his arm—a girl that definitely was not the girlfriend he had told us about the day before. That sight, together with my encounter with the masked man the night before, made me question loyalty.

To me, it seemed that people were disloyal everywhere I turned. But what did being loyal even mean? And if they were disloyal, were they suffering the consequences of being so? Was I suffering the consequences—or rather, reaping the rewards—of being loyal? Or was I being loyal to an illusion, clinging onto something that wasn't meant to be? Something that wasn't mine to have?

In any case, I could see clearly how, amidst life's multitude of questions, loyalty to ourselves and personal growth must take precedence. In which case, misplaced loyalty might be holding me back.

WHY ARE PEOPLE NOT MORE LOYAL?

I messaged him without thinking, without considering the weight of the question or the time difference.

The German:
ACH MANÖNNCHEN...

SOME ARE.

SOME ARE NOT.

**AS LONG AS YOU DO WHAT YOU FIND
TO BE OK...**

**YOU SHOULDN'T CARE ABOUT OTHER
PEOPLE'S BEHAVIORS.**

I didn't care all too much about other people's behaviors, but I cared about my behavior—and his behavior. His heart seemed guarded, wrapped in walls that kept me at arm's length, and I found myself constantly grappling with the question of how he truly felt about me. It was as if we were dancing on the edges of vulnerability, with only fleeting moments of sweet words and kind gestures that gave me glimpses of what *could* be.

Despite the uncertainty, however, we grew closer with each passing day, spending hours on video calls, exchanging dozens of messages every day. He was attentive, his presence was comforting, and I could see he cared about me. Nevertheless, two questions gnawed at me: Was I being greedy for wanting more than what he could offer? Did I genuinely believe in a future for us?

The girls and I had one more full day and night in Shanghai together, so we headed to The Bund—a promenade in a historical district along the Huangpu River, known for its impressive view of Shanghai's towering skyline.

Although the weather was fine, a thick layer of smog floated in the air, seemingly strangling the skyscrapers that dotted the surroundings. The gray skies and gloomy atmosphere seemed to mirror my own emotions for, out of the blue, existential doubts crept in.

Looking at the murky river flowing by and the faint outlines of boats drifting, I wondered what was the point of being here; what was the point of carrying on? Adventure, self-discovery, healing, clarity—my purposes were coated by something, strangled like the buildings.

"Cuz-y, look! Smile!" my cousin's energetic voice snapped me back to reality.

She bounced around with a huge smile, beckoning to a woman and her husband, who pulled out his iPhone to take a picture of us.

"Yes, yes! Everybody come see!" S shouted, gathering a crowd around us.

"Erm, what are you doing?" I asked, slightly uncomfortable but unable to suppress a smile.

"It's Paris Hilton!" she called out to the crowd, pointing at me.

"These people are never going to believe that," I chuckled.

But apparently I was wrong. S directed a line of men with cameras and phones as they snapped pictures of me posing with their wives.

After a few minutes, she wrapped up the photoshoot. "Paris has to go now! Bye!"

"You're a clown, you know that, right?" I told her as we walked away giggling, arm in arm. "A clown. But I love you."

We kept strolling along the promenade, chatting, smiling, and joking, while others captured their moments by the waterside.

Suddenly, I noticed that my melancholy had vanished—even though the smog still blanketed the sky. I looked at my cousin, at her big smile and the skip in her step. Ever since we were teenagers, she had had this unbelievable talent for finding joy even on the darkest of days. Her funny, outgoing character made her stand out in any crowd, attracting people like bees to honey—and the whole Paris Hilton episode was a reminder of that. She spread laughter wherever she went and I admired her for it.

The following afternoon, the three of us made our way to the train station. We grabbed some food from a nearby café, its hectic atmosphere a stark contrast to the bittersweet mood settling in. As we sat at a small high-top table, we shared soggy sandwiches and noodles. Laughter was punctuating the air as we reminisced about the unforgettable memories we had created. With each bite we took, the weight of the impending goodbye loomed larger. Z was staying in Shanghai for a few months. This had always been the plan—the whole reason we came up to do this specific part of the trip together—but now that the moment arrived, it felt like leaving someone behind.

"Next time you see me, I'll be fluent," she laughed, her eyes sparkling with determination.

But beneath the laughter, there was a flicker of sadness that mirrored my own.

When it was time to part ways, outside the station, Z pulled me into a tight embrace.

"Thank you for allowing me to bring you to China," I whispered, tears brimming in my eyes.

She held me a moment longer before pulling back with a grin. "Promise me you'll take care of yourself."

S, sensing our melancholy, tried to lighten the mood. "Don't worry, we'll all figure out what we need, and then we'll reunite," she said, optimistic as ever.

My cousin wrapped an arm around my shoulders, offering silent comfort as we watched Z walk away, her figure slowly receding into the crowd.

Roughly fifteen minutes before the scheduled departure of our overnight train, S and I headed to the platform. The train, with its sleek exterior, looked more modern than the Trans-Siberian Express but was not nearly as futuristic as the bullet train we took from Beijing. Excited about the prospect of an overnight trip and giving S a little taste of my past couple of weeks, we showed our tickets to one of the officers standing near the open door.

"No," he said firmly.

"No?" I asked, puzzled.

"You, late," he explained with a stone face.

S and I exchanged looks. The doors were wide open, and the platform clock indicated we still had twelve minutes left before the train's departure time. We wondered if we had misinterpreted something. The tickets were almost entirely in Chinese.

"Fifteen minutes before departure, no more entry," the officer stated.

"What?!" I exclaimed in disbelief.

I attempted to plead and negotiate, both nicely and not so nicely, to no avail. My ears rang, my heart throbbed, my throat clogged. We were less than five feet away from the door—which was open—and we were not going in. *How were we supposed to know?!*

Back at the ticket kiosk, I managed to get some of our money back, and before I knew it, S and I stood outside the train station again, staring into the night with no place to go. It took me a minute to collect my thoughts. Realizing there was no other option, we started brainstorming a new plan. Our first priority was to find a safe place to get a grip on the situation.

We spotted a beautiful five-star hotel nearby and the staff was kind enough to let us sit in the lobby and connect to Wi-Fi. A quick online search showed there was a flight to Hong Kong at 7:30 a.m. the next morning. I had never heard of Juneyao Air before, but after reading a few reviews, it looked safe enough. Besides, it was cheap, so I purchased two tickets.

Next, we stepped outside and hailed a taxi bound for the airport. On our way, I felt a sudden urge to lift our spirits and somehow prepare us for what was going to be a very long night. I asked the driver to make a pit stop at The Bund, where we had walked the day before. This time, the place was dark and there was nobody around. Yet the smog was gone—or imperceptible at night; the skyline covered with dazzling lights. I watched Shanghai glimmer as the taxi sped along. *There is beauty around us*, I thought to myself. *Even when there are challenges. Even when things don't go according to plan.*

•

In the rideshare from the airport to our hostel, Hong Kong presented itself in a subtly distinct manner compared to mainland China. It was like trying to catch a fleeting thought —an intangible quality. As we crossed a bridge, I noticed the blue waters below and the sleek cityscape ahead. There was something familiar about the tall buildings rising against the steep hillsides, almost Riviera-like, evoking memories of the Côte d'Azur, though much more modern, with an aura of high technology pervading the scene.

Our Uber driver mentioned that the majority of people here spoke Cantonese, unlike the mainland where Mandarin was widely spoken. Hearing him talk about his homeland there seemed to be a distinguishable and palpable sense of pride in being a resident. Though it's technically a part of China, he said, most locals would assert that it's more like its own country. It operates with a degree of autonomy that sets it apart.

After a short power nap, we headed to Din Tai Fung, which was quickly becoming our go-to spot because of their xiaolongbao and sautéed garlic spinach. Originally a Taipei chain, they took it to the next level in Hong Kong with one of their branches even earning a Michelin star. Somehow it was still surprisingly affordable compared to what we knew such a recognition meant in Europe.

We then set off toward Times Square, which, although smaller than its counterpart, buzzed with the same exuberance —a hub of activity where shoppers flock to upscale boutiques and trendy shops. Amidst the lively atmosphere, a colossal AT-AT from *Star Wars*, meticulously constructed from LEGO bricks, stood towering over the scene. The upcoming release of a new *Star Wars* film had set off a global promotional wave, and it was fascinating to see many of the world's iconic cities partaking in this shared excitement.

Navigating the pedestrian-friendly area in the Causeway Bay district, the energy of the crowd was infectious, making it easy to feel at ease. People around us enjoyed the Christmas lights twinkling in the reflections of our eyes and the neon lights casting their glow on Christmas ornaments hanging from the trees.

The night embraced us with a gentle warmth as we kept strolling. Having traveled considerably further south, we were now stepping into the beginnings of summer in December. Unlike Shanghai's colder, brisker air, Hong Kong's climate was milder, more temperate. The heavy Canadian coat I had been wearing was slowly becoming an unnecessary accessory.

Knotting my coat around my waist by the sleeves to let the pleasant evening touch my skin, we took Fashion Walk back to our hostel. A golden bathtub filled with Moët & Chandon champagne bottles literally invited visitors to "bathe in luxury," as high-fashion art installations followed one after another. When a Christmas tree made entirely of Kurt Geiger stilettos came into view, I paused and looked around. I had seen many holiday decorations in the coldest of cities, but right there, breathing in the warmth, was the first time I really stood still thinking about where I would be for the holidays. It was going to be the middle of summer in the Southern Hemisphere—quite different from the dark, cold days of December we had always known.

S, standing next to me, had a similar realization. "It's going to be a very different holiday season this year, cuz-y," she said, grabbing my arm.

The following day, one of our roommates recommended we visit Victoria Peak, also known as The Peak. Standing at 1,811 feet on the western half of Hong Kong Island, it proudly holds the title of the tallest hill on the island. Only a twenty-five-minute bus ride from our hostel, we arrived at the Peak Tram Station. There, we boarded the Peak Tram, a funicular railway renowned for its steep ascent and panoramic views.

As we settled into our seats in its historic wooden interior, the tram rattled to life, our noses pressed against the large windows. In operation since 1888, it was the first cable funicular in Asia, so we were told. Lurching forward, the world outside transformed. The lush tropical vegetation—ferns, ficus, palms, and orchid trees—slowly gave way to tall buildings emerging from the greenery.

Steadily climbing higher during the less-than-ten-minute ride at a steep incline, the city began to unfold beneath us, skyscrapers gliding past at seemingly impossible angles. With our ears popping and slight nausea settling in, my mind struggled to make sense of the distorting perception of verticality. This illusion, we learned, was a visual phenomenon where the high rises on the right side appeared to lean toward The Peak as we climbed, caused by the tilt of the tram and our reclining position.

As we reached the top, now at a bird's-eye view, we took in the scene, droplets from the clouds gently grazing our skin; it felt much chillier than anticipated at this elevation. Even with the low-hanging clouds, we could still see the skyscrapers nestled against the hillside, their glass and concrete facades reflecting the muted light, with the contours of the tall buildings across Victoria Harbour emerging from the mist.

Seeking refuge, we entered the avant-garde Peak Tower and strolled around its hallways past the many restaurants and shops. In one of them, S caught sight of a small bowl of fruit for sale.

"I haven't had fruit since I left Holland!" she exclaimed, clutching the bowl.

I laughed, but it was true. Being on the move constantly, it was often difficult to find fresh fruit, especially in places where we couldn't read signs or menus—unlike here, where much was in English.

Spotting an artisan café next door, we decided to pop in for a hot chocolate. With steaming cups in hand, we stepped back outside, savoring the rich, creamy chocolate as we strolled around the tower. The mist continued to cover the city and the air remained moist. I looked at the towering landscape below and beyond and imagined how jaw-dropping the views must be on a clear day, with the sun illuminating the vibrant colors of the city and the azure waters of the harbor.

Back at sea level, we spent the afternoon leisurely strolling around, opting to walk instead of taking public transport back to Times Square, S still clutching her precious bowl of fruit. Determined to savor it in the perfect spot—a park or a lush garden, somewhere with meticulously manicured hedges and artful statues, a true sanctuary—we followed the tram line along the road to orient ourselves. If we kept an eye on that, we couldn't get lost. Our plan seemed to work; however, the tram line cut through many streets, not parks or gardens—at least not where we were walking.

Then at a turn, S spotted a temple, hoping it would provide the perfect spot to peacefully enjoy her fruit. She dashed across the road, and I quickly accelerated to catch up with her. It was in the midst of this maneuver that I heard a sudden squeal.

I paused, and there it was—her once-cherished fruit bowl, now a bunch of exotic fruit strewn across the asphalt.

We burst into laughter, her hysterical reaction causing us both to nearly lose control. Still, deep down I saw the incident as a reminder: life's opportunities must be seized when they appear—for if we wait too long, they might be gone forever.

On our last day, we learned about the Symphony of Lights, an event that transforms the skyline of Hong Kong every evening at 8 p.m., featuring a synchronized performance of lights on the buildings. Eager to experience it, we crossed the harbor for the best view. Sometimes, stepping back allows you to see things from a different perspective. We took the subway to Tsim Sha Tsui, navigating through the bustling streets of Kowloon until we reached the Avenue of Stars. The dark, sparkling waters framed the cityscape of Hong Kong Island, poised to dazzle the night with its brilliant display.

Anticipation filled the crowd as we gathered along the lengthy promenade. The skyline alone was a stunning sight, but then something magical happened. A brief moment of darkness swept over the scene, silencing the chatter of the crowd. And then, one by one, the towering skyscrapers turned into an array of colors, like a choreography of lights. The synchronized dance of these illuminated buildings, set to the backdrop of traditional Chinese melodies and modern electronic beats, made the crowd hush.

Basking in the afterglow, we crossed the river once more and headed to the infamous Lan Kwai Fong district for some beers. The streets were a non-stop party, a delightful kind of mayhem, bright, blinding neon signs beckoning tourists into their lively establishments. Unlike the meticulously curated clubs and nightlife we witnessed in Shanghai, Lan Kwai Fong felt refreshingly accessible to everyone. There were no guest lists, exclusive elevators, or extravagant hallways with dazzling shark tanks—just straightforward, good old-fashioned fun for everyone.

Still buzzing from the night out, I was caught by surprise when, upon returning to the hostel, I received the following messages:

The German:
HONEY!

I'M CRAZY ABOUT YOU!

AND I MISS YOU...

SWEET DREAMS!

It was a somewhat rare display of emotional expression from him, leaving me rather perplexed, wondering what had prompted this sudden outpouring of affection. Was it my subtle distancing since arriving in Hong Kong? Or merely the passage of time? The growing physical distance between us? Or, perhaps, something entirely different? I couldn't be certain, and while the messages made me feel good, they also cast a shadow of uncertainty. As his return to Germany for the holidays approached, I felt an increasing urge to fly there and have a face-to-face conversation. Not to give up on my journey, but as a way to gauge if the connection still held strong in person, if it was worth the continued investment of time and energy. I had to know.

The next morning, we headed to Hong Kong International Airport where a flight awaited to take us first to Sydney, Australia, and from there to Queenstown, New Zealand.

It was a significant day—December 5th, a day celebrated in the Netherlands as *Sinterklaas*. This holiday, distinct from Santa Claus, featured Saint Nicholas, Santa Claus' brother, who resided mostly in Spain and made a yearly visit to the Netherlands with his steamboat for a few weeks, delivering presents through the chimneys. Or so I had been told.

If you behaved well, you could leave your shoe by the fireplace with a carrot for the horse, and the next morning a gift would magically appear—some days. This anticipation lasted until the final night, when a loud bang on the door signified a visit. My mom and I would huddle together, eagerly gazing out of the bedroom window.

We would search the rooftops, our eyes wide, as if trying to catch a magical moment. The darkened streets held an air of mystery, lit only by the moon, and every rustle of the wind seemed like a hint of something extraordinary.

It was a tradition, a time when imagination soared and the boundaries between reality and enchantment blurred. That small window, a portal to a world of childhood magic, made every December 5th unforgettable. We would all gather, singing songs and writing poems for each other. Those days were gone too.

Thankfully, S always had a knack for lifting my spirits. At the airport, she found a Christmas tree in our departure terminal—a little festive surprise in the midst of our wait.

"Give me your shoe," she said, sounding quite mischievous.

"What do you need my shoe for? Are you expecting *Sinterklaas* here at the airport?" I smiled.

Placing both our right-footed Nike sneakers under the tree, she stuffed them with our plane tickets to Australia and New Zealand.

"Check it out!" she exclaimed. "It might not be a chimney, but hey, it's our version. These are the presents we're giving ourselves this year!"

PART THREE

BREAKING POINT OF THE SOUL

New Zealand

After nearly ten hours flying from Hong Kong to Sydney with Qantas, a quick plane change, and another three hours with Air New Zealand, we soared over the stunning mountainous landscapes of the South Island. New Zealand had always held a special place in my heart. First because I'm a huge *Lord of the Rings* fan. But also due to its name—Dutch cartographers were inspired by a province in the Netherlands called *Zeeland* —which created a peculiar kind of familiarity that, somehow, bridged the incredible distance between my origins and this country on the opposite side of the globe.

As we descended into Queenstown, the plane shuddered and jolted through turbulent air, with narrow valleys and the Southern Alps below creating unpredictable wind currents. Despite the bumps and sudden drops, I couldn't tear my eyes away from the view. Rugged mountains reached skyward, their jagged silhouettes forming a striking contrast against the clear blue sky. Some peaks were crowned with snow, glinting in the sunlight, while Lake Wakatipu shimmered below like a sapphire. The turbulence was intense, but the unfolding landscape, like a living postcard, made every bump worth it.

Only a fifteen-minute ride from the airport, the hostel was situated on a hillside along the gleaming lake, from where a short, pleasant walk led us to the heart of Queenstown.

As I strolled along the tranquil shores, a light breeze carried the scent of pine and earth. A clean silence wrapped around me, broken only by the gentle lapping of water and the distant tune of an acoustic guitar. Here, the weight of my worries felt miles away, unable to catch up.

The rhythm of life slowed, and a thought crossed my mind: *I could live here.* In this place, so far removed from everything I had known, I envisioned a life unburdened by the chaos and clutter of the past. The isolation was mine to have, free from stressors. With the fog in my mind dispersing, I inhaled the crisp, invigorating air by the water's edge.

It was a proper Sunday—unhurried, serene, familial—and it seemed like the entire community had convened on the central beach, lugging barbecues and coolers brimming with refreshing drinks. A mellow medley of music flowed from multiple speakers, harmonizing with the echoes of laughter that danced in the air. The festive atmosphere was infectious, and we were eager to partake in the collective joy.

We went to a small supermarket and bought a freshly baked baguette, a selection of spreads and some ice-cold Dutch beers, setting up for our impromptu picnic. Bags in hand, we found an empty spot on the beach, where the sand was a mix of fine grains and smooth pebbles. The light, earthy color of the shore contrasted with the dark waters of Lake Wakatipu. We took off our shoes, the ground cool and slightly rough beneath us.

Settling down amidst the lively crowd, we opened our picnic, passing the baguette and spreads between us, savoring the ice-cold beers. Watching the families and friends packed tightly around us, I felt a connection, as if we were part of a community that simply loved life. S and I exchanged smiles, both lost in the simplicity of the moment.

"I wish every Sunday could be spent like this," I said, glancing at the distant mountains. "Or every day, really."

The thought of living here, so far from everything I knew yet feeling so familiar, crossed my mind again.

"Do you think it would ever get boring?" she asked, sighing.

"I don't think so," I shook my head. "Not with moments like these, not when the world feels just right."

The following day, I was blindsided by a sudden mood swing. Despite being aware and appreciative of where I was, I could also see that the accumulated fatigue and emotional baggage from the journey was beginning to catch up with me. All I really wanted was to cocoon myself in the warmth of the bed.

S, on the other hand, was planning an exciting adventure with a man she had met a few months earlier. In six weeks, they would head to Thailand, where an exquisite, romantic island with luxurious amenities awaited them.

While I genuinely felt happy for her, seeing her plan materialize also sparked a cascade of thoughts about my own situation. I wondered why her man was willing to take such a bold leap—flying all the way from the Netherlands—while the German seemed perfectly content to keep things casual, exchanging daily snippets of vulnerability without ever hinting at taking a step forward. The contrasting experiences painted a vivid picture, causing me to yearn for a deeper connection, more profound conversations, and, ultimately, reassess the path this relationship was taking.

I wanted someone who could share not just my stories, but my life. Someone who would stand beside me through the ups and downs, no matter how difficult or uncertain it might get.

There and then, it became clear to me: I needed to find the strength to open up my heart and have an honest conversation with him about where we stood and what we both wanted.

I called him and shared my plans—I intended to travel to Germany in two months time so that we could see each other in person again. Importantly, I emphasized that this wouldn't mark the end of my adventure; it was just a chance for us to gain clarity and take our connection to the next level.

I suppose a part of me was expecting him to be as excited as I was. I mean, how often does someone offer to traverse the globe just to be with you? However, his response left me unsure and a bit perplexed.

He said he wanted to see me, but the way he worded it made it seem like he didn't want me to give up my dreams for him, as if he was leaving me the choice to decide if all of this was truly worth it. On the one hand, it felt noble and honorable, I suppose. On the other hand, it was far from what I had hoped for. In any case, we left it at that for the day.

That night, sleep escaped me. Instead of waiting for the following morning to revisit my decision, I felt an urgency within. I wanted to go to Germany, to take that leap and see where it would lead. My mind was a whirlwind of thoughts, a clash of desires and fears, because, many times, I had told myself that I wouldn't give up anything for a guy.

I remembered the panic I felt on the Greyhound bus and the unease on the Trans-Siberian train. I didn't want to be in this state, but I couldn't shake off these feelings. He had become intertwined with my journey, a kind of safety net that I had put in place along the way. I needed to know what we could be if we had one more day together.

What if there was something beautiful left to explore? Or what if this was meant to be a lesson, a chapter of growth? Perhaps he was there to help me find balance as I ventured into new countries, a supportive presence in spirit.

Every new place I traveled to, I felt a sense of security knowing I could reach out to him upon arrival, share my experiences. Throughout our conversations, it was like he eased the weight of processing my mother's death and the struggles of my teenage years. He knew just what to say in the hardest moments, bringing me comfort—a welcome escape when memories and emotions threatened to engulf me.

But I also had to be honest with myself. Was I using him as a shield, a way to avoid fully processing my past? Was I relying too much on the prospect of love instead of working on my own healing and self-improvement? Either way, I had to see him again. Every fiber of my being was screaming a resolute *go*.

At the crack of dawn, I noticed an incoming message on my phone—at last, a voice note from him.

"Darling, right now I am getting ready to start my day, but first, I need to talk to you about your plans to go to Germany. You're investing so much in us, and I'm sure I can't give you everything you deserve. Imagine you coming to Germany. I'll be really busy, and you'll be spending hundreds of Euros to visit me, probably only to be disappointed because I'm not the man you need me to be. Even if we see each other again, we both knew there wasn't a future for the two of us when we first met, didn't we? I know I'm not the best friend by saying this, but I don't want you to hate me. That can't happen to us, so I think it's better that we don't meet in two months."

As I listened to his message, the bed I was lying in ceased to exist, and I felt like I was floating through space. My phone screen was the only source of light in the room, surrounded by darkness. A tear rolled down my cheek as I processed his words. "I can't give you everything you deserve," "I am not the man you need me to be," "no future." His voice resounded in my mind, more tears fell. I began to sob softly, trying not to wake anyone else.

How could he sound like he never saw a future while I felt so differently? And how dared he suggest that it would be better for us not to see each other, just so I wouldn't *hate* him? "That just can't happen to us." What the hell is happening to us? What does this mean? How is today different from yesterday? And *friend?!* "Not the best *friend*" right now? Is this a joke? Is this the end, then?

I listened to his message again. His voice sounded different from all the other times we had spoken. He sounded rational and distant. Not in the mood to answer him with a voice message, I responded with a text.

UH...

I AM SO CONFUSED RIGHT NOW.

I THOUGHT YOU LIKED ME.

Still with a lump in my throat and fighting back tears, I tried to regain my composure as I read his response.

The German:
MANON, I LIKE YOU!!!

I LIKE YOU A LOT.

Yeah, not helping, I thought to myself. *How can you "like me a lot" and say all that at the same time?* I could see how going all the way to Germany just to figure out if any of this was real was a bit much for most people, but I also couldn't waste more time investing in something that was nonexistent. Nevertheless, if he really didn't want to see me, then that was it. I had to move on.

I AM GOING TO CLIMB A MOUNTAIN.

Those were the only words left within me. Perhaps the challenging trek to the peak of Ben Lomond that morning would offer me the clarity I so desperately needed, keeping me from prolonging this conversation and potentially uttering words I shouldn't.

It was still morning when S and I disembarked the gondola, after ascending nearly 1,500 feet, and stepped onto the dirt track. We turned a hard left, with the trailhead for our three-and-a-half-hour hike to the summit just around the corner, and the towering 5,735-foot mountain presiding over it all.

The path started off wide and well-trodden, lined with hardy tufted grasses and scattered rocks, gradually narrowing as it wound through patches of forest. The scenery was beautiful—dappled sunlight filtered through the canopy of trees, creating a play of light and shadow on the ground. Yet I was grumpy, mulling over the conversation earlier that day. Deep down, I knew the answer was simple. The German was right. I deserved more, and he couldn't give it to me.

We trudged on, reaching the saddle—a broad, windswept expanse, covered in thick tussock grass that stretched out like a green carpet, nestled between lower slopes and the peak. The higher we went, the more barren the vegetation became, and the heavier the atmospheric pressure weighed on me.

I noticed my strides growing more forceful, my breath wavering. I watched my red Nikes navigate the changing path, from smooth trail to loose rocks. I felt sad, deflated, detached.

Nearing the final stretch toward the summit, my thoughts suddenly halted. I stopped walking and finally glanced up, taking in the surroundings. The wind grew sharper, and the sun beamed on my cheeks.

"They're taking the hobbits to Isengard!" I caught myself saying much louder than I had intended.

S gave me a puzzled look.

"Cuz-y, did you just snap out of your thoughts to quote *Lord of the Rings*?" she asked, grinning.

Indeed, I had. Looking around, I felt like I was stepping right into the world of Tolkien, or at least Peter Jackson's cinematic vision of it. The *Lord of the Rings* holds a special place in my heart, mainly because the films were released during the final years of my mother's life. I vividly remember the weekend she fell ill, a weekend my brother A and I spent together in Amsterdam. We watched the first and second films at his house, and then in the evening, we went to the movie theater to catch the third installment. Little did we know, that week would lead to a scan revealing my mother's brain tumor.

As her illness progressed, I clung to those movies. They felt like a link to the last day of my life without worries, a magical world where some could live forever. For my birthday a few months later, as she bravely battled her cancer, my mother gifted me the One Ring and the Evenstar, an Elvish necklace symbolizing eternal love.

To me, they weren't just two pieces of jewelry; they were tangible reminders of the love, strength, and hope that my mother wanted to convey. These were the last gifts she gave me before she passed away.

"I know those films are important to you," S said, as if reading my mind, "I miss her too, you know."

I looked up at the sky, drawing strength from my memories —pictures of time in my mind. The brief pause fueled my grit, my determination reinvigorating me.

As we resumed our ascent, I finally felt connected to the world around me—and to my body—again. Soon the relative incline turned more vertical, prompting us to use our hands and scramble our way to the top, toward a large, flat and somewhat angular slab—the pinnacle of Ben Lomond. With one final push, S and I climbed up and sat down on the cold schist.

Up there, protected against the chilly wind by my Canadian coat, I looked down at the varying shades of bright blues, lush greens, and the earthy tones of rugged terrain. Hills rolled in every direction, the lake weaving its way through; wisps of clouds adorned the sky, drifting like fluffy sheep. *Nature is so majestic*, I thought. *And I am just a small part of it.*

Suddenly, the weight of daily concerns seemed insignificant. It was as if the universe had conspired to bring me to this very moment. I felt a surge of energy, a primal urge to unleash all the emotions that had been building inside me for years. A part of me wanted to scream, releasing all the pain, frustration, and hurt that had been accumulating.

I stood up, as if I could spread my wings and take flight, the breeze gently caressing my cheeks; my hair dancing around my face. At that moment, I reinforced once again that the power to shape my future rested solely with me. The decisions ahead were mine to make—and that's exactly what I was going to do.

•

A five-hour bus ride took us from Queenstown to Dunedin— a city renowned for its strong connections to Scottish culture, nestled on the southeast coast of the South Island, adjacent to the Otago Peninsula.

As soon as the bus pulled up to Dunedin Railway Station I understood why the building was the most photographed in the entire country: dark basalt and light limestone formed a striking contrast against the lushest green hedges, accentuating the asymmetrical structure with a tall clock tower rising prominently on one side.

After settling into our hostel, we went for a walk—as usual. We came across The Octagon, a lively square, technically an octagon, lined with inviting, nostalgically European looking terraces, and took a seat at one for a meal and a glass of wine.

People strolled leisurely, glancing at teenagers jumping into a fountain and capturing playful moments on their phones, bright bouquets of flowers in hand. Laughter and chatter filled the air, broken only by the occasional splash of water. There was a graduation day vibe in the air, and we speculated if indeed something was going on at the nearby university, the oldest in the country.

When we returned to our hostel after our outing, I received unexpected messages. From my ex-boyfriend. Our sparse and sporadic contact, mostly around small life updates and getting our affairs in order—bank accounts, money he owed me as we went our separate ways—hadn't been very pleasant. But it was his birthday.

X:

HEY, IN ALL SERIOUSNESS. I AM SORRY FOR HOW I TREATED YOU.

YOU DIDN'T DESERVE ANY OF THAT.

I let myself drop onto my bunk bed. A small glimpse of the guy I had once loved revealed itself. Where had that guy been?

I remembered a moment right before my trip. I had stopped by his parents' house, for I had promised to return the silverware his mother had given us. He had moved back in with them, and he was home when I stopped by. His mother and sister warmly welcomed me and invited me in for tea. They even called upstairs to ask if he wanted to join us, but he declined and remained in his room. When I left, his mother asked him once more if he wanted to bid me goodbye, and his response was a simple "No." After six years together, he couldn't even muster a hello or goodbye.

Ironically the best months we had ever had were in the final year of our relationship. I hadn't mourned the loss much; I didn't even shed many tears after parting ways with him for the last time. My tears were for the frustration of being deceived, for returning to an empty apartment in Amsterdam after I believed I was building a life with someone, and for the uncertainty of starting over, questioning whether I would find love again. But my tears were not for losing him. I had shed enough tears over him leaving, then begging to come back, during the years he was in my life.

But now, as he apologized, I was reminded of many good things, too. No matter how turbulent our relationship had been, he had given me a home when I didn't have one, providing support in times of despair. I wondered, if he hadn't been unfaithful, would I have had the courage to walk away?

I closed my heavy eyes, grateful for choosing my own path and prioritizing my happiness over staying entangled in a relationship where I clearly never belonged. I pondered how many more men might become fleeting chapters of my journey, each one imparting a lesson before I could move forward, until that stable, "let's grow old together" kind of love—a love with someone who wouldn't hinder my progress and wouldn't flinch when I declared my readiness to board a plane for them.

The following morning, we went on an excursion around the Otago Peninsula. We had been told about the astonishing wildlife in that area; the Yellow-eyed Penguin held a particular fascination for me, and I hoped to catch a glimpse of one— hopefully more than one—and many of the other animals this region is known for.

Our first stop was a clifftop viewpoint near the Royal Albatross Centre at Harrington Point, offering a sweeping view of the cliff's rugged extension, where a lighthouse stood at the edge, gazing out over the vast ocean below. The sky bore a somber shade of gray, laden with clouds, and the ocean rested in a deep, dark hue.

"This is the home of the world's sole mainland colony," our guide pointed at the horizon.

Then I saw, observing them in their natural element, heaps of Royal Albatrosses soaring gracefully, their massive wings effortlessly slicing through the wild currents of the sky. They screeched, glided, swooped down to the cliffside, and took off again. We, the audience, fell silent and watched.

After being ushered back onto the bus, a short drive took us over rolling hills dotted with grazing sheep before stopping at a penguin conservation reserve. From a gravel parking lot, we descended a hiking trail toward the ocean and followed our guide through native bushland.

Just as we rounded a bend, there it was: a single Yellow-eyed Penguin, the rarest in the world, standing in the middle of our path. We halted and hushed, trying not to disturb it as it cleaned its coat. Our guide quietly led us around.

I hadn't expected to spot one so readily, so far from the shore. Nor had I expected to see such diversity of wildlife—not only a waddle of penguins, but sea lions, fur seals, and birds—when we finally reached the beach. I could hear comments and the click of cameras; everyone was fascinated by the simple yet somehow majestic sight of wild animals lounging around. Among them, I spotted a baby fur seal, and then another, and another. My entire body warmed up; my mind cleared. Cuteness soothed the soul.

As I stood there, listening to the gentle yet assertive rhythm of the waves, it suddenly occurred to me that this was the Pacific Ocean. Exactly three months had passed since I heard the sound of these waters, back on the sands of Santa Monica Beach in Los Angeles. Three months—a seemingly brief span of time, but oh, how much had transpired. I recalled that day in Santa Monica when I leaped for joy, running through the shallow water near the shoreline. And here, once again, I found myself leaping in the sand, not out of exuberance but in celebration of the immense distance I had covered—both in miles and self-discovery.

The moment lingered with me even as we returned to the hostel, high on the day. Then, my phone pinged.

The German:
GOOD NIGHT, MY MANÖNNCHEN.

Still calling me "yours," huh? I thought. I didn't belong to anybody. I belonged to the world.

•

Cromwell was a quick pit stop on our way to Mount Cook. The bus dropped us off at the edge of town, far away from our hostel and with no taxis in sight. Walking amidst rows of crisp apple trees, each glistening in the sun, we spotted a car in the distance.

"Should we stick our thumb out and try hitchhiking?" S asked, a mischievous grin on her face.

Hitchhiking had always been on my bucket list, and if there was ever a place in the world to give it a shot, New Zealand seemed like a safe bet. Still, my mind was clouded with horror movie scenarios. Before I could even second-guess, S waved at the approaching vehicle.

"Where are you girls headed?" a friendly-looking young couple asked.

We gave them the address of our accommodation.

"Jump in the back!" the woman said with an inviting smile.

We hopped into the car, placing our trust in the universe and in the couple. They were backpackers like us who had rented a car, which did ease my nerves a bit. As we drove, they asked about our trip, making small talk that further calmed me, though not completely.

Nothing happened. They dropped us off in front of our lodgings and drove away. But even after we were safe and sound in our room, I could still feel the adrenaline coursing through me. They were complete strangers, after all, and we were in an out-of-the-way place.

The following day, we took another bus to a wooden lodge at the base of the Southern Alps in the town of Mount Cook—a delightful private haven overlooking the mountain of the same name, furnished with neatly made split-king beds and even a proper bath. Needless to say, our first order of business was indulging in a luxurious hot soak, accompanied by multiple cups of tea and cookies. We then retired to bed; the next day would require energy. I dozed off quickly and peacefully, snug beneath soft linens, but not for very long.

Vivid dreams interrupted my slumber, weaving a complex tapestry of emotions that I struggled to navigate. A recurring figure emerged—my mother. She appeared in fragments, distant and elusive, like a faded memory. I could see her, but her voice remained muted, lost in the vast expanse of my subconscious. I woke up. Somehow, I knew that these dreams reflected thoughts and feelings inside me.

I clung to the darkness behind my closed eyelids, hoping to unravel the meaning behind my mother's presence. What was she trying to tell me? The question lingered, blending with the remnants of my dream. I yearned for clarity, for a glimpse into the messages my unconscious mind desperately attempted to convey. But for now, all I could do was keep my eyes shut, hold on, and wait for the answers to reveal themselves in due time.

Jolting awake a few hours later, I felt the dwelling weight on my soul and knew I had to walk it off. After a quick breakfast to refuel, S and I grabbed our purses—not our daypacks, as we probably should have—and stepped out the door, ready to find adventure.

Confident in our ability to navigate, we set off on a nine-and-a-half-mile out-and-back hike, with the weather gray and the Alps snow-covered. It took us thirty minutes to walk through a grassy stretch from our lodge to the trailhead of the Hooker Valley Track, which wound its way through the valley to Hooker Lake, offering stunning views of Mount Cook, or *Aoraki,* as it's known in Māori, New Zealand's highest peak.

The cloudy sky cast an eerie atmosphere over the trail, and small snowflakes began to fall softly. But it didn't dampen our spirits, on the contrary. We twirled around with our coats zipped open, catching the delicate flakes on our noses as we looked up, embracing the weather rather than letting it wear us down.

"How far do you think we should go?" S asked, trying to catch a snowflake with her tongue.

"All the way, cuz-y! We go all the way," I replied, swirling around once more, as if the weight on my shoulders would fall off if I kept spinning.

We hiked along, crossing suspension bridges that swayed underfoot, with rivers and streams popping up at every turn. It was unpredictable, exciting. Finally, Hooker Lake unfolded ahead of us. The snow had stopped, revealing patches of blue in the sky as we settled on two small rocks, the wind sweeping over the matte mint-green lake.

"Do you think we'll ever find it?" I asked my cousin.

"Find what?" she replied, turning to me.

I shrugged my shoulders. "The place we're supposed to be. A place where I can leave the pain behind."

"If anyone can make their dreams come true, it's you," she said, her eyes sparkling with warmth.

"Dreams," I mumbled. "If only I knew what that meant."

•

In the morning, we headed back to Queenstown, where we would catch a flight to Auckland the next day. Everything was going smoothly, though not exactly according to plan.

We had accepted a ride from three Australian backpackers —whom we met at the lodge—in a camper van, and canceled our safer, yet much less adventurous, bus ticket. Aside from embracing the spirit of the moment, there were no further surprises as we reached our accommodation and checked in.

That is, until we stepped into our dorm to find two British lads, dressed as comic book characters Batman and Robin, standing in the center, their backpacks overflowing with costumes. They immediately began thrusting their colorful, neon-lit costumes at us, pestering us to come join them for a party. But we were not in the partying mood and had a flight to catch the next day, so we declined. This didn't mean we were immune, however. One is never immune when sharing a room with seven other people.

Around midnight, Robin stormed into the room, bumping into furniture, growling and mumbling, undoubtedly under the influence. He hurled himself onto the lower bed of the only unoccupied bunk and, as his intense breathing suggested, fell asleep right away. The room's occupants collectively rolled over in their beds, muffling groans of annoyance and adjusting their blankets in an attempt to recapture sleep. There was a moment of silence. Then, the door opened again.

"Ah, that must be Batman!" I exclaimed.

"Bat-man?" a girl with a French accent asked as she entered the room.

Everyone who was now awake laughed.

Holding a flashlight, she walked up to her bed, where she found Robin passed out. She shed all her clothes, and lay down next to what appeared to be a stranger to her. My eyes met those of a girl across the room. She looked as bewildered as I was.

Once the atmosphere settled and the room returned to darkness, we tried to get back to sleep. But not for long! A strange rattle came from outside, prompting someone to turn the lights on. I sat up, grabbed my glasses to see better, and directed my gaze toward the open window of our ground-floor room. Batman was hanging halfway through it, only his head and shoulders visible above the sill.

"Just use the door, man!" someone shouted.

Batman struggled to pull himself up but didn't want to use the door. Flailing his arms, he tried to wriggle through.

The girl with the French accent got up—still unclothed—and helped him inside, prompting the comic heroes to share a bed before climbing up to the bunk above them.

At about three in the morning, unable to get back to sleep, I went up to the common room to call the German. When I told him about my night so far, I felt my phone buzz. On the screen, a message from my cousin, who had been sleeping on the bottom bunk below me.

S:
HE PEED ON ME!

I hung up the phone straight away and ran back to the room, fuming. I slammed the door open and saw S, even angrier than I was, sitting on the edge of her bed while Robin stood next to her, holding his private part, with more of his pee than I ever wanted to see all over the place.

Scanning the room, my eyes landed on my red Nikes, my faithful companions, completely soaked. A greater force took over, and before I knew it, my hand landed on Robin's face.

Given that there was no staff on duty, we had to wait until the hostel owner arrived to report what happened. Obviously, he was not happy, especially considering that neither Batman nor Robin were guests—they had been trespassing. He called the police.

"She beat me up!" Robin squealed, his finger pointing at me when the officers arrived.

"He peed on my cousin and our belongings in the middle of the night, officers," I countered.

"They did what?" said the female officer. "They urinated on you and then you struck him?"

Admitting to a police officer that you have hit someone can be a precarious move—who knows the local laws?

With a subtle smile, I looked at her and, in a hushed tone, whispered, "Maybe."

"Good girl," she responded with a quick nod, then shifted her attention to Batman and Robin.

"I believe you lads owe these girls some compensation," the other officer declared sternly.

Batman mumbled something under his breath then handed over a one-hundred New Zealand dollar bill.

"That should help you girls clean up and maybe grab a meal," the male officer said, both officers grinning before settling into their police vehicle and driving away.

•

The ocean breeze tousled my hair as we gently navigated the waves. Even in Auckland, the northernmost major city and the country's largest, we found a way to combine the concrete buildings with the natural beauty of nearby Waiheke Island, just a forty-minute ferry ride away. I let my eyelids fall shut, surrendering to the gentle sway—a soothing lullaby from the Hauraki Gulf—as the afternoon sun warmed my skin, the scent of sunscreen adding an exotic touch.

Armed with a picnic basket brimming with a freshly baked baguette, assorted cheeses and plump olives, we disembarked and headed for one of the white sandy beaches. Sailboats dotted the horizon as we settled in, toes buried in the sand. I felt a surge of self-assurance, mastering the art of navigating the unknown, which led me to this spot with its turquoise waters and few others around.

My moment of peace shattered as my phone buzzed—a local prepaid SIM card now made navigating easier, but it also tethered me to my device in places I didn't want to be connected. It was an incoming video call from the German.

I shifted my camera to show him my view, expressing how at ease I felt. New Zealand offered a perfect blend of cityscapes and nature, a balance of noise and total silence I didn't know I craved.

"Tell me, will you end your journey in Germany?" he asked, catching me off guard.

"Well, why don't you tell me?" I shot back, dripping with sarcasm.

Nearly two weeks had passed since he advised against my visit to Germany, yet here he was, posing this question. His fluctuating emotions were as confusing to me as they were to him—indecisiveness choking our conversations.

We maintained a daily dialogue, as if nothing had changed, yet everything had—except my heart, which still raced every time I saw him on my screen.

"I can see how you look at me," he said, breaking the silence between us. "Your eyes reveal more than your words ever do."

At a loss for how to continue, I silently ended the call and shifted my gaze to the clear waters where a boat caught the wind in its sails. As I watched it glide toward the open ocean, determination began to form within me. Suddenly, I understood what inevitably lay ahead: Germany, a journey that might signify some clarity or perhaps it meant the end.

The choice was clear. Life is too short to bear the weight of wondering *what if.*

•

The flicker of torchlight carved shadows into the night as we walked up to Tamaki Māori Village, a place steeped in the customs and heritage of New Zealand's indigenous people—one of the main experiences of Rotorua, in the center of the North Island. As we gathered at the entrance, a young man from our group was chosen to represent us in the *powhiri*, the traditional Māori welcoming ceremony. He stepped forward, towering Tawa trees looming overhead, the air thick with anticipation.

A warrior wielding a staff-shaped wooden weapon with a pointy end stood before us, his face and chest covered in traditional tattoos. He made sharp, intimidating sounds, his eyes bulging wide. With a commanding gesture, he beckoned all the men in our group to step forward. They complied, stamping their feet and moving their arms in unison, tasked with protecting the women. Then, with a swift motion, the warrior laid down his weapon. Our representative accepted the challenge by picking up the token laid before him—a sign of peace.

With the formalities complete, we were invited deeper into the village, passing a small river to an empty clearing in the woods. The atmosphere grew tense when five Māori warriors, their bodies and faces adorned with intricate tattoos called *moko*, appeared before us, wearing traditional black garments. For a moment, they were silent, still, their intense, unwavering eyes locked onto ours.

Then, with a sudden burst of energy, they erupted into a powerful *haka*. Their voices boomed in unison, rhythmic chants reverberating through the trees. Feet stomped the earth, sending vibrations through the ground as their faces contorted into fierce expressions—tongues extended, eyes wide with passion. It displayed strength, unity, and ancestral pride, challenging and welcoming us simultaneously—the raw energy nailed us to the damp forest floor.

After the electric spectacle, we were ushered into a small amphitheater, where we learned more about the culture, dances, fights, weapons and survival techniques.

Adjacent was the dining area, where wooden tables groaned under the weight of roasted meats, vegetables and sweet bakes. The smell of earth and fire mingled with the scent of the feast as we learned that most of the food was cooked underground using a traditional *hangi* method; red-hot stones heated in a pit infused the ingredients with rich, smoky flavors.

"Kia ora," an elder woman greeted us, her flax skirt swaying as she approached.

She leaned in, her tattooed face close to my cousin's, who instinctively took a step back.

"What's this all about?" S whispered, uncertain.

"Kia ora, meaning hello or welcome, is more than just a greeting in Māori culture," she spoke softly. "It's part of the *hongi*, a ritual that involves gently pressing our noses together, sharing the breath of life."

As the elder closed her eyes and pressed her nose to my cousin's three times, they exchanged breaths in an intimate moment, nearly close enough to feel each other's heartbeat.

S then turned to me. *"Kia ora,"* she said, pressing her nose to mine, deepening my connection and admiration for New Zealand.

Eager to explore more, we set out the next morning on a day tour to see some of the region's highlights. Our first stop was Lady Knox—a geyser with a small spout atop a white silica mound, surrounded by tall evergreen trees that created a lush, natural enclosure.

At 10:15 a.m., right on the dot, a park ranger poured a bag of surfactant—a soap-like substance—into the geyser's narrow opening. A chain reaction broke the surface tension between the hot and cold layers below, rapidly building pressure.

Our eyes fixated on the spout as plumes of water soared sixty-five feet into the air. Standing at that fenced-off platform, the vertical water glistening like a spraying champagne bottle, I thought about how Lady Knox was provoked to reveal her strength and potential.

"Do you think she wants to be awakened every day?" I turned to S.

"Sometimes all we need is a little push, cuz-y!" she replied, her hands mimicking the motion. "Just a nudge."

I returned my gaze to the geyser, watching as it rose up intensely but not violently. It was breaking free rather than bursting forth.

We then headed to Wai-O-Tapu Thermal Wonderland—a geothermal park renowned for its colorful hot springs, often seen as manifestations of the earth's energy and, by some, considered sacred. To explore the area, we set off on one of the walking paths of the Thermal Track, weaving our way through bubbling mud pools, steaming vents, and bright green and yellow mineral deposits crusting the rock edges.

Halfway through, the Champagne Pool stretched out beside us, a large hot spring heated by geothermal activity, bursting with orange, green and blue hues. Its name comes from the pool's constant effervescence. However, it's not a pool for swimming—the water is far too hot and contains toxic gasses and minerals, making it dangerous to enter.

We sat there for a while, at a roped-off edge, watching it bubble nonstop. It reminded me that, deep down, there was always movement, growth, transformation—something I could draw strength from.

Afterward, the bus brought us to the permanent *Lord of the Rings* movie set, Hobbiton, located just outside the town of Matamata, marking the end of the tour. As we walked along the same paths as Frodo and Gandalf, through lush green hills and winding sand trails, the meticulous design of the hobbit houses became apparent: their round, brightly colored doors inviting us in. I had expected the set to be small, the houses tiny, in keeping with the hobbits' stature. But to create the illusion that hobbits were small, the houses had to be quite large for filming. Conversely, some were designed smaller—not for hobbits—but to make the wizard Gandalf appear towering in comparison. It made the landscape even more whimsical and allowed my thoughts to wander freely.

Strolling through Hobbiton made me feel closer to my mother, as if she were walking beside me. She wasn't a fan of the films per se—some parts were too violent for her—but Hobbiton was different. There was peace, joy and family, everything she wanted for me. A place to escape, to fantasize about, far from the reality of her illness; it was also a shared memory, something we both held dear.

After her passing, the world continued to evolve, and I kept accumulating new memories—memories she wasn't a part of. In that sense, on that day, Hobbiton became a bridge to the past, transporting me back to that final year with her. And whenever this happens, I'm grateful.

●

Arriving in Wellington on Christmas Eve, we barely managed to slip into a supermarket for some essentials before the early store closures. It felt surreal to be experiencing summer in the Southern Hemisphere during the holiday season. Our hearts yearned for cups of hot chocolate with marshmallows and the snug comfort of a blanket by a crackling fire.

When we woke up on Christmas Day, there were no gifts under the tree, no stockings by the fireplace, and no family to hug other than each other. Looking at our phones and scrolling through social media, everyone else seemed busy celebrating—except for us in that hostel.

The atmosphere felt heavy with melancholy, a shared sentiment among the few fellow backpackers who found themselves in the same boat. Then, as we all sat in the living room, an Italian traveler broke the silence.

"That's it," he declared, his voice cutting through the stillness. "I'm not sitting around for all of us to be miserable. It's Christmas!"

Curiosity piqued, we turned our heads to see what he would do next. He stepped into the large kitchen and started digging through the communal fridge, looking for options to cook a festive meal. Along with others, we quickly joined in, eager to contribute ingredients or share what we had brought.

He began cooking spaghetti and meatballs topped with Parmesan cheese, while someone else brought out butter and bread rolls. We uncorked two bottles of wine.

I watched as the kitchen filled with laughter and the aroma of spices, but my heart felt heavy. Thoughts of the German, now back in Germany, drifted into my mind. He had shared his plans for elaborate family feasts and cozy pajama gatherings beneath the Christmas tree. The contrast stung, intensifying the ache that settled in my chest.

It was everything I longed for yet felt so far out of reach—something I hadn't experienced in years. In the Netherlands, I had often felt just as isolated. The violin I used to play had fallen silent, our family torn apart, the warmth that once filled our home had turned to stone. I missed the days when we could come together, share laughter and love as we once did.

Instead, I found myself in this bustling kitchen with people I had never met yet had so much in common with. I watched them making the most of an otherwise colorless day.

"Merry Christmas!" we cheered as we gathered around a big rectangular table outside, plates filled with food, raising our glasses.

None of us was an island anymore; seven travelers from different corners of the world came together, breaking bread and enjoying delicious pasta—igniting the spirit of the holiday season.

After the Christmas quiet, Wellington gradually stirred back to life: stores opening, sights to be seen again. We took advantage of the little time we had left to visit the national museum of New Zealand, commonly referred to as *Te Papa Tongarewa,* "container of treasures" in Māori.

The museum sat along the waterfront, offering stunning views of the harbor. Inside, we immersed ourselves in exhibits that highlighted the country's unique ecosystems, storied past, and dynamic culture. We admired it, especially after having seen so much of it in a few short weeks.

In one of the halls, surrounded by interactive exhibitions designed to make art and culture accessible and enjoyable for everyone, a large magnetic board displayed an array of words waiting to be rearranged into poems. Embracing the ethos of Dadaism, which often celebrates the absurd and encourages creative expression without constraints, I decided to give it a try, even though I was no poet.

To my surprise, I found myself completely immersed in the simple act of shuffling words, so much so that I zoned out, letting the pieces dance by themselves, until the following poem unfolded:

Carve color like blue stars
Go shape snowflake or moon
Where that woman flood
With their grief
Perhaps time hold the twilight
Dance to me

I gazed at what I had created, shuffled together. I couldn't quite ascribe it a coherent meaning. Nevertheless, a profound significance flooded over me. It was almost as if the words carried a message from myself to myself; something, I mused, related to sculpting opportunities, like an artist carving out different forms from a piece of material. These opportunities can take varied shapes, just as stars come in various shades of brilliance. And in the midst of life's struggles and sorrow, akin to a flood of tears, there exists a glimmer of hope. Time, like a gentle hand, cradles the twilight between day and night, reminding us that even close to darkness, a flicker of light persists. This light, when seized, bestows a profound sense of vitality and purpose.

It was as if the poem spoke to the essence of life—the beauty that emerges when we embrace each moment and make it our own.

After collecting our backpacks, S and I walked through the swarming corridors of the airport toward arrivals, wondering if my Dutch friend, M, who had been living in Sydney for a while, would be there to greet us.

"We'll probably need to grab a taxi or Uber," I told her.

"I am telling you," she said, grinning and confident in her instincts for these things. "Your friend is going to be right here waiting for us."

It turned out her intuition was right—as usual. There he was, amidst the crowd at arrivals, waving at us and smiling.

"Oh my goodness, he is here!" I squealed, dropping my backpack, running toward him, and hugging him tightly—a warm embrace from home in a foreign land.

As soon as we made plans to go to Australia, he had been my first call, hoping we would be able to reunite. He knew what it was like to be in a long-distance relationship with the life we lived before, the friends and family we left behind—he understood what it took to pursue something different.

We had been friends since our teenage years, when we both worked at a small liquor store in my hometown, determined to save for our futures. As time flowed, he embarked on several international adventures, traveling from the United States to Sri Lanka and the Philippines. Although life often led us along separate paths, our friendship remained unchanged; every time we met, it was as if no time had passed, and the echoes of shared memories resounded warmly between us.

But meeting here, after all we had experienced, added a new dimension to our friendship—one that didn't exist before. Back then, when we worked together, it was all just a dream.

"I can't believe you're here!" I exclaimed.

"Well, I couldn't possibly let you two wander around this city without a proper welcome now, could I?" he replied.

The following day—which just so happened to be December 31st—we headed to Bondi Beach, a popular destination east of Sydney known for its golden sands and famed surf breaks.

We were gifted a warm, clear morning. The South Pacific Ocean glistened, and the streets buzzed with people clad in flip-flops and swimwear, some carrying surf and bodyboards.

Seated on the sandy shore, M and I engaged in hours of conversation, trance music playing from our portable speaker. We clinked our lime-infused cold beers, a toast to our reunion.

"I am so happy we are finally here," I said, resting my head on his shoulder, feeling the warmth of the sun and his presence on my skin. "What's next for you?"

"I don't know," he replied, his gaze drifting toward the horizon. "I'm just happy here—at least until my visa runs out. There's always more to explore after that."

I nodded, remembering our shared dreams from years ago.

"We always talked about traveling, about not getting stuck in the mundane. Do you think we're doing it?"

"Absolutely. Just look at us," he laughed, a hint of nostalgia in his eyes. "We used to stock shelves together, dreaming about faraway places. Now we're here, experiencing it together."

"Oh man, I have missed you." I squeezed his arm.

"What a time to be alive," he smiled. "I love you."

In the evening, we returned to his place nearby to prepare for what promised to be a long night. From there, we took a train to the Sydney Harbour area, where some of his friends invited us to a pre-fireworks celebration.

After a brief visit, M glanced at the clock on his phone.

"We've got to keep moving!" he urged, seeing everybody scrambling to find rides—Ubers, taxis, anything—to head to Pirrama Park, which offered a view of the Harbour Bridge.

Our group—now five people—was too big to share a cab, so we knew we had to split up. The streets were crowded with others rushing to get to their midnight destinations on time.

"Make sure that the girls get there!" M yelled, ushering us into a vehicle, entrusting his friends to get us to the fireworks.

The car crawled forward, I fidgeted nervously. I had always dreamed of spending New Year's Eve in Australia because of the show they put on in Sydney. Missing the fireworks I had seen on television for many years was not an option.

"We need to get out here!" one of the guys sitting next to the driver said as the car screeched to a sudden halt.

"Here?!" S questioned.

We peered out the window: an ocean of people flooded the park and the wharf next to it, blocking every potential vantage point for a clear view of the bridge.

"Yes, here!" he urged. "We have to run!"

I glanced at my phone: eight minutes to midnight. I grabbed S and jumped out of the car, following the two guys through the crowd, unsure where we were heading.

A minute into our rush, both guys began disappearing into the crowd, and S, more accustomed to running than I was, glanced around mid-sprint.

"Someone is following us!" she exclaimed.

Breathless and now slightly panicked, I asked, "Who?!"

"A man!" she shouted, still sprinting. "Run faster!"

Suddenly, a forceful yank on my ponytail threw me off balance, nearly toppling me to the ground.

"Give it to me!" an angry man's voice shouted from behind.

"What are you doing?!" I shouted back, grabbing my hair and struggling to wriggle free.

"Where is your friend?" he asked in a heavy accent. "The one who was with you."

Two burly guys came to my rescue, grabbing the man by both arms and pulling him away, freeing me from his grasp.

"I am calling the police!" he shouted as he grappled with the guys, his eyes bulging out, his face flushing crimson.

"Did someone take something from you?" I asked the man, trying to comprehend the situation.

"Police! Police! Police!" the man continued to roar.

We didn't know what to do. What had happened? Did M's friend owe this man money?

S and I stood there, frozen, until one of our protectors said, "Go, run!"

Without a second thought, we scrambled away from the enraged man, stumbling and bumping into people, trying to settle our pounding hearts. Eventually, we reached a viewpoint overlooking the iconic Sydney Harbour.

I glanced at my phone again—one minute to midnight. The air thickened, the urgency of the moment pressed in like a tide. I took a deep breath, muffling the hubbub and finding a quiet corner of my mind to reflect on the year that was fading.

So much had transpired. The ten-year anniversary of my mother's passing incited a resurgence of grief. I ended a long-term love, letting go of the familiar routine and the supportive relationships I had cultivated with his family. I parted ways with my childhood home, the apartment in Amsterdam where I was building a new life, my sense of stability. Even some cherished friendships frayed and drifted apart.

But, in a way, I also woke up. Or rather, the urge, the need, for a fresh start woke me up somehow. It was a strange and unexplainable feeling, this desire for a clean slate. It wasn't about right or wrong; it was about intuition, about creating the space to grow, making room for new experiences and opportunities. All with the goal—which, to a certain extent, I had achieved—of discovering or reimagining feelings and sensations that touched the depths of my soul: love, or something like it.

Excited, I turned to S.

"Can you believe we're here, ringing in the New Year?"

"I know, right?" she grinned. "It's like a dream come true."

As the clock neared midnight, the crowd began to count down together. "Ten! Nine! Eight!"

The collective energy was infectious, and we joined in. "Seven! Six! Five!"

My heart raced in anticipation.

"Four! Three! Two!"

S and I held our breaths, eyes fixed on the harbor.

"One! Happy New Year!"

The fireworks burst forth in a dazzling display, painting the sky in colors, illuminating the night. Each explosion seemed to hold a story of its own, a symbol of the collective hopes and dreams for the new year. As the vibrant hues danced across the water, people cheered and applauded, instilling me with optimism that even greater things awaited.

When the fireworks came to an end, I hugged my cousin tightly. *This is it*, I thought, *another fresh start*.

•

The new year might have turned a new leaf, but all I wanted was to lounge under a blanket and lose myself in movies. The rain drummed softly outside as I sank deep into the couch cushions on our last day at M's house in Bondi. In his presence, I felt a rare kind of safety—there was no need to put on a happy face. He understood me in a way that made it easy to just be, even if that meant indulging in romantic comedies.

We put on one of my favorites, *Letters to Juliet*. The male lead's charm was irresistible, his words weaving a romantic tale that left me yearning.

"Just message him," M said, as if reading my mind.

"Yes, cuz-y, you deserve love like *that*," S added, pointing at the television screen.

Torn by romantic struggles, I reached out to the German, babbling about true love.

The German:
OUR STORY IS VERY ENDEARING TOO.

**ALL I WANT FOR YOU IS TO FEEL
EMPOWERED AND BE HAPPY.**

Endearing—that was one perspective. I couldn't muster the same sentiment. Not anymore. It didn't feel particularly endearing when he suggested I should *not* come to Germany, effectively shutting the door on a future between us. Perhaps our story had been endearing once, but now it was anything but. True endearment, I realized, would be a man who dives fearlessly into passion and commitment—unconditionally.

Rolling my eyes at my phone, I tried to refocus on the film. I longed for that kind of love—that Hollywood, picture-perfect, almost-too-good-to-be-true kind of love. A man who effortlessly utters the right words and genuinely means them. Someone intelligent, engaging, unafraid of love. But I knew life wasn't a scripted movie. It was real, often unpredictable, and not concocted by someone else's imagination. Still, I couldn't shake the desire, setting myself up for failure with unrealistic expectations. I sank deeper into the cushions, pulling the blanket over my head. M sat down beside me.

"You know you can always come find me, right? Whenever you need me—anywhere in the world," he said gently, pulling the blankets off my face.

"Thank you for letting us stay here." I snuggled up against him, feeling grateful and comforted but also weighed down by the thought of leaving.

"I'm sorry I wasn't able to catch up to ring in the New Year together," he continued. "And I'm sorry about my friends. They should have paid the cab driver properly."

"You have nothing to be sorry for," I said, shaking my head.
"Where's your travel diary?" he asked. "I'll write in it."
And he did.

*It still feels like yesterday that we stocked shelves together
at the local liquor store. No matter how I felt when I
clocked in, I always left my shift with a smile on my face.*

My eyes glided over the text, feeling nostalgic about how he
described some of the times we shared in our friendship. He
had known me when I was in such a different phase of my life.

*Whenever I reflect on forging my own path, I realize
how much of a role you've played in it—as an example, a
pillar of support and a true friend.*

A tear escaped as I soaked in his words. Before seeing him in
Australia, I hadn't realized this was how he truly felt. I had
contributed something, yet never seen it.

*Your enthusiasm, ideas and positivity bring joy to people
all over the world, and for that, I couldn't be prouder of
you. Never change.*

As much as I had been blinded by all the emotional turmoil
of the past, he looked beyond it and really saw me. It was on
moments like these that I wished I could pack up the people I
cared about the most and plant them near wherever I would
end up—creating a community strong and supportive, a place
where we would rise together.

*No matter how infrequently we meet, it will always feel
like our first day together, stacking shelves. I love you
dearly—until we meet again.*

•

Checking into our hostel in Airlie Beach, Queensland, a two-and-a-half-hour flight from Sydney, S and I were immediately enveloped by the laid-back, tropical vibe of this coastal town. Known as the gateway to the Whitsundays—an archipelago of seventy-four islands sprinkled like gems across the Coral Sea—Airlie Beach offered a pleasant base before embarking on an island adventure. We were in no rush.

As night fell and the warmth of the day faded, I drifted into a deep sleep, a depth that births the most vivid dreams—both wondrous and nightmarish—akin to traversing a dark tunnel with no clear endpoint. Perhaps it wasn't a tunnel at all, but rather a void, a pitch-black abyss of nothingness. Loneliness and being alone intertwined—two distinctly different things, both truths in this boundless void. Everything consumed by the darkness, unresolved emotions swirling without color—each feeling magnified, suffocating, nauseating. A profound bitterness within me, a pervasive sense of loss, fermenting.

"Wake up." A voice cut through the dream.

"Wake up."

It echoed in the darkness with a warm familiarity. Years had passed since I last heard this voice, yet I remembered it clearly. It was a part of me.

"Mom?"

I peered into the darkness of my dream, straining to see.

"Wake up."

The command grew louder, jolting me awake. For a while, I lay there, my gaze fixed on the underside of the bunk bed above me, trying to make sense of what had happened. She had yanked me out of that suffocating abyss, that bottomless pit—why? Her voice was so clear that she could have been whispering into my ear. It was as if she had descended to check on me, weaving a protective cocoon.

When daylight finally poured in, I strolled through town and wandered into a nearby bookstore. Amidst the shelves, a mindfulness-promoting coloring book caught my eye. With my mother's voice still echoing in my mind, I decided that I would spend the day with myself, embracing mindfulness by coloring the pages. It seemed like a good way to navigate out of the lingering darkness.

I picked up the book and a fresh set of color pencils and returned to the hostel, settling in a hammock hung between two tall palm trees. Hours drifted by, just me, and the coloring book with its intricate shapes and lines, soaking in the gentle warmth of the sun. Life still felt tangled and messy, but in that moment, bringing color and structure to those pages was all I could accomplish. And so, that's what I did.

Two days later, we were finally ready to go to the legendary Whitsundays. We had booked a boating and island-hopping adventure with two nights at a private resort nestled on a picturesque piece of waterfront land. Rumor had it that even actress Nicole Kidman had rented out that same spot while filming in Australia in the past. If it was good enough for her, it was certainly a remarkable accommodation for us.

Instead of taking our backpacks, we were given distinctive orange reusable waterproof bags and were told to pack only the most essential items.

We arrived at Abell Point Marina at 1 p.m. and hopped on a forty-foot catamaran. As I settled into one of its seats, a sense of tranquility and comfort enveloped me. The water had always been where I felt most connected, oddly grounded amidst the ebb and flow of the ocean's force, as if it washed away my shadow—there was light again.

As we motored out of the marina and cruised farther from shore, the boat glided smoothly over the waves, the sound of the engine mixing with the splash of water against the hull. I leaned against the railing, feeling the cool spray of the sea on my face, joy bubbling inside me.

We briefly stopped; some swam, while others snorkeled. I simply sat there, feeling the boat bob beneath me, staring at the rippling clear blue waters all around.

"Can I grab you a wetsuit?" the captain asked.

"There is a time and a place for everything," I mused.

"It's nice to see," he remarked as he took a seat next to me, "someone who appreciates the beauty of just being out here on the water."

In the late afternoon, the catamaran made its way toward our accommodation—a place technically on the mainland but so secluded it was virtually inaccessible by land. And even by boat, getting there was tricky: the water grew so shallow that we were forced to drop anchor about fifty feet from the shore, wading in with our orange waterproof bags held high above our heads.

One of the resort staff members waited on the beach and guided our group of twenty-eight people to a spacious building—Paradise Cove Villa—surrounded by lush coconut palms and hammocks swaying gently in the breeze.

After settling in, we were invited to a buffet-style dinner featuring roasted chicken, fresh seafood, tropical fruits and local desserts. S almost cried with happiness as her eyes glided over our options.

Long dining tables were set up outside, but we grabbed our plates and chose to sit on large outdoor cushions scattered across the deck. The resort was luxurious yet grounding, with an indoor-outdoor style of living so secluded it felt as if nothing could disturb the peace.

After cleaning up our plates, I returned to the deck, dropping onto that same cushion, not a shred of stress on my mind as the night settled in. S chatted with a fellow traveler, while my eyes fixated on the darkening horizon.

Watching the shimmering stars, radiant as small flashlights illuminating the velvety night sky, I was transported back to Mongolia. There, the night was brutally cold, the air biting at my skin, but the stars—countless, vivid—were unforgettable, with the entire Milky Way visible.

Here in Australia, the experience was different—warmer, more comfortable in the soft summer air, barefoot on the deck. The stars were just as mesmerizing, but the contrast in setting made the moment feel both familiar and entirely new —under the same stars, yet worlds apart.

I lay down, noticing my body tingle in gratitude, just as it had so many times throughout this trip. Behind me, a guest strummed an acoustic guitar, while others sat on the porch and played card games, laughing and shooting the breeze.

My cozy bed wasn't far, but I had no wish for comfort—or sleep. I simply wanted to lay there, under the night sky; lay there counting the stars. Lying there until dawn.

Birdsong awoke me slowly the next morning. I took a moment to listen to the melodies as I watched a small lizard poke its head around the beam of my bed. Then I woke up S, and we made our way to the kitchen.

As we chatted over a breakfast of scones, scrambled eggs and banana smoothies, she pointed out how remarkable the day would be—exploring the Whitsunday Islands and getting closer to the edge of the Great Barrier Reef.

"Are you going snorkeling, cuz-y?" she asked, brimming with excitement.

Diving here had long been on my bucket list, but my ears had always been sensitive to pressure changes, so snorkeling would have to do.

"Today is the day, cuz-y! Today is the day," I said, getting up and making my way to the beach.

We waded back through the water to our catamaran, which was able to get closer to the shore that morning. Once the whole group settled into their seats, we surged over the waves.

This catamaran with no masts or sails, often referred to as a power cat, featured larger engines than its sailing cousins. Its powerful motors allowed for higher top speeds, enabling us to visit multiple sights throughout the day.

As the crew navigated to find the best snorkeling spots, Manta Ray Bay came into view, nestled off the coast of Hook Island. It was surprisingly quiet, with few other boats. The lush greenery and rocky outcrops of the island framed the bay, while its turquoise waters shimmered in the sun, contrasting beautifully with the deep blue of the Coral Sea beyond.

Dressed in a snug wetsuit and swimming fins, I dove in, kicking my feet softly to propel my body along the surface. Below, not even fifteen feet down, colorful fish swam slowly and unconcerned through and around nooks, crannies, and holes in the coral. The reefs varied greatly: from sprawling, fan-like structures swaying gently with the current to tightly packed clusters that resemble underwater gardens.

Sunlight filtered through the glassy water, illuminating the living canvas beneath me. I dove deeper, swam close to the reef, scrutinizing its cracks and edges, then resurfaced, filling my lungs before heading down again.

Whenever I submerged, the water compressed every inch of my body. Yet what I felt wasn't pressure but release. I moved my limbs effortlessly, oblivious to the density of the saltwater and the weight of gravity. Gliding like the manta rays for whom the bay is named, I swam respectfully and silently, careful not to disturb the life around me, becoming one with the sea and its inhabitants.

Back on board, I settled at the boat's railing for a while. My black wetsuit glistened under the drops of water before I took it off and dried in the sun, now in my bathing suit.

We continued on to Whitsunday Island—the largest in the archipelago—and headed straight for Whitehaven Beach, located on the eastern side. This stunning almost four-and-a-half-mile-long shoreline is renowned as one of the most beautiful beaches on Earth. Composed of extremely small, silica-rich quartz. The ultra-soft sand was the whitest I had ever seen—blinding me without sunglasses.

We had an hour and a half to explore, and we instantly dropped down at the waterline, wiggling our toes and fingers to feel the texture. The sea lay almost still; the only sound the gentle lapping of waves as they kissed the shore. The water's clarity made it appear colorless where it met the sand, gradually shifting to turquoise as it deepened, with distant islands on the horizon.

S and I jumped up, dashing through the shallow waters, letting sand and saltwater tangle in our braided hair. The beauty of this place felt surreal and irresistible—like being stranded on an uninhabited island, quiet, peaceful, where only light and brilliance existed.

In the shallow water, we lay down again, the gentle waves barely submerging our backs, with only a few other people around. S reached for my hand.

"Thank you, cuz-y, for encouraging me to take this leap," she said as we cherished this beautiful moment together.

When our time was up, our catamaran repositioned slightly to moor in Tongue Bay, a small bay just north of the beach.

A sign in the sand directed us toward a twenty-minute trail to Hill Inlet Lookout, where we hoped to gain a different perspective on the island.

The trail wound through a lush, shaded rainforest, my flip-flops kicking up sand as butterflies accompanied us along the way. Gentle inclines gave way to steeper sections, but the path remained manageable, offering occasional glimpses of the coastline through breaks in the trees.

As we approached the top, the dense forest parted, and we stepped onto a raised platform. My eyes widened, and my jaw dropped at the sight below. A blend of turquoise waters and shifting white sands painted the landscape. The unique patterns swirled and constantly moved with the tides.

"What does the sign say?" I asked S, who stood near a small information point.

"Wind and waves shape this land," she started.

"Does it say how?" I was curious.

"The currents tug at the grains, pulling them northward to the shallow banks and swales," she read. "And once the sand is gone, it will be gone forever."

As I took in the view, I felt a bittersweet tug at my heart. This moment, just like the shifting sands below me, wouldn't last forever. I realized that even if I returned, I would never be able to see exactly what I saw then. It reminded me of life itself. You can go back—back to family, lovers, a home, a place, a feeling—but sometimes all there is is forward, as it will never be as it once was.

When we set sail back to the resort in the late afternoon, I sat on the deck, my gaze trailing over the moving waters. In the background, Xavier Rudd's *Follow the Sun* played through the boat's speakers:

"Follow, follow the sun
And which way the wind blows
When this day is done

Breathe, breathe in the air
Set your intentions
Dream with care

Tomorrow is a new day for everyone
A brand new moon, brand new sun"

The soulful tune swayed with the gentle rhythm of waves, each verse seemingly a call to action. "In which way the wind blows," the phrase echoed in my mind. I would go wherever the wind would carry me after Australia.

•

As soon as we arrived in Melbourne, I was eager to reconnect with the Australian girls I had met in Ottawa three months earlier. After we dropped our bags in our room, they came to meet us at the hostel.

"It's so great to be in Melbourne," I said, greeting them.

They laughed. "It's not Mel-*born*," one of them corrected with a smile. "It's Mel-*ben*! Just like Edinburgh is not called Edin-*burg*, but Edin-*bra*."

This little linguistic quirk stuck with me, not just because it's one of the top contenders for one of the most commonly mispronounced cities in the world, but because it highlighted how much of a place's—or person's—identity is wrapped up in the way it's spoken.

I related to that feeling; after all, most people mispronounce my name unless they speak French or Dutch, *Meh*-non, Ma-*noon*, Mah-*naan*, Ma-*nana*, *Ba-nana*—I have heard it all. To me, there is a certain respect associated with trying to learn a pronunciation, a piece of what makes someone who they are.

Discovering a place through the eyes of those who call it home enhances that comprehension. It's more than just seeing the sights; it's about understanding the subtleties, like the correct pronunciation of a name or the hidden gems locals cherish.

For me, traveling is about these moments of connection—learning the little details that give a place its unique character and being welcomed into a way of life that locals experience every day.

The girls led us through the Central Business District, stopping at the State Library of Victoria to show us the La Trobe Reading Room inside, which featured a grand domed ceiling soaring overhead and natural light pouring in.

Back outside, the combination of modern glass skyscrapers and neoclassical columned buildings left me wondering how the city had accomplished such a harmonious blend of historic and new. This architectural mix stunned me once more when we reached the Parliament of Victoria, with its wide-stretching tall columns—commanding respect against the overcast sky.

The weather began to turn as we made our way to a lively corner of the city near the river, brimming with art galleries and museums. Seeking shelter from the drizzle, we stepped inside one of the many exhibition halls. Surrounded by large paintings and white marble statues, one of the girls turned to S and me.

"There's this thing we love doing here," she whispered with a grin.

"Oh, really? What's that?" I asked.

"We become part of the art!" she exclaimed, grabbing her friend, dashing toward a canvas, and striking poses as if they were characters in the painting.

As polite Europeans, S and I stifled our laughter, worried a security guard would ask us to pipe down. But no one came. In fact, no one seemed bothered by the sudden commotion, or the human addition to the baroque-looking artwork.

We carried on, moving from one hall to another, choosing our favorite artworks then freezing into the depicted poses. We held our arms high in the air. We strangled each other. We knelt, dropped dead, contemplated, danced, and transformed into maidens, royals, explorers, and even David and Goliath.

Gradually, other visitors took notice, their attention drawn away from the paintings to us, becoming spectators to our impromptu performance. This went on for a good forty-five minutes, and once we finally reached the exit, all four of us finally burst into laughter. Outside, the rain had stopped, and I was left with the sensation of having stumbled upon a fresh perspective on art—one that not only appreciates the intricacy of landscape pieces like Monet's *Water Lilies,* but also works depicting the essence of human life.

After saying goodbye to my friends, who were only able to meet up with us for the day, S and I began strolling back to our hostel. As we turned a corner, another work of art caught my eye—a gleaming Formula 1 race car.

As a lifelong F1 enthusiast, I was immediately drawn to the Red Bull Racing car, pressing my nose against the glass to examine its design. With the Australian Grand Prix set to open the 2016 season in Melbourne, anticipation hung in the air, especially with the Australian Daniel Ricciardo driving for Red Bull.

I had high hopes for Dutch talent Max Verstappen, who was impressing at Toro Rosso, Red Bull's junior team. The dream of hearing the Dutch national anthem on a Formula 1 podium felt within reach, especially if Verstappen got his shot in this Adrian Newey masterpiece.

As a child, I often listened to the German national anthem on Sunday afternoons, cheering on the legendary Michael Schumacher, one of the greatest F1 drivers of all time.

At six years old, my father took me to Monaco on a race weekend for the first time. Dressed head-to-toe in Ferrari race gear, standing high on a hill that overlooked the yacht club and street track, I was captivated by "Schumi," as I fondly called Schumacher, and the roar of his red Ferrari. He was my hero. I admired how fearless he was, always pushing himself to go faster. Watching him race made me dream big and want to be brave like him. Wearing that racing suit, I didn't just feel like a fan—I wanted to be in the car, to feel the speed, the rush, like I could take on anything.

It was no surprise that, after gazing at the Red Bull race car for a while, a wave of nostalgia swept over me, bringing back treasured memories of my family gathered in the living room, watching Formula 1 on Sunday afternoons—simple, magical moments of quality time. The joy of dressing up as Schumi, the shared laughter running around the coffee table with my grandparents pretending to be driving a race of our own... I could still hear their voices, see their smiles, feel their warmth.

Sadly, after my mom passed away, those cozy Formula 1 Sundays vanished, leaving me without yet another one of our beloved traditions.

One day, I thought to myself as I stood before that Red Bull machine encased in glass on a sidewalk in Melbourne, *I would resurrect those traditions, surrounded by the roar of F1 engines, in my own newly established home.*

Our last day in Melbourne arrived, signaling the end of my time with my cousin.

"Let's go out for dinner," she suggested, eager to make the most of our remaining moments together.

We scoured the internet for a place to eat and found exactly what we craved: Swiss cheese fondue.

Entering the restaurant, we felt instantly transported to the Alps. We settled into our seats and inhaled the nutty aroma of Gruyère. Without hesitation, we exchanged a glance and knew exactly what we wanted, placing our shared order as soon as the waiter approached.

When he returned to our table, setting a fondue pan atop a small burner, steam rising enticingly from its surface, along with two ice-cold beers, we dove right in, dipping slices of baguette, broccoli and cauliflower into the bubbling pot. For a few minutes we were silent, the rich blend of Emmental and Gruyère oozing with each bite.

"I'm so proud of you," I said, setting down my fondue fork.

"For taking a chance to change the course of your life, and for trusting me to stand by your side as you leaped."

"Oh, cuz-y. I don't know if I ever would have done it if you hadn't shown up at my door, sharing your plans and nudging me to rethink my own," she chimed in. "I bet you won't miss me talking in my sleep every night!"

We both laughed.

Her humor, her lightness of being, her confidence—having her by my side provided me with much-needed strength and fun when I needed it most, even when I didn't know I needed it. The sadness of parting and anticipation of our individual journeys weighed equally on both of us.

"Are you excited about your romantic Thai getaway?" I asked.

"I can't wait to indulge in luxury!" she squealed. "A private jacuzzi overlooking the ocean, Muay Thai boxing lessons, soothing massages and total pampering!"

"Sounds like a dream!" I gazed at her, a soft smile spreading across my face as I imagined her joy.

"How about you, cuz-y?" her tone turned serious. "Will you be okay out there in the big world?"

"Always."

As night fell in Melbourne and we returned to our hostel, we shared one more long hug before heading to bed—better to say goodbye now, since I had to slip out in the middle of the night to catch an early flight to Perth. I held onto her tightly, at peace, that we would both go our own way.

While having a constant companion was reassuring, solo travel offers an entirely different experience, and ever since New York, I hadn't been alone. Traveling side by side with my cousin—and my friend Z before that—with so much history and love between us, I always had that extra set of eyes. It was comfortable. But being alone, without anyone who knew me, sparked something different. No one was watching me at my most vulnerable, allowing me to be unapologetically true to myself. In that state I discovered a drive to learn more—not just about people, experiences, and cultures, but also about myself when there was no one left to hold my hand or lean on. It's just me and the world—with my heart open to whatever lies ahead.

"Remember, I'm never too far if you ever need me," I told S, hugging her one last time.

"I know. I love you, cuz-y," she replied, holding me even tighter.

"I love you too."

·

My plane from Melbourne left at 7:15 a.m., arriving in Perth three hours and twenty minutes later, at 8:35 a.m.—a perk of flying from east to west. At arrivals, amidst joyful reunions and clattering luggage carts, B, an Australian girl I had first met in Las Vegas, was waiting for me with her sister.

"Hey, hey, hey!" I sang, as I fell into her arms.

"Welcome!" she said, before introducing me to her sister. "You have to tell us all about your travels since I last saw you."

"I will tell you everything you want to know." I laughed.

Being with her, I wasn't technically alone in my travels. Yet I had arrived alone in a city I had never been to before, open to experiencing the life of someone I had spent only two days with, but whose light shone so brightly that I eagerly accepted her invitation.

"Let's start with *brekkie,*" B suggested.

"Start with what? Breakfast?" I inquired, still not used to how Australians abbreviate words, so many words, even after two and a half weeks there.

"Yes!" she grinned. "You'll quickly catch on to how we do it in *Straya.*

After a proper Australian *brekkie:* crispy bacon served with grilled tomatoes, freshly poached eggs, and zesty lemony avocado toast—my friend took me to her family home, where I would be staying for two weeks.

The house was located in Dianella, a large suburban home on a quiet street. Tall trees lined the driveway, and flowers bloomed by the white steps leading to the front door. Her mother, a warm and elegant woman, was there to welcome me, with a beautifully arranged board of Dutch specialty cheeses waiting in the kitchen.

They took me on a tour of the premises, and when she showed me the room I would be staying in, I almost cried of happiness. It was good enough to avoid hostels for a while, but to have my very own bright, spacious room with a large bed— that was a refreshing escape from the constant awareness of others in my personal space.

"Stay as long as you need, dear," her mother said, handing me a towel and hugging me warmly. "You must be exhausted after all your travels."

Exhausted was an understatement. I don't know if it was the weight of my backpack or all the emotional baggage I had accumulated so far, but when I sat on the airy bed and rubbed my hands on the white linen, it truly felt like the weight of the world was lifted off my shoulders.

"Yes, we'll let you get some rest," B said, probably noticing my weary eyes.

"Ah, by the way," she added as she closed the door. "Are you still in touch with that guy? The one from Niagara Falls?"

Just after my date, I had breakfast with her in New York City, where our paths had coincidentally crossed again. She was the first who had heard the whole story, and together we reveled in the romance of it all. Back then, having a new friend to share those emotions with made all the difference.

"Sure am," I replied. "But it's a bit...complicated."

Little did I know, when I uttered those words, just how complicated it was actually going to get.

As I buried my head into the pillows, my phone rang—an incoming video call from *him*.

"We need to talk," his voice sounded out of sorts.

"Hello to you too," I replied, sensing this wasn't going to be good and bracing myself for impact.

"I am seeing someone." He went straight to the point, now sounding uneasy as he rubbed his furrowed brows.

"You're *seeing* someone?" I replied, my body going numb.

"You actually met her in Canada, the day we met. One of my friends," he elaborated.

"Huh?"

"She obviously knows all about you, so it doesn't seem fair to not tell you," he continued.

I remembered—a petite brunette. He had mentioned her before, but nothing significant, just ordinary conversations about friends hanging out in Canada.

Yet once, recently, he met up with her for dinner in a German city that wasn't his, and there was something about him not telling me until I asked that made me feel insecure— that nagging feeling creeping in, that intuition. I asked him why he hadn't mentioned it, and again he brushed it off as "just friends," making me sound paranoid. I forced myself not to think much of it because there was trust—so much trust— between us, or so I believed. My head spun, and a cold wave hit me like a brick: trust was not given, it was earned.

"So," I said after a couple of seconds, my mouth seemingly moving out of its own accord. "You're choosing her over me?"

He didn't answer; instead, he played the "you deserve more than I can give" card. It was an excuse he had used before, but this time, I wasn't willing to listen. I had wasted enough time in this state of uncertainty. For the sake of what, hope? And if so, hope for what? What was the desired outcome?

I felt a knot forming in my throat. I tried hard to hold back the tears I didn't want him to see, but eventually, I couldn't contain it any longer. The walls started to crumble around me, and without them, the harsh echoes of the piercing voice of the woman my father brought into my life rushed back in, always belittling me over the years—words that had made me feel small, miserable, worthless.

Throughout this journey, I had longed for a home, and meticulously pieced together thoughts of a new life, or at least what I envisioned it could become. Yet, with just a few words from the German, it all came crashing down once more. The imaginary house I had constructed thus far, trying to rebuild what was broken, didn't have a solid foundation. It didn't yet stand its ground.

"I gotta go," I said, unable to see where to go from there.

"I really don't want to lose you," the German pleaded.

His words barely registered; my mind was overwhelmed, trying to make sense of what was happening, which only added to the confusion. He said he was seeing someone but he didn't want to lose me—all on the same call. What was he playing at? And more importantly, why couldn't I simply let go of him, even after all the clues?

When the call finally ended, a heavy weight pressed on my body and mind. I forgot about my urge to make sense of things. I just wanted to shrink into a tiny ball and lie there. I just wanted to endure it.

When I walked into the kitchen the following morning, B's eyebrows shot up.

"What happened?" she asked. "Have you been crying?"

I gave a rundown of what had happened overnight, feeling guilty and ashamed for bringing sadness into the home that had welcomed me with so much joy. It felt all-consuming as I struggled to summon a smile.

"You need to visit the farm," her mom suggested as we were having breakfast. "It'll be a blast!"

"The farm?" I inquired.

"Yes, it is our family's, a few hours south of here. You girls could all go together, make a road trip out of it. It's very quiet and surrounded by beautiful nature, you might even spot some kangaroos!"

The idea was very appealing, venturing to remote locations intrigued me, especially given how I felt. So I accepted their invitation.

Only a few hours later, we drove along a narrow road in Mumballup, where dense forest gave way to stretches of farmland. Only a few farms dotted the landscape, most with their own access roads. Turning right, we continued along a dirt track. The trees were vibrant green, while the rolling hills of dry pasture shimmered golden as far as the eye could see.

We pulled up in front of a house surrounded by tall trees, their thick branches and abundant leaves creating a private corner in the vast landscape. It was very different from the farms I had known growing up—much larger, drier, untamed.

After a comforting cup of Earl Grey tea, B and I strolled through the fields. She showed me the empty livestock pens and, in the distance, countless sheep dotting the horizon, grazing.

"Look!" She paused and pointed toward the treeline ahead of us, yet far away.

I turned my gaze in the direction she indicated, and there they were.

"Kangaroos!" I exclaimed at the sight.

They hopped from tree to tree, fast like a Greyhound yet smoothly, as though springs were hidden under their paws.

Then they disappeared behind the trees as we walked across the field, trying to get closer and improve our chances of seeing more.

The sight of those wild animals roaming free grounded me somewhat. Standing in the middle of the open field, I closed my eyes. The only audible sounds were the gentle creaks of the dry, hay-like grass beneath our feet and the faint whispers of the wind. When the breeze picked up momentum, I imagined nature's dance surrounding me, the lyrics of *Colors of the Wind* playing in my mind, fictional leaves swirling in circles and stirring the serene atmosphere.

These were the moments I sought while traveling, again and again—moments of self-realization, when I understood that I alone must take charge of my life. No one could provide a safety net or choose my next steps; I had to trust in my ability to pave my own way. Truly, when I looked closely, the one who had broken my heart the most was myself. I had set unrealistic expectations, clung to illusions, attempting to fill a void and escape the task of facing my pain and darkness. It was sometimes simpler to focus on someone else than to delve into my own depths, fearing what I might uncover.

The breeze tousled my hair, and I tilted my head to the sky, slowly opening my eyes. I thought back on how fortunate I had been in my upbringing and the opportunities that came my way. I realized how much of a disservice it would be to let a loss, a person, or an event dictate my pain, holding me back. *This is where I craft my plan.* I told myself. *The time is now.*

Three days later, I called my cousin and updated her on the German situation. I expected her to be stunned, but she surprised me with her own revelation.

"Mine's a bust too!" S exclaimed.

"Wait, what?"

Her dreamy Thai escape was supposed to be idyllic, filled with love—palm trees, sandy beaches, massages, and amazing food—but the reality was far from what she expected. He turned out to be uninterested and dull. Granted, they hadn't had much in-person time before her departure, so anything could happen. Still, I had seen his messages—as she had seen the ones the German sent me—and given all the time spent on calls, the words exchanged, and the heart emojis sent, I would have never guessed he would be that way. It was difficult to acknowledge that after hyping up these men for months, everything went pear-shaped in the same week.

"What now? What's next?" I asked her.

"I'll probably stay on the island for as long as I planned," she replied.

"And then? What's the plan?"

"I don't know, cuz-y. Heading to Koh Phi Phi. Want to join me there?" she suggested.

"Done!" I exclaimed without really thinking it through, suddenly seeing a light at the end of my tunnel of sadness.

Despite my intentions to be on my own, her invitation seemed to be exactly what I needed—what we both needed—before starting what would essentially be a new phase.

The next day, a missed call from the German dragged me back into his orbit, again. This time, however, I was fed up; fed up and determined to take some form of control.

Before calling him back, I went online and booked my flight from Perth to Phuket, Thailand. I also purchased a multi-city ticket that included flights from Thailand to Finland and from Finland to the Czech Republic, bordering Germany, for my return to Europe—without hesitating.

"I'm coming to see you," I asserted when he answered the phone minutes later. "I've made up my mind."

"I'm not sure if that's the best idea," he replied, hesitant as usual.

"I don't really care. After all this time, I owe it to myself to close this chapter. You said you liked me, you hurt me, and now you owe me the time."

"I do like you! But coming here doesn't make sense. I never wanted to hurt you."

I wasn't entirely sure why I needed to go, but I did. I had built an idea of him in my head—this rare creature—and I needed to confront that illusion, to check whether I had been irrational or if there was some truth to it. I needed closure, a real conclusion, instead of him vanishing from my life as if he had never been there. More than anything, I wanted him to see me—not to rekindle anything, or maybe I did, I wasn't sure—but so he could face what he had lost. My anger demanded that he take a good, hard look.

"I already booked my tickets. I will be back in Europe next month," I informed him.

"If that's what makes you happy, I won't stop you," he said.

"You're damn right you won't," I responded.

He smiled. Then, after a couple of seconds, he shifted gears. "So, what do you want to do while you're here?"

"I'll figure it out," I replied, feeling the pressure ease from my chest.

Five days later, B took me to Cottesloe Beach, a white sandy stretch roughly thirty minutes from her place.

I rarely got my hair wet when swimming in the sea, but somehow, the Australian waters lured me in every time—crystal clear and pleasantly warm.

Drifting on my back in waist-deep water, I gazed up at the sky. My thoughts, seemingly swaying with the motion of the Indian Ocean, eventually led to the realization that I only had three days left in Australia. Suddenly, a tinge of sadness crept in. *I could stay here,* I mused, thinking of the comfort this big island had offered me.

When I finally stood up, my feet on the ocean floor, and looked around, I was completely astounded by what I saw.

"Eh, there's a shark!" I exclaimed, signaling to B who was wading deeper into the water.

"You're joking, right?!" she yelled back, nervously. "That's not funny, Dutch!"

"No, seriously, right there between us!" I pointed out the small fin cutting through the water.

"Oh my, lead the way around it!" her tone shifted swiftly.

"Head right! My right, your left!" I shouted urgently, while stepping backward toward the beach myself.

She swam as fast as the shallow water allowed, her feet half wading, half kicking up spray. The distance to safety was about fifty feet, but it felt like miles. I could hear her agile movements while I continued slowly stepping back, keeping my eyes glued to the fin—just in case it came closer.

When we reached the safety of the shore, the shark's fin drifted lazily toward deeper water.

"Looks like a baby!" B gasped, dropping down in the sand. "Still, that...was way too close."

I sat down next to her, still processing. As much as I loved being in Australia—the beauty, the space, the wildness—the nagging thought that everything wanted to take me out was hard to shake. Sharks, spiders, even kangaroos.

It was a slow, quiet morning at Perth Airport as the sun began to rise on my final day. Standing in front of departures, I held B tightly, thanking her for all the warmth, love, and glee she and her family had given me. Being part of their home, even for just a few weeks, brought me closer to a semblance of belonging and emphasized the importance of living joyfully and spreading kindness. It felt like a blessing.

After clearing security, I reached for my travel diary tucked in my backpack's small front pocket, where B and her mother had written a message.

*Thank you for being so happy and for reminding us
what it means to be a traveler. You are so alive and full
of spirit that it is a pure joy to be in your company. Keep
smiling that beautiful smile!*

You are always welcome in our home.

Their words lit up the pages, warming my soul as I tracked
them with my fingers. It had been a whirlwind of emotions,
especially at the beginning, but I was glad that they saw my
bright side as well. Their words were like a mirror, showing me
that, despite the grief and heartbreak, my love for life remained
unwavering.

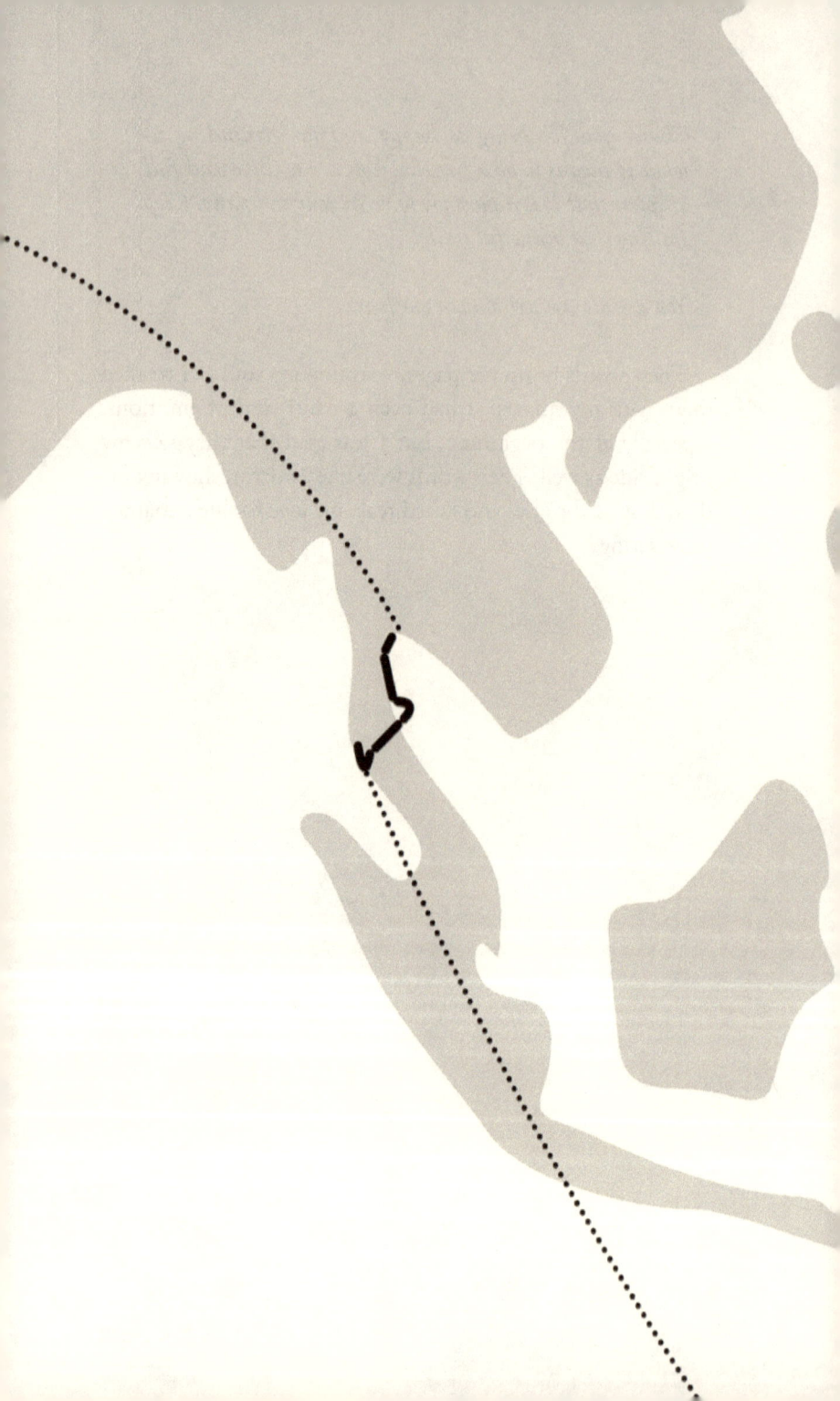

PART FOUR

DON'T WAIT FOR TOMORROW TO COME

Thailand

Soft sunlight breached the curtains of my Phuket hostel room, illuminating scattered backpacks and towels. I reached for my phone to check what time it was; the screen showed 8:41 a.m., February 1st—the day my mother died.

Emptiness filled my stomach immediately, just as it had on every February 1st for the previous eleven years, and many other moments when I thought of her. Yet this time, the void seemed even larger, or deeper, because I was unable to visit her grave. Once again, I realized how much I was still hurting, still processing.

I sat up, rubbed my eyes, and glanced around the room. Nine others were still asleep, but two roommates had already started preparing for the day ahead. As was my habit in dorms, I struck up a conversation with them—T, an American from Minnesota on a four-month backpacking adventure, and H, a Canadian in her mid-twenties, traveling before resuming her teaching job in China. I hoped to spend the day around town and then head to the beach, so I invited them to come along.

We kicked off with a visit to a busy local market. Every stall we passed drew us closer with pungent aromas—grilled meats, spicy curries, sweet banana roti, and sizzling skewers galore. The smells made the dishes even more tempting, and though I'm usually wary of street food, I considered giving them a try.

That is, until I spotted a tray of fried insects and skewered scorpions. It reminded me of the Hot Pot restaurant with live shrimp on sticks in China and I immediately lost my appetite, abandoning the idea altogether.

We navigated the narrow, cracked streets of the market for over an hour, sharing stories, laughing, and joking around as if we hadn't just met. We had become so comfortable with each other that one market stall owner mistook the American and me for a married couple. *The last thing I need is a husband*, I thought to myself. Yet he and I played along. It was harmless and funny, which actually made me feel good, knowing that our bond appeared so solid and genuine.

The beach was just a fifteen-minute walk from the market place—tangled telephone wires overhead, with scooters and tuk-tuks zipping by. After a sharp turn and weaving through the lively crowds of Bangla Road—some already drunk by daylight—we arrived at a palm-fringed coastline that opened into a pristine cove with turquoise waters.

The three of us bought a coconut from one of the kiosks on the sand, sipping its water through a straw as we slowly walked along the shoreline. Finding a nice spot to sit, we stopped to contemplate the surroundings.

The Andaman Sea stretched ahead of us, tranquil but for some tiny chop stirred by the midday breeze. The calls of seabirds and the occasional cuckoo sang all around us. We remained in silence for awhile, watching, absorbing.

Little by little, I started to feel something churning within me, something heavy, pressing to come out.

"Today marks eleven years of my mother's death," I blurted out, almost without control of my words.

February 1st had always reminded me of the importance of honoring her memory and keeping her spirit alive. One of the ways I found to do that was by sharing stories of who she was and what she meant to me—so that's what I did.

I told them how she always welcomed me home from school with tomato soup, pancakes, sliced cucumber, or a grilled cheese: a *tosti*—all my favorites because she knew the kids weren't always nice to me. I told them how we would snuggle up on the couch to watch our favorite soap every night and how she brushed my hair every morning. I told them about her unconditional love and selfless nature, how she always cared for others, often at her own expense, and how she had the gift of turning even the simplest little things into something extraordinary. I told them how I missed her the most on rainy days, and during winters. I told them that the sky hadn't been as blue since she passed, but as of late, with every mile I traveled and every challenge I overcame, I was getting closer to her, or solidifying her presence within me, and I was beginning to notice the indelible hue again.

"I hope I will never have to know how you feel today," T said between one of my stories. "But I can relate."

He then explained how his mom had faced a tough battle with breast cancer. He had to watch it unfold from afar while studying abroad in New Zealand, the months filled with uncertainty as the chemo drained her energy. Yet she fought for her family, so much so that she and his dad flew across the world to visit him. They climbed mountains together—both literally and figuratively—creating cherished memories along the way, even as she put up the fight of her life. Thankfully, she was doing much better. But still, I sensed he had tasted the anguish and fear of potentially losing a mother, his love for her unmistakable, much like mine.

The air suddenly grew even heavier, harder to breathe. I lay down in the soft sand. H reached out and gave my hand a reassuring squeeze, while T leaned back, resting his head on my stomach. Our emotions intertwined, weaving our separate experiences into one shared grief. Staring up at the cerulean sky, I searched for my mother among the clouds.

"She is out there, watching over you every day, I'm sure of it," H added warmly, following my gaze up.

"I know you were so young..." T said softly. "But...if you had one more day with her, what would you say?"

For a moment I stayed silent, processing his question, then I closed my eyes before answering.

"I would ask for her advice, her hopes, her dreams; I would want her to tell me all the things about life we didn't have the chance to discuss. I would ask her how she felt when she knew she was losing us, when she was losing herself. How was she ever able to let go? But it was okay that she did, when she did, taking away the pain she had fought so hard against... I would thank her for everything: for who she was, for inspiring me to be better, for showing me the way...and..." A tear rolled down my cheek as the earth absorbed my pain. "I would tell her how much I love her."

●

Hopping on a ferry from Phuket to Phi Phi Don, the largest and main island in the Phi Phi archipelago, I realized I might have overpacked—or maybe mispacked—for this part of the world. My Canadian winter coat and Siberian hat hung on my backpack as the sun beat down on the upper deck, ironically representing how past choices weigh on the present—and the inevitabilities of long-term travel.

As soon as we docked, I spotted a slender figure leaping excitedly, arms flailing—it was my cousin. I rushed off the ferry and into her embrace, feeling that familiar—yet never fading—warmth upon meeting a loved one.

S guided the way to where we were staying. It was a small beach hostel with open-air common spaces, ensconced on the white sand, overlooking the blue waters of Loh Dalum Bay and the rowboats that floated on its surface.

It might not have been a five-star resort, but stepping on the sand straight out of bed surely added character. And as the day faded, the beach burst into life with bonfires, DJs and live performances creating an electric and upbeat atmosphere—a sort of parallel reality.

Many travelers sought Thailand for the opportunity to shed inhibitions and embrace life unbound by restrictions or, quite often, accountability—even if only for a few days. And while a part of me appreciated this fervor and freedom, what truly mattered was being reunited with my cousin.

During this transition of no longer being attached to a guy, it felt special—almost essential—to have each other's support. It made it easier to recognize that despite our yearning for love, our greatest strength lay within ourselves.

At daybreak, S and I headed to a charming little beach café just outside our dorm room. We settled on a rustic wooden bench and watched the rowboats sway as we waited for our breakfast.

There was something enchanting about the sheer simplicity of the moment—the salty hair and sandy feet, although not the cleanest, made me feel carefree and happy.

"We have a big day ahead of us, cuz-y!" S said, wiggling.

"Oh yeah?" I laughed. "What did you cook up?"

"I met five Dutch guys before you got here! I overheard them talking and you know me, cuz-y—we've been mates ever since."

"Of course you did," I said, unsurprised. "Are we meeting up with them today?"

"You'll see! I have it all taken care of. Just go with the flow!" she teased, unable to sit still.

As we waited for them to show up, I relaxed my shoulders, trying to surrender to the *laissez-faire* atmosphere. Out of the corner of my eye, I noticed a young lad stumbling out of the hostel and making his way toward us.

"Blimey!" he exclaimed in a thick British accent, as he sat down at our table. "What 'ave I dun?"

"Are you alright?" I asked, realizing he wasn't who we were waiting for—the accent gave him away.

"I don't know what's got into me..." he mumbled, glancing down at his legs.

We followed his gaze and spotted a large, see-through piece of plastic taped to his skin.

"Did you get a tattoo?" S asked.

"I think I did!" he exclaimed, bewildered. "I must 'ave done it last night... It's my name! It looks real, doesn't it?"

The Dutch guys walked up, and all but one sat down. The one who remained standing placed a hand on the British lad's shoulder, noticing our compassionate stares.

"You alright, mate?" he asked.

"Blimey! It's upside down," the Brit replied.

Our new friends looked confused, while S and I chuckled.

"At least everyone will know your name!" she quipped.

"Oh boy, oh boy, me mum is going to kill me," he sighed, then stood and shuffled away, head down.

The five Dutch guys turned to us and properly introduced themselves.

"What was that all about?" one of them asked.

"Oh, just a fellow traveler shedding his inhibitions," I said, shrugging my shoulders. "So, what are we up to today?"

They invited us to join them for a boat ride. Boats? That was a no-brainer. One of them approached the bar to grab us some drinks, while another pointed to a long-tail boat, its colorful hull resting against the white, warm sand, with a Thai man waving at us as he awaited our arrival.

With welcome cocktails in hand—Piña coladas served in coconuts decorated with pink flowers—we sailed to Monkey Beach, a nearby shore famous for its playful macaques. I got chatting with the Dutch guys; it turned out four of them had flown in to accompany their friend who had been away for months, his most recent visit being Shanghai.

"No way!" I exclaimed. "Shanghai was one of my stops too! I dropped off a friend there after a train journey from Moscow to Beijing, and then Shanghai."

"You took the *train?*" he asked.

"Absolutely," I said, grinning.

"No way," he continued, perplexed. "I met another Dutch girl in Shanghai who also took the train!"

I couldn't believe it. The odds seemed astronomical, but to our surprise, we both mentioned the same name at the exact moment—the name of my friend Z. Only days before, he had seen her while visiting one of his friends, who had met her there because the same company had arranged their stay. Suddenly, it felt like this group had entered my inner circle, and we were destined to have a great time together. They cracked open a large ice chest filled with Chang beers and raised a toast to the serendipity of it all.

After ten minutes and ten beers, we eased onto Monkey Beach, stepping out of the long-tail boat and into the shallow water, our feet sinking into the soft sand as we waded to shore. A troop of macaques, aroused by our arrival, darted along the rocky outcrops, chattering loudly as they scurried closer to the water's edge. One little monkey sat down in front of me, looking deep into my eyes. In an almost human-like gesture, it pointed at an empty beer bottle. One of the guys handed the bottle to the monkey. It grabbed it with both hands, held it up, closed one eye, and peered into it with the other, as if inspecting its contents. Then, the macaque shook the bottle, ensuring nothing was left inside, before tossing it at my feet.

Thinking it might want to play, I filled the bottle with ocean water and handed it back. The monkey seemed hesitant as it took the bottle from my hand, sniffing it cautiously and emptying it right at my feet. It gave me this longing look. I couldn't quite decipher if it wanted the beer, knowing that wasn't what it was offered, or if the monkey was engrossed in this game of fill-and-empty that we had started. Regardless, I felt a genuine bond—almost friendship—and trust; it didn't seem scared of me at all.

Next, we sailed to the iconic Maya Bay on the uninhabited island of Phi Phi Leh, a site that had soared in popularity after featuring in the movie *The Beach* with Leonardo DiCaprio. Known for its stunning visuals—tropical waters nestled amid encircling limestone cliffs—this bay held a special allure. If not for the surrounding boats, it truly felt as though I had been brought to a distant, deserted island.

As soon as we came to a stop in the middle of the bay, the propellers cut and the boat drifted gently, we all leapt off the bow into the emerald-green water. Coral reefs and clownfish swirled beneath me. The beach itself was distant, the water closer to shore murkier. I floated in the middle, pretending I had discovered this paradise on my own. I blocked out the noise, the towering cliffs rising above me. For a moment, everything stilled, and I wondered if this was what it meant to be truly free—adrift, yet anchored in the present, with no demands or expectations tugging at me.

•

Lounging on Loh Dalum Beach a couple of days later, we decided to take a recommendation to visit Koh Lanta for a couple of nights. Renowned for its quiet beaches and laid-back environment, it promised the perfect escape from the more tourist-heavy Phi Phi Islands.

After we boarded the ferry the next morning, a salty breeze whipped through my hair and I settled against the rail on the top deck. The sun's rays filtered through the clouds, offering a gentle warmth without beating down on us—a welcome relief on the unshaded deck. I glanced around. Some travelers looked tired, likely recovering from late nights, while others kept the party going, playing loud music through speakers and passing around beers.

When the boat pulled away from the dock, my attention shifted to a guy who wasn't trying to rest or join the party. He sat just a few feet away, leaning against the rail, just as I was, sketching in a small notebook. He seemed to crave solitude, but when he caught my gaze, he smiled.

"What are you sketching?" I asked, curious.

"Just doodling. I'm an artist," he said, closing his notebook and putting his pencil behind his ear. "Actually, not quite...I want to be an artist. I'm an artist at heart."

I studied his facial expressions as he spoke.

"I'm tired of being an engineer," he continued softly.

"An engineer? They get to sketch sometimes," I said, trying to connect the dots.

"I left it all behind, it didn't make me happy," he replied, his gaze shifting to the open waters.

A native of Canada, he had a muscular build, dark hair, and a disarming smile. Yet there was also something contemplative —almost tormented—about him. I recognized it, felt it.

He wasn't made for the corporate rat race; he longed to unleash his creativity, to think in colors and bold strokes, to recreate the magic of a landscape or a bear dashing through a lake. As he spoke, I could see the world through his eyes; it was clear that he found wonder and beauty in the everyday.

In turn, I shared stories about my childhood, my reasons for leaving. He admired it, encouraged it, his soothing presence making me feel understood, appreciated. I could tell he missed his family too.

"It takes courage, you know," I said. "What you're doing—making this change, following your heart."

"I'm in my late thirties now, older than anyone else on this boat," he said. "If not now, then when?"

Those words unearthed thoughts, reminding me of how fleeting and fragile life is.

"Don't let that make you feel different." I shook my head. "For some people, it's not a matter of *when*. It's *never*."

And just like that, I became part of his story, as he had become part of mine, supporting each other's choices as we strove to become the truest versions of ourselves.

I glanced around the boat again, taking in the faces around me. We were all seeking something, but what we sought was different. Like people searching for treasures in a hidden cave, each of us was drawn to a specific glimmer or glow.

My cousin and I, in search of our own little daily indulgence, wandered around Koh Lanta after arriving and stumbled upon a small salon offering a "zen Thai experience." As soon as we stepped inside, the locals greeted us with warm smiles, ushering us to comfy armchairs and offering us tea.

Within minutes, we were having our nails done, listening to their passionate conversations about the island's charm, and learning about the best places to visit during our stay. They recommended Diamond Cliff Beach, describing it as a perfect recipe for calming the mind. Their enthusiasm? Contagious.

But first, they were determined to calm our bodies. After our pedicures, toes glittering and gleaming, one of the women led us through a long curtain with intricate embroidery that divided the salon, revealing the massage area. S and I settled onto our designated beds.

When another curtain closed between us, I realized this would be my first Thai massage—a traditional practice combining yoga-like poses, stretching, and pressure-point techniques. The therapist uses their hands, elbows, knees, and feet to apply targeted pressure while guiding the recipient through a series of stretches and movements, all while remaining partially clothed.

Even knowing this upfront, when a slender Thai woman climbed on top of me and started massaging me with her knees and elbows, I was still surprised and chuckled. Behind the curtain, I heard S have a similar response.

"Is she crawling over you too?" she whispered.

"Yeees..." I groaned, attempting to relax as my head was squashed into a face donut.

My back had been sore for quite some weeks; I could feel the knots where my backpack had pressed against me during hikes and long walks. And of course, sleeping in a variety of hostels, trains, planes, beaches and buses hadn't done it any good either.

"Very tight," the petite massage therapist said, digging her hands and elbows into my shoulders with precision.

"Yes, ow, very tight," I grumbled.

After another couple of minutes, she reiterated, "Very, very tight."

I tried to relax and let her do her magic, but I could feel how tight my muscles were—more like tough shank than a tender filet mignon.

"Wait one moment please, I know what you need," she said, noticing that her small hands and slight weight weren't doing much. "You need strong, big."

In a way, I was the one to blame for what happened next.

Before the massage, I filled out a questionnaire indicating no preference for the therapist, which I remembered when she walked out of the room. After a few minutes, the curtains rattled again. I lifted my head—a tall, intimidating Thai man with tightly pulled back hair and a face sculpted like bronze walked toward the table. He looked like an ancient warrior.

"Hi," I said, hoping he was there to help rather than kill me.

"Focus," he said with a firm but gentle voice.

I looked down and took a deep breath, unsure I wanted to feel what I was about to feel. After a moment that felt like an eternity, he slowly started folding my limbs into various positions—legs to glutes, arms behind back, crossing my legs with my knees bent as he leaned on top, gradually applying pressure. He rolled me onto my side, pushing my knees toward my chest, stretching my spine. He had me sit up, twisting my torso and pressing my shoulders while he anchored me from behind. I had no choice but to follow his movements. It wasn't too painful per se, but the whole time I was thinking, *I didn't know my body could bend like this!*

"You okay, cuz-y?" S asked from behind the curtain.

"Yep, yep," I said, holding my breath as I felt the knots releasing.

After he freed me from his firm grip, the therapist crawled on top and used his feet, knees, and elbows to push the tightness from my spine out to the sides, tracing my shoulder blades and lower back. I closed my eyes, listening to my body.

"All better, you will see," he said, stepping off the bed and opening the curtain.

Carefully, I started moving off the massage table. Once I stood up, I couldn't believe what I felt: my shoulders didn't hurt anymore, my neck could turn freely, and even my calves felt like they could run a marathon.

"Take better care of yourself," the Thai warrior said with a grin before he slipped out the front door.

Outside, I floated through the streets, amazed at how little resistance the air offered. My body had never been this light—and to a certain extent, neither had my mind and spirit. They had even braided my long blonde locks! I felt reborn, like a ribbon in the wind—unshackled, unrestricted, and flowing freely.

The next afternoon I video-called my dad, and the woman in his life joined the conversation. Her kindness toward me—a rare occurrence, often harboring ulterior motives—suddenly seemed possible with me on the other side of the world.

For my dad's happiness, I had long accepted her presence in his life, yet it didn't imply friendship between us. That, to me, might be too much. Nevertheless, I celebrated the semblance of a normal conversation on that call, hoping that perhaps one day we could peacefully coexist—two individuals tolerating each other's existence. Still, just hearing her voice cut through my being like a knife. I had to find a place to lick old wounds.

S and I hopped on rented Vespa-style scooters, two hostel mates taking the handlebars, toward Diamond Cliff Beach. We parked at the top of the cliff and descended steep, uneven wooden steps to a secluded beach, tucked against the rock walls with tropical vegetation spilling over the sand.

Strolling along the deserted beach as the sun began to set, a calmness embraced my being. The towering cliffs formed a protective barrier around the small beach, creating a hidden sanctuary from the outside world. I felt invisible, free to let my thoughts drift unrestrained without fear of judgment. The rocks, standing tall and solid, seemed to promise that here, all my secrets could unfold, carried away by the wind and waves, lost in the quiet of the cove.

I stopped by the shore, picked up a stick, and began sketching in the sand. Setting aside any intention or goal, I allowed my creativity to run wild. Smooth lines eventually connected. They formed the figure of a horse, its tail flowing and mane sweeping upward with the energy of a gallop.

I dropped the stick and stared at it. The figure came from within me, a visual representation of the emotions that had been silently stirring in my heart. I suspected these emotions were brought to the surface during the call with my dad.

As a teenager, I spent hours on end at the local stable, riding and grooming my pony. When he retired due to old age, at my mother's request, my father gifted me a magnificent young black horse called Vaya con Dios.

"The horse—buy it for her, please," she told him two weeks before she passed.

In the dark days that left me motherless, I played the song *Vaya con Dios, my darling, Vaya con Dios, my love* by Les Paul and Mary Ford relentlessly, hoping my dad understood the message amidst my grieving adolescent chaos. And he did.

Whether it was an attempt to bring joy back into my life or not, it succeeded. I remembered the day the horse arrived. He was three years old and I was thirteen. The moment I gazed into his dark, shimmering eyes, I felt an unspoken dependence and I knew I wanted to raise him. I fell for him instantly—and deeply. He too had lost his mother, yet there he stood, tall, noble, and steadfast—he had survived. His strength became my inspiration. I saw a reflection of my own resilience in him.

Vaya con Dios became my rock, my balance. He filled a void that lingered; a void that no other human relationship seemed to fill. In moments of despair, I would bury my face in his neck, and he would rest his head on my shoulder as many tears rolled down my cheeks. He was my confidant, my protector, my bright light in the darkness and the only one I could fully trust. He once defended me by swiftly launching a boy off his bicycle after an insulting comment; it took only one quick strike with one of his legs. He had my back, and his friendship was one that would never betray me.

In the most unloved era of my life, the person I cared for the most was entangled in a relentless power struggle between me and the woman in his life. The cherished dinner conversations with my father morphed into heated debates because this woman made it her mission to counter, reject, or invalidate every topic we discussed. Her mere presence catalyzed conflict, casting me as an outsider, a bystander to my own home. I would sit at the table, silently wishing for the ordeal to end.

Such a toxic atmosphere prompted me to seek solace in greater independence, with the horse remaining my silent refuge. As I got older, I gained more freedom and immersed myself in my studies, further minimizing my time at home and finding a temporary reprieve.

But then, just when I thought I had created a safe space, Vaya con Dios fell critically ill. Thankfully, my dad stood by me through it all. He gazed into the horse's eyes and resolved to give him every possible chance. Despite the twenty percent odds of survival, he made it through surgery. Yet the road to recovery stretched long and strenuous.

I can still see him, standing in the specialized stable at the equine hospital, surrounded by IVs and bandages. He entered surgery as a robust, muscular young horse and emerged frail and delicate. His eyes, as intense as ever, seemed to implore me to fight for him while silently conveying how much strength it took to endure. A year of painstaking recovery followed, and eventually, we returned to our beloved sport, dressage—literally, getting back in the saddle. I never imagined we would compete again, but the horse seemed as determined as I was to move forward, to live.

Another year passed, and life gradually brightened. I thrived in my academics, tapping into my strengths to push myself further. Taking those initial strides toward independence. I dedicated every spare moment to a part-time job, saving for a significant goal, each achievement bolstering my confidence.

Somehow I had transformed all my emotional baggage into a reservoir of newfound energy, a driving force to change the trajectory of my life.

With time, I sensed more control, and the world appeared full of opportunities. I wanted to explore that world, discover my purpose, grow, learn, and delve into the vast unknown. If I were a caterpillar, that would have been the moment I felt empowered enough to emerge from my cocoon, find my wings, and take flight. Throughout every endeavor, this horse, even in the midst of his own pain and recovery, served as a steady handrail, preventing me from unraveling, guiding me to rise above challenges.

On a beautiful September day in the Netherlands, the sky painted in a soft blue with a gentle early fall breeze, Vaya con Dios and I trotted under the late afternoon sun. Everything felt perfect; we were a harmonious unit, flawlessly gliding in a steady gallop. He gave his all, and for an instant, it felt like I could ride in that calmness forever.

Then, in the blink of an eye, Vaya con Dios collapsed—his knees buckled and he fell forward, twisting sideways as he turned. My feet hit the sand beneath me. I swiftly dismounted and tried to help him rise, stroking his shoulder. His knees sank deeper into the sand, and I dropped down beside him as he gently pressed his nose against my leg.

"What's wrong, buddy?" I whispered, my voice trembling.

He responded with a slow blink and shifted his nose toward his stomach, indicating the source of his discomfort before attempting to rise onto his hooves, one by one. He managed to move toward the stable, taking careful, small steps, leaning against me, shoulder to shoulder. As soon as he smelled his spacious stable, he briefly quickened his pace, but then sank back to his knees, lying down in the soft bedding.

Throughout the night, my dad, stable friends, and I took turns walking alongside him—soothing his anxiety, reducing gas buildup, and preventing him from rolling onto his back, which had caused his critical illness two years before. I caressed him, kissed him, and sang songs until the glimmer in his eye began to shine a little brighter. He seemed to improve.

In the middle of the night I went home, trying to sleep but tossing and turning, while a village of people kept watch over him. If the local veterinarian ran out of ideas, we would need to return to the equine clinic, and I knew that if we did, it would be our final journey together.

Early the following morning, during my work shift at the local liquor store, I received a message from my dad: the horse was deteriorating; he no longer wanted to walk, sinking into his bedding with dark, weary eyes. My boss, understanding the situation, promptly released me from my duties and I rushed out the door, while my dad loaded the horse into our trailer.

Together we drove to the clinic. At some point, the silly horse managed to break free from the ropes that kept him looking out of a small window, facing forward. He turned around and stuck his nose out through the large open space between the loading ramp and the roof, then twisted his head to look at me in the back seat of the car. There was a sense in the air, as if he *understood*—this was his final chance to take it all in, to inhale the fresh air. He had mustered the strength to stay on his feet, savoring every moment—the trees, the birds, the green Dutch countryside.

Once inside the clinic, he willingly lowered himself onto a thick layer of hay in the specially prepared intake stable. I followed suit, settling beside him, providing a comforting space for his large, friendly head to rest on my lap.

As my dad spoke with the veterinarians, the undertone suggested it was time to bid farewell. But how does one say goodbye? I grappled with guilt for all the times I told him about my dreams of exploring the world and how I longed to get away; I never intended to leave him behind.

"It's okay, buddy," I reassured him.

He sighed heavily, as if sensing the inevitable, struggling to lift his head and meet my gaze.

"It's okay... You were strong for me; now, I have to be strong for you," I whispered, cradling his head close to my chest.

In my mind, I played his song.

"Now the time has come to part, the time for weeping"

"Vaya con Dios, my darling
Vaya con Dios, my love"

"Wherever you may be, I'll be beside you
Although you're many million dreams away"

"Now the dawn is breaking through a gray tomorrow."

In a pivotal phase of my life, when I needed him the most, he stood by me. It felt as if he had entered my world with the sole purpose of guiding me through that challenging period. Just as my life started to brighten, he departed, as if he nudged, "Fly high and far now."

That day, he died in my arms.

"Vaya con Dios—Go with God."

Sitting on that Thai beach, thousands of miles from home and four and a half years from that shattering episode, I looked at the drawing again, its lines now connecting beyond the sand. The phone call earlier that day had indeed unearthed past emotions—the suffocating pain of being a young girl trapped by grief, vying for her father's love and attention, and losing my horse and friend, my anchor and refuge from the daily complexities of home.

As the night descended during the scooter ride back to the hostel, I sensed a change within myself. It became clear to me that if I was to remain stuck in the grip of past feelings and harboring grudges, the one to suffer the most in the long term would be me. I wasn't sure exactly how, but I had to overcome that pain, liberate myself from what was holding me back. There was work to be done.

•

When we reached the mainland by ferry in Krabi, we hopped into a compact white van. It had three rows of seats for travelers heading to the east coast. We sat down in the first row with a Canadian guy. Behind us sat three bearded Norwegians, and behind them, two clean-shaven Austrians.

Noticing the energy in the group, the driver turned the music up, reggaeton beats rattling the windows. S, ever so energetic, started laughing and dancing in her seat, pulling the boisterous Norwegians into the fun. Meanwhile the two Austrians, eager yet reserved, smiled but didn't budge, their quiet demeanor intriguing me.

After three hours in the van, we reached another ferry dock. The Canadian and Norwegians went their separate ways when we got out of the van, but the Austrians joined us on the same ship and we struck up a conversation. They turned out to be brothers from Graz, a city I only vaguely knew because of Arnold Schwarzenegger.

My only visit to Austria involved a winter sports vacation, where skiing, to me, meant lounging in the sun on a mountain with a lemony Radler beer in hand, wearing ski shoes only because I attempted a single descent.

"You should visit Graz sometime!" the older brother said.

"Don't tempt me," I cheekily replied. "When I commit to something, I mean it."

"She sure does!" S chimed in, wiggling her eyebrows at me, a mischievous spark lighting up her face, then throwing the same expression at the brown-haired, brown-eyed stranger, who looked like he could belong to a boyband of tall, smooth-talking teddy bears in lederhosen.

Continuing our conversation, I discovered he wasn't in a lederhosen-wearing boyband. In fact, he worked at a law office while pursuing studies to become a lawyer. I enjoyed a good debate, so I challenged him with questions about morality and criminal justice. We talked for two hours, teasing, laughing.

When the ferry briefly docked at Koh Samui and he left to explore the island with his brother, I wished S and I hadn't made plans to continue on to Koh Phangan. Nevertheless, we exchanged contact information, and he promised to find me in a few days.

"Nice guy, huh, cuz-y?" S teased, giving me a little nudge at the shoulder.

I shrugged. "I suppose," I said, thinking no one minds a bit of attention from a handsome stranger.

Two days later I called my dad for his birthday. After we hung up, I sat at the beach in front of our bungalow and gazed at the ocean, recalling the joy I felt as a child, interlocking my little hand in my dad's big hand—our special sign meaning "I love you unconditionally, even when it goes unsaid." He had always been my role model, someone who rose from the streets of post-World War II Rotterdam, working hard to provide a better life for his family. We had always been inseparable.

When my mother passed away, I wanted—and needed—to rely on him even more for support. And we did lean on each other; that is, until other women began throwing themselves at him—shamelessly, relentlessly. Though I was a child, I wasn't blind. Many visited under the guise of checking on us but were, in fact, tugging at his attention and taking time away from our grieving process. Obviously, I didn't welcome the distraction. I wanted my dad to be happy, and even my mother would agree that he deserved a chance at a second life and more love, but not like this, not while the flowers on my mother's grave were still in bloom.

S called my name, snapping me back to reality. I wiped away my tears and followed her to our room, where we changed into bathing suits and headed out for a swim.

"Do you think the guy will come for you?" she inquired as we walked to the pool overlooking the beach.

"Who?" I asked her, still somewhat weighed down by the call and the memories it evoked.

"The guy! The Austrian!"

"We'll see." I shrugged.

While he did mention he would come find me, you never know. People often make promises they can't keep, so I wasn't going out of my way to set a meeting spot. Besides, there was nothing wrong with my cousin and me lounging in the sun, gazing at the serene sea and the tall palm trees. If he showed up, it would be an added bonus to a day that I intended to live fully and presently.

Not even two hours later, a tall shadow stole my sunlight.

"I promised," the Austrian said, standing by the pool where we were sunbathing.

It was a refreshing change to have someone follow through on a commitment—just as I always intend to do. In fact, it was *so* refreshing that I straightaway began contemplating the idea of adding a pit stop to Austria to my itinerary. After all, I would be in Germany in less than a week, and Austria was just a skip and a hop away... *Slow down*, I thought, catching myself getting ahead of myself.

After some flirtatious chatter, we decided that the four of us, including his brother, would join the five Dutch guys—who just so happened to be on the island as well—for a night out in the Thai jungle at the Jungle Experience.

All nine of us agreed to wear green—a groundbreaking creative choice—and with plenty of time before it started at 10 p.m., we took the Austrian brothers shopping. A store with neon green shirts hanging out the door had everything we needed to go with the theme, including neon green flower headbands—the finishing touches—for S and me.

"The green monkeys!" one of the Dutchmen yelled at the top of his lungs as we approached the fire pit outside their bungalow, raising his beer.

"The green monkeys!" everyone echoed as we "clanked" our plastic wine cups and beer bottles together.

After warm-up drinks, we caught a *songthaew*, a pickup truck converted to carry people, to the heart of a dense jungle in Baan Tai. Everywhere I looked, shades of green blended with bright neon lights among the trees, and as we passed through the gates, loud deep house, trance, and techno music surrounded us from various directions, sending vibrations through the ground beneath our feet and causing the palm leaves to sway. I felt a flutter in my stomach, pulsing in time with the rhythm.

Inside, we followed a winding trail flanked by tiki torches, their flickering flames casting playful shadows on the vibrant foliage, leading us deeper into the jungle toward the pulsating main stage. A multitude of people had already flooded in, dancing energetically, with a laser show overhead.

Sticking together as a group of nine proved challenging. The Dutch guys and my cousin vanished into the crowd, drawn by the lasers after ordering buckets overflowing with drinks—literal buckets filled to the brim with a beverage. Even the Austrian brothers split up, leaving only the older one by my side.

"We'll find them later. Come on," he said as he grabbed my hand and guided me down a different path.

There was a turn, a clearing, where black lights illuminated a wall of neon drawings. We entered—my eyes squinting to adjust to the contrast of colors and darkness, then widening as the scene came into focus.

Inside, rows of eight-foot-tall black canvases stood one after another, showcasing glowing examples of art. Bodies gleamed under the black lights; faces, arms and torsos adorned with the same intricate designs I had seen on the canvas walls. Dragons curled around shoulders, suns stretched across backs, phoenixes and hearts flared on arms and chests, and even Batman symbols glowed in vibrant blues and yellows on faces.

A friendly lady gestured toward her laid-out blanket and brushes on the ground.

"Sit, sit!" she encouraged.

"Yes, sit!" the Austrian nudged, and we both settled onto the blanket.

"What are we doing here?" I asked, feeling a bit out of my comfort zone.

"Dragons, for good fortune," the woman replied, swiftly finishing the Austrian's left arm before turning to mine.

Minutes later, our arms were covered in fiery scales of yellow and orange, our hands resembling skeletal claws in the same hues. We radiated under the fluorescent black lights, which were strung on bamboo poles, our arms, neon green shirts, and the flowers in my hair glowing brightly.

We ventured back into the crowd to search for our friends and family. Seeing one of our Dutch companions, he reassured us that my cousin was safe but said the younger brother was still missing.

"Let's go. Let's go find your brother," I said, grabbing the Austrian's arm as we headed to a smaller stage.

After scouting every corner, we finally spotted him holding a massive bucket of drink with colorful straws.

"There he is!" I pointed.

The Austrian smiled, no longer concerned.

"You will make a great mother one day," he observed, his eyes fixated on me.

Before this journey, I rarely explored potential relationships during a night out. However, meeting so many different people from so many different places was showing me that I could let go and open up more—without straying from my underlying values. I craved spontaneity, willing to stretch my limits, and in that moment, I wanted what I wanted—him.

In the midst of the jungle, with dragon scales painted on our arms, neon lights overhead, and music vibrating through our bones, he caressed my face and kissed me, passionately, gently. Everyone on this journey was there for a reason, his kiss igniting a truth: I was enough, and the right people would always appreciate who I am.

It was nearly noon when S and I finally woke up groggily, our stomachs growling louder than any other morning. We headed to the charming waterfront restaurant of our bungalow hotel, ordered hamburgers and fries, and sat at the tables, feet in the sand, soaking in the silence and the ocean view.

Still, I couldn't shake the awareness that this marked our last day together—again. The following day I would head to Bangkok to continue on to Europe from there, while S would stay in Thailand a little longer before traveling to Indonesia.

After our breakfast we walked over to some nearby shops, browsing fluorescent pink accessories and outfits fitting for the occasion—it was Valentine's Day. Bags in hand and arm in arm, I glanced at S—beautiful as always, even with the humid heat showing on her face, her hair damp.

When we were little girls, I often felt overshadowed by her beauty, humor and charm, convinced I would never measure up. But as we matured, we found ourselves side by side—just as we were now, walking down that street in Thailand, and as we had in China, New Zealand, and Australia. We faced life's challenges and grew stronger together, learning not just about the world, but about ourselves. No longer in her shadow, we basked in the sunlight—both literally and metaphorically.

After going out with the usual crew—the Dutchmen and the two brothers—S and I returned to our bungalow hotel in the wee hours of the night, the Austrian following suit.

With my bags packed and ready for the 7:30 a.m. departure to Bangkok, I asked him to join me for a chat by the pool.

"I will be waiting for you right here," he said, nodding as he settled into a pool chair overlooking the Gulf of Thailand.

I went to say goodbye to S, who was standing in front of our room, her lips curled downward in a slight pout.

"These moments never get easier, huh?" I said, wrapping my arms around her.

"I am so glad you came to Thailand, cuz-y," she squeezed me tightly. "You have to tell me everything about Germany when you get there! Show him what he'll never have."

"I will." I chuckled and rolled my eyes. "Sweet dreams cuz-y, I love you."

"Safe travels! I would say goodnight to you too, but...it looks like your night isn't quite over yet," she winked at the Austrian sitting by the pool.

"Could still be a good night," I said mischievously, then laughed and walked away, back to my solitary path.

I took a seat next to the Austrian on the lounge chair, his arms wrapping around me as we gazed over the water. The silhouettes of distant fishing boats blinked in and out like fireflies on the dark horizon, their dim glow mirrored by the gentle waves. The warmth of his skin and the faint, sweet scent of sweat filled the air between us. I could hear his breath sync with mine as a deep stillness settled over the world, our world, broken only by the rhythmic hum of insects behind us and the waters ahead. He caressed my face like he had before and gazed into my eyes as a soft breeze rustled the palm trees above, cooling the heat of his kiss.

Night transitioned into twilight, the sky shifting from inky black to soft purples and pinks, heralding the sun's ascent over the sparkling water.

"Is this it?" he asked. "Do you have to leave?"

I didn't have to do anything, and moments like these made me question why I was returning to Europe at all. I wasn't planning to return; it was merely the next place my heart felt compelled to go. I had shared every detail with the Austrian about the German before we kissed in the jungle. I wouldn't have engaged in that moment without laying bare my plans.

I wasn't seeking a fleeting romance, and I left it to him to decide how he wanted to handle the information regarding my impending journey to Germany. I extended the same courtesy to the German about the Austrian—perhaps unnecessary, but transparency was my guiding principle.

"So...why are you flying back if you're not sure this is the end of your trip and he's not a new beginning for you?" he asked, his big brown eyes fixing on me.

The truth was, I wasn't exactly sure. Perhaps it was because I detested unfinished business, especially after investing so much time, energy, and heart.

As I attempted to explain my internal conflict, the Austrian remained interested and balanced—guiding me through my emotions.

Once the sun finally showed itself, we hailed a taxi from the bungalow's alleyway to take him to his hotel nearby and me to the ferry harbor.

"The trip was meant to be an odyssey in the fullest sense of the word, an epic journey that would change everything," he said, holding the car door open as he was about to step out in front of his accommodation. "It's from my favorite book."

Jon Krakauer, *Into The Wild*. I smiled. His understanding of my journey gave me pause, making me wonder if I should go to the ferry at all.

Before closing the door, he leaned in one last time and said, "Find me in Austria?"

"You got it," I nodded, still smiling.

PART FIVE

EVERYWHERE BUT
MOVING BACKWARD

Germany

"Berlin?! I am in Berlin?" I said out loud, startled awake as the plane sat still on the tarmac, glancing around at my fellow passengers.

"We sure are!" someone in my row broke the silence.

My flight destination was Prague, but given the snowstorms over the Czech Republic, the crew deemed it safer to divert to Berlin. Bad weather may have been the official reason for my detour, a part of me wondered if the universe orchestrated this diversion just to give me some time to think.

Perhaps it wasn't about disembarking, but simply about touching down here after all the conversations of the past few months. I longed for a moment of clarity—something that could signal destiny or, perhaps, the comforting familiarity of home I hoped to find in due time.

Czech Republic

Once the snowfall ceased, the plane finally continued on to Prague, where I would eventually get a bus to Nuremberg in the southeast of Germany. Just before we took off, I shared a snapshot of my impromptu stop in Berlin on one of my social media accounts. Then, I turned my phone to airplane mode.

A few hours later, as I lay in my hostel bed resting, I reached for my phone again to check what I had missed. A giggle escaped me when my screen lit up, and I started reading the incoming messages.

The German:
  YOU ARE SO CLOSE TO ME.

The German-Croatian:
  ARE YOU IN BERLIN?!

The Austrian:
  YOU ARE SO CLOSE TO AUSTRIA NOW!
  PLEASE WAIT FOR ME TO COME HOME.

After two nights in Prague, the desire to head to Germany had dwindled. Still, I couldn't deny the anticipation; it was clear that, deep down, I cared a great deal. And the irony wasn't lost on me—it had been precisely four months since I last saw the German at Niagara Falls in Canada.

As I hopped on the bus to Nuremberg and settled into my seat, texts from the Austrian made my phone buzz.

The Austrian:
  ARE YOU ON YOUR WAY TO NUREMBERG?

  MAYBE YOU WILL FIND "HOME" THERE.

  WITH YOUR GERMAN.

His sassy tone came through even in writing. Yet I couldn't decipher if he was joking, expressing a hint of jealousy, or simply mocking me. The nuances were lost without facial expressions and sounds, and my tendency to overanalyze every word sent my way only fueled my nerves.

Seeking solace, I reached out to one of my best friends, C, whose insights had always brought clarity. His advice was simple yet powerful: be myself, stay honest, just as I had been throughout my travels. The people I met had no preconceived notions. They just discovered the unapologetic, candid, life-loving version of me who had become an unstoppable force of nature.

The German:
ARE YOU ALMOST HERE?

I WILL BE WAITING FOR YOU.

My heart pounded. After four months, I was about to see *him* again. Staring at the phone screen, I reflected on the rollercoaster of emotions we had ridden—the intensity that ignited and eventually faded into a choking pain.

He had fueled my flame, only to extract the air from our shared electronic space across numerous time zones. Once the oxygen ran out, I surfaced like a phoenix from the ashes, ready to face the truth deep inside: the real pain I had clung to.

For weeks I cried, finally releasing emotions I had bottled up for so long—emotions that had nothing to do with him. Layer by layer, I peeled back the parts of myself I had kept hidden—the parts my love for him had masked, softened, and protected from emerging. I had to confront the real pain I had buried within, eventually.

Anxiously shuffling in my favorite bus seat—the seat right behind the driver on the opposite side, that offered the most panoramic view—we rolled into the station in Nuremberg.

He couldn't see me yet, but I spotted him instantly: leaning casually against his dark silver Mercedes-Benz, clad in a deep red winter coat. His perfectly styled hair and welcoming smile that had once captivated me in Montreal remained, though that electric spark I had vividly felt four months ago had clearly dimmed. I had rehearsed this scene countless times in my mind over the last couple of months—from passionate reunions to sassy encounters where I flipped my hair, exuding a newfound confidence—but this was no scripted movie moment. The unfolding outcome was a mystery only the future could unveil.

As the bus came to a full stop, I found it hard to believe I had traveled such a distance for this moment. Stepping onto the asphalt, I looked up to meet his gaze; he smiled and embraced me in a tight hug. I felt his cheek against mine and closed my eyes, seconds passing, our longing finally ending, as people shuffled past us at the bus station. With his arms around me, my soul took a step back, as if I could see myself standing there. My heart, calm instead of racing, told me clearly—the loose ends were tied. There had been all this build-up, all this fantasizing, and when you fantasize for too long without taking action, it becomes exactly that—a fantasy.

That evening, we went to an Italian restaurant, reminiscent of the last time we shared a meal together at Niagara Falls. He had that same amused grin, but it didn't have the same meaning.

"I knew I would see you again," he broke the silence.

"You did, huh?" I said, picking up my glass of Prosecco. "You didn't work very hard for it."

"You know I'm very busy, but I never thought I could stop you," he said, also taking a sip.

"If I didn't show up, wouldn't everything just have been a waste of time?" I asked him. "Wouldn't you ever wonder..."

"No," he said resolutely. "None of it was a waste of time."

I raised my eyebrows, waiting for him to say more.

"I wanted to be on this journey with you," he continued.

"Yes," I said, taking another sip. "Just not *with* me."

A candle flickered between us, the flame that once was now feeble, interrupted, running out.

"Manönnchen..." he shook his head. "You have dreams that will never be mine. I have no doubt you will have everything you set your mind to. You don't need me holding you back."

Across the table, as we savored our Fettuccine Alfredo, I gazed at him. The depth of my care for him was undeniable, a sentiment that had grown while I shared every inch of my journey, mind, soul, and heart with him. However, I couldn't *feel* it anymore—and that's precisely why I had come here.

"So...are you happy?" I asked, a hint of mischief in my eyes.

"I'm not talking about her," he mumbled.

"Well, that's promising." I leaned back, crossing my arms.

I enjoyed watching him squirm. The look on his face alone, as he faced accountability for his choices, made the detour worth it. Any lingering resentment I had for the pain he caused slipped away. I was right to come here—at least from where I was sitting. Some things can only be seen face-to-face.

I could have gotten back on a bus and left. Instead, he suggested I stay and explore the city for a few more days, which I accepted. After all, we had shared so much, and he had played such a significant role in my journey.

The following morning we strolled through Old Town, its cobblestone streets leading us past market squares and historic fountains. I had always wanted to visit Nuremberg for its rich history and well-preserved architecture. It did not disappoint. Walking there, the towering Nuremberg Castle caught my eye, perched on a hill and watching over the city with a quiet, imposing presence. Beneath the beauty, however, I couldn't shake the weight of the city's darker history.

Later, as clouds moved in, we visited the Nuremberg Trials Memorial, where the shadow of the Nazi regime loomed heavy, sending chills down my spine. Walking through the halls where war criminals were tried, I was reminded that Nuremberg's history isn't just one of charm, but also one of atrocities, reckoning, and justice.

Leaving the weight of the past behind, we made our way to a chic cocktail lounge—the atmosphere shifting dramatically. Some of his closest friends were already waiting at a table by the window. It was strange walking in, being among them, knowing they probably knew everything about me—and about us. Yet they all welcomed me warmly, hugging me and kissing me on the cheek. Their gestures instantly dispelled my discomfort, replaced by an overwhelming confidence I didn't know I possessed. Like I finally knew the woman I was in the company of men, and that I had nothing to be ashamed of.

"So, how can you let this one go?" one of them said, smiling broadly and winking at me after only a few minutes.

My German mumbled, visibly uncomfortable. I chuckled.

As we sat together, sharing stories, the night outside the window dark and the city twinkling, I could only speculate about their thoughts on the situation. In the end, it didn't really matter. I had achieved what I came here to do—I had found the closure I needed.

"I'm in a lose-lose situation," the German said as we walked home later.

"You are, huh?" I questioned, glancing at him.

"I can't win with you, and I can't win having you here with others."

He probably wasn't wrong, and I tried to empathize. I knew, just as he did, that I had to continue on. Everything that needed to be said had been said; there was no point in staying another night. When we returned to his apartment later that evening, I began packing my things.

"Where would you go at this late hour?" he asked with a concerned look on his face.

"I'll figure it out." I smiled. "I always do."

He dropped me off at *S/U-Bahn* station Hauptbahnhof—the largest in northern Bavaria—with hundreds of options to leave, to move on. By the entrance, we hugged. Our bodies were close, yet there was no warmth—it felt final.

Forcing myself not to look over my shoulder, I walked away, leaving a version of myself behind, standing in the cold.

Inside, commuters were walking and running, weaving between the many platforms as I made my way to the ticket booth. Unsure what direction to go in, I reached out to a girl I had met a few years earlier while studying English at UCLA in Los Angeles. I was aware that she lived in the vicinity with her parents. Luckily, she responded instantly and they kindly let me stay the night at their house.

Once aboard the train, I opened my travel journal—the German had left me a note.

Dear Manönnchen, I just want to say thank you for all the time you spent with me around the globe, even if I wasn't there with you. I truly enjoyed every single minute.

When the train started moving, I read the last sentence: *In the future we can laugh about everything that happened!*

His note appeared somewhat light, airy, not reflecting the depth of my own experience—but, of course, he was entitled to his own perspective. Besides, he was never one to use many deep and meaningful words, and I, in turn, had a tendency to overthink written messages. In any case, that marked the end. They were the final words of a chapter.

After one night in Munich and a two-day stop in Salzburg, I boarded the train to Graz—where the Austrian had returned home to. As the train chugged through the Eastern Alps, a *Sound of Music* song played on constant repeat in my mind.

> "Edelweiss... Edelweiss...
> Every morning you greet me
> Small and white, clean and bright
> You look happy to meet me"

Austria gifted me a unique kind of happiness: I was joyful, lighthearted, excited. Outside the window, green and snow-covered hills rolled by. I snapped a picture, sharing it on social media. Soon, my phone pinged with a notification.

The German-Croatian:
YOU ARE ACTUALLY GOING TO GRAZ?

Yes, why? I thought to myself. Why were some people still surprised that I followed through on the things I said I would do? Was I sure I could survive the Siberian train? Was I sure about traveling for such a long duration? Was I sure about staying in all those hostels? Was I sure about staying with *strangers?* Rather than caution, it felt like they were doubting me. Even those who supported me didn't always seem to have faith in my decisions.

However, when a message like the one from the German-Croatian arrived, I did ask myself—*where was the end?* Yes, to a certain extent I was floating around; there was no specific goal, direction or destination. But even when I missed my family and friends, nothing seemed more uninspiring than returning to the Netherlands with a lingering sense of incompleteness—unaccomplishment. If I were to settle down now, I wouldn't have the opportunity to shed my anger, and the haunting pain would persist in my sleep.

As I walked out of Graz Hauptbahnhof, I saw the Austrian waiting for me at the parking lot—also leaning against his car. There's something about guys leaning against their cars, trying to appear calm and composed, as if to contain their nerves while awaiting a woman's arrival. It's full of unspoken tension, in an effortlessly charming way.

He pushed off the Audi, his smile widening in recognition, the sunlight catching in his warm eyes. My heart didn't slow. He stepped forward, arms wide open, and I melted into a hug, feeling the reassuring strength of his shoulders.

"It's really you," he said, his voice rich and inviting.

"It's so good to see you," I admitted, pulling back slightly to meet his gaze.

He chuckled softly and lifted me off the ground without warning, spinning me around as laughter spilled from my lips.

Seeing him again made me think of how some people enter our lives at specific moments in time and in particular places for a reason. A part of me wondered if there was meant to be a continuation to our relationship, or if our intense connection had stayed behind in the Thai jungle. Then I looked at him, at our surroundings. There was no need to answer that just yet. I was open to figuring this out as we went along.

Before heading to his place, we stopped at a traditional Austrian restaurant to savor some local specialties. We ordered *Spinatknödel*, delicious spinach dumplings with Parmesan, and *Wiener schnitzels*, crispy breaded veal served with potato salad, all paired with a pint of ice-cold beer.

Sharing a meal proved to be a great way to catch up, as it not only kept my hands busy while talking but silenced me just long enough to listen attentively. I noticed how his gaze shifted constantly, avoiding direct eye contact at times. He had exuded such confidence in Thailand, one of the things I liked about him. But now I sensed a different energy, making me realize how layered some people are and how much there was yet to discover about him and myself.

"So...you didn't stay in Germany?" he put down his cutlery.

I shook my head, trying to catch his gaze. "I did not."

"Any plans to go back to Germany?" he fiddled with the red cloth napkin on his lap.

"I will not," I said resolutely.

"Very well then. Austria is way better anyway," he said as he stopped fidgeting and looked up.

Finally, I saw that glow in his big brown eyes—the one I had captured in Koh Phangan, the glow that captivated me, lured me in, *hooked* me. He turned away and winked at the waitress, an older lady wearing an apron, and she brought over a warm plate of *Kaiserschmarrn*—fluffy caramelized pancakes dusted with powdered sugar. He had read my mind.

"I am never nervous about anything, but picking you up from the train station had me on edge," he confessed.

I chuckled. "Why?"

"Wouldn't you like to know," he said mischievously.

He settled the bill, pulled back my chair, and offered his arm to guide me from the restaurant. Under the stars, we walked side by side, ascending the steps and slipping through the door of his apartment. Once inside, he closed the door with a soft click, pulling me close as if we were finally free to explore the spark between us—the magnetic pull, the fire. The world outside faded, leaving only the heat and the unspoken desire flickering in his eyes.

From that point onward, we glided into a harmonious connection; conversations flowed naturally, as though we were two parts of a whole, finishing each other's sentences, and I felt safe in his presence. The days passed with remarkable ease, not least because of the effort he put into ensuring I had the best experience. He took me to Schlossberg, the historic hilltop fortress overlooking the city, where we marveled at the panoramic view. He held me close, keeping me warm as the chilly breeze swept over us. We strolled through the charming streets of the old town, the aroma of freshly brewed coffee wafting from old cafés adorned with colorful flower boxes, even in winter. He pampered me with caviar and champagne, indulging in the region's finest flavors over leisurely lunches and decadent dinners. He introduced me to his friends, we went to a local wine bar and danced in candle-lit cellars. I felt appreciated, having been treated so lavishly. I saw a side of Graz I would have never seen. But also, I saw a part of him that, for better or worse, I was eager to encounter.

During this time, the German checked in on me multiple times. I felt flattered and, to a certain extent, vindictive—he had forfeited the right to know my whereabouts, my activities, and the intricacies of how I navigated breaking free from stagnation. My priorities had changed, and I was happy with where I was. Perhaps that was the step I needed to take all along. I had always been fixated on the past, feeling the weight of creating a better future, often losing sight of what was right in front of me. Now I was determined to make every day count.

One of those days, the Austrian surprised me with a drive to an undisclosed location. The busy streets of the city soon turned into smaller roads; buildings, parks, and petrol stations gave way to rolling hills. Near Riegersburg Castle, I spotted a whimsical building with a prominent sign reading *Zotter Schokolade*. Even with minimal German comprehension, it was evident that chocolate awaited inside.

"Is this your favorite chocolatier?" I inquired.

"You'll see," he replied with a mysterious smile. "Just wait."

As we entered the main building, I felt like Charlie and the Chocolate Factory—surrounded by rich aromas, flowing chocolate fountains, cacao nibs and rows of glistening chocolate bars. Instead of calling it a factory, they named it a theater, where the process of crafting chocolate unfolds like a live performance, engaging all my senses.

We set off on a private tasting tour, watching every step of the production through huge glass partition walls as the guide explained the process from bean to bar. Finally, we reached a hallway where we had the opportunity to taste every variety of chocolate made by the company. With tongs in hand, we playfully scooped morsels and fed each other, the sweet flavors melting on our tongues. His eyes lingered on me, sparkling with anticipation as I savored each bite, slipping in kisses whenever he could as we moved together, glued as one. I couldn't have pictured a more fun and creative way of showing me the countryside.

Turns out that wasn't the only surprise he had in store for me. The next morning, I woke up, and he was gone. Strolling around in my pajamas, I searched his apartment for a clue to where he had disappeared. When I got to the kitchen, I found a handwritten note—*Went to change my car, be right back*—and next to it a bowl of muesli with yogurt, an omelet, whole grain bread, and freshly pressed orange juice. It was nice to be cared for, but what did he mean by changing the car?

"Well, well, well," I said when he came back a few minutes later. "I thought you had left me here."

"Ha," he chuckled, then added, nonchalantly, "I had to go get the Porsche."

"Oh, of course, *The Porsche*," I replied mockingly. "And what, if I may ask, do you need the Porsche for?"

"Just be ready in thirty minutes," he said with that all-too-familiar grin.

Why couldn't this man just tell me where we were going?! And what in the world did we need a different car for? I got ready quickly, trying to contain my excitement, and half an hour later, there we were, heading out of the city again and into the mountains west of Graz.

"I want to show you our cabin," he said excitedly while we drove up the winding roads.

"Our cabin? You know that's how most horror films start, right?"

He chuckled. "Does our time together look like a horror film to you?"

"Touché." I looked at him, amused.

After an hour-long drive, a charming wooden mountain cabin emerged in a forest—a classic Austrian chalet with a sloped roof and reddish-brown details. The entire plot was blanketed in five inches of snow, with pine trees standing tall, their branches bowed under the weight. Since it was the first time I had seen so much powder in months, I dropped to the ground and pulled the Austrian down with me, lying there together as snowflakes landed on our noses.

"I love how you appreciate the little moments," he sighed, brushing snowflakes off my eyebrows. "It makes me pause and be more intentional, more in the moment."

I grabbed his hand in response.

Once inside the cabin, it wasn't much warmer than outside. He handed me a blanket and turned the fireplace on, the light crackling sound already making the room feel less cold. This was a far cry from how I had envisioned my day when I woke up, and I didn't know why he was going to such lengths to impress me. After all, we had first crossed paths in a scrappy old van in Thailand. As much as I relished how he took care of me, sustaining this constant stream of fun and extravagance did not seem like a realistic expectation. And I couldn't just stay there, could I?

We sat on the wool carpet, snuggled between the heavy blanket and the fireplace, snowflakes falling outside the window. I looked at him, tracing every inch of his face.

"Even the smartest fall in too deep eventually," he said, staring back at me intently.

"I will leave for Vienna tomorrow, then go home from there," I mumbled. "But I don't want to..."

Five days of living together had shown us how compatible we were—or could be. We communicated easily, laughed constantly, and I started to think: *Yes, I could get used to this.* But then I thought of my journey—how I had buried my pain by running from it. And it opened my eyes: compatibility alone doesn't build a great relationship, neither does love. I didn't even know if I was ready to love again, truly love, before untangling the knots of my past. I couldn't ask him to walk that road with me, to hold my hand, no matter how much I wanted that.

"It would have been so much easier if we had just left what we had in Thailand," he said, breaking the silence.

His comment blindsided me; the gears in my brain worked to process not the meaning of the words, but what he meant by them. Perhaps it would have been easier. Austria had brought us into a third dimension, and I wondered, from his words, if while he was lifting me up, he was also *falling*.

I grabbed his hand again, wanting the moment to last, etching it in my mind as I felt his fingers caressing mine. Despite my head telling me it was the end, I couldn't shake the feeling that it might not be. Our connection was smooth, painless, drama-free. It seemed silly to just walk away from it —I didn't want to walk away from it.

Before going to bed, he borrowed my travel journal to write me a note—following the tradition. Yet, his note was one I particularly treasured.

Liebe Manon, you are a human of which there aren't two in the world, lively, intelligent and incredibly beautiful to see. I am quite likely not the only man you have enchanted with your smile.

I read every sentence twice, trying to unpack its meaning before moving on to the next. He wrote about the days we had, etched in his memory, and to not lose sight of each other.

And if that does happen, if we do lose each other out of sight, I'm confident you will find your way.
In Liebe ♡

The snow turned into rain. I listened to the pattering against the window, unable to sleep as his words echoed in my mind. What would it take for me to see clearly through the fog? Where must I go to envision what I am supposed to do?

The next morning, he had to attend a court session for a legal case, and I had a Flixbus to catch.

"Thailand is really over now," he said, sighing in the taxi.

The moment reminded me of our last goodbye, dropping him off at his hotel before continuing on to the ferry boat in Koh Phangan.

"I suppose it is." I nodded.

Before getting out, he whispered, "Will you miss me?"

"I'll be back," I said in an Austrian accent, jokingly referring to Arnold Schwarzenegger's *Terminator*, trying to lighten the mood of the moment.

Upon boarding the bus, I realized that the phrase "I'll be back" carried more than casual weight—it held the weight of a commitment. I tried to listen to my inner voice, wondering if what I had said was a genuine promise or merely a jest. Did I want to be back? *Yes,* yes I did.

I leaned back in my seat and smiled as the plane soared into the sky, destined for Rotterdam The Hague Airport. It had been thirteen flights, numerous bus rides, and a mix of many trains and ferry boats since I last set foot in the Netherlands, but now, the sense of home no longer lingered, and the house of my upbringing was no more. Yet home was still home; despite any uncertainties, my family's love awaited me.

Of course, that didn't make the practical side of my return much easier. It required all my courage to ask the woman in my father's life to help me surprise him. She assured me she would be waiting at the airport, although, to be honest, she was the last person I wanted to see upon my return. However, if she was willing to help me, perhaps we could turn a new leaf. It might be the right time to make amends and see if she, too, was open to the same.

Looking out the window as we descended, the green fields below resembled an abstract canvas reminiscent of Dutch painter Piet Mondrian—geometric shapes and lines dividing the landscape into blocks of varying shades. Those lush farm fields were special to me. None matched the vivid colors of the Netherlands on a clear day, neatly sectioned by canals, dykes, and waterways, dotted with clusters of windmills.

To my amazement, the woman was indeed waiting for me. She squeezed my arm, my hands burdened with baggage, and said hello. Then we walked out of the airport in silence and settled into her car, in silence. I never knew which version of her would show up, so it was always better to start off quietly and see what unfolded. But then, as we neared the house, I was prompted to ask her—hesitantly and cautiously—if she would film my father's reaction. After some reluctance, she agreed.

The moment we parked on the street, I hoped my surprise was worth the awkward airport arrival, which would have been warmer if I had told my family I was coming home.

The anticipation of seeing my dad again, after missing him so much, was akin to the rush of a rollercoaster just before the drop. I stealthily crept behind a low wall in front of his house, careful to stay out of sight. My heart was in my throat as the woman entered the side door, closing it behind her.

I crawled from the wall to the cool brick beneath the kitchen window, edging along and keeping my head down until I stood by the door, hidden from the transom window beside it, close enough for a quick knock.

Slowly, the door creaked open again, and my dad poked his head outside to see what was there.

"My daughter!" he exclaimed, his voice cracking. "Oh, it's my daughter, my daughter is home!"

I leaped forward and embraced my father tightly, burying my face in his shoulder. If there was any sense of true home left, this was it.

That week, I quickly noticed that my father wasn't himself. Winter's chill had dimmed his usual shine and charm, as though a shadow had fallen over him. Witnessing him in that vulnerable state always unsettled me. It was a stark reminder that, being born later in my parents' lives, my time with him would be significantly shorter than that of my much older brothers. Despite the sadness and anxiety these circumstances stirred within me, I was determined to cast a ray of light on his days and shower him with love.

However, staying at his new house—which I had only seen once during the planning stages of its purchase—felt strange. To me, the move didn't just represent a move to a new home, but a move away from my childhood memories. Unlike the previous house, which held fragments of our family's past, memories of my mother, and visions of happier days, the new house felt alien, sterile, and kind of surreal. The modern decor boasted clean lines and cool colors, a stark contrast to the warm hues of our former residence. I tried to remind myself that I wasn't moving in; I was merely staying temporarily, trying to figure out my next steps. And in the end, the main thing was that my father found happiness in this new space, even if it didn't feel like home to me.

Sadly, in the days that followed, I quickly slipped back into avoiding the place altogether. I went to several parties and gatherings, savored delightful lunches and brunches with friends in Amsterdam, and relished my godparents' amazing charcuterie plates and warm company.

Cozy evenings of cheese fondue and deep conversations with my brother filled me with contentment, and the idea of visiting my other brother in Normandy, France gave me something to look forward to in the near future. The love of those who truly cared for me made me feel secure, grounded, like I didn't need anything else, at least for a little while.

The only place where the weight of the past clung to me was my father's new house. The initial kindness displayed by the woman in his life on the first day quickly faded, plunging us back into an unpleasant routine of butting heads. While my father remained supportive of my personal journey, in her eyes, my travels were a waste of time, the result of an allegedly spoiled and unhinged child unwilling to accept her mother's passing. Although she was right that my globetrotting was a quest to confront the grief that weighed me down, it was also a means to delve deeper into the anger embedded in my bones from years of mistreatment.

Countless times I faced discouragement, often being told by her that I couldn't accomplish certain things simply because I was deemed not smart or pretty enough—never direct, always covert, masterfully pushing to aim lower.

Others—teachers, peers—weren't always kind either, but her words cut the deepest. The impact of these comments lingered, and it even extended to a moment years ago when I introduced a boyfriend. She later insinuated his friend was a better match for me, as he aligned more with what was considered "my type"—less popular, more awkward, and a bit chubby. The friend was an incredible human. However, this woman couldn't fathom that a handsome, popular guy would genuinely be interested in a person like me.

Her comments diminished me—subtly, insidiously—even when my father was around. Her tone sharpened when he looked the other way. While I understood the need for her to assert her presence in my old house, in the new house, a place she had more ownership over, I hoped she might feel secure enough to dispense with constant competition. But no.

On one of those days, I retreated to my attic bedroom after a late dinner. Even if it didn't have a door, I appreciated the clever utilization of the typical Dutch architecture with its distinctive gable roofs; it was cozy, a small haven.

As I sat on the bed, unable to sleep, I contemplated my next steps. Suddenly, my phone buzzed with a message. It was *her*.

W:
TURN THE LIGHTS OFF.

OF COURSE, I WILL TURN THEM OFF WHEN I GO TO BED.

I replied quickly, thinking of the light that was still shining in my space. But maybe she meant the lights downstairs? I went down to confirm and found the entire house in darkness. Returning to the attic, I texted her again.

YOU MEAN THE LIGHTS IN THE ATTIC?

YES. TURN THEM OFF NOW.

Those words, that order—as if I were a teenager again. Yes, it was her home, and maybe it was bothering her, but surely it wasn't unreasonable to keep the lights on a little longer until I decided to go to bed. Was she really staying up just to make sure I did? Was I really bothering her that much? Anyway, to avoid drama, I switched off the lights.

I lay in the darkness for a couple of hours, still unable to sleep. *This is it*, I thought, *I can't stay any longer*. I grabbed my phone and booked a bus to Paris, and from there, another bus to Normandy to visit my oldest brother and his family before ultimately departing again to...I wasn't yet sure where. The only thing I was sure of was that my healing process was far from complete. I needed to keep moving forward—anything but moving backward.

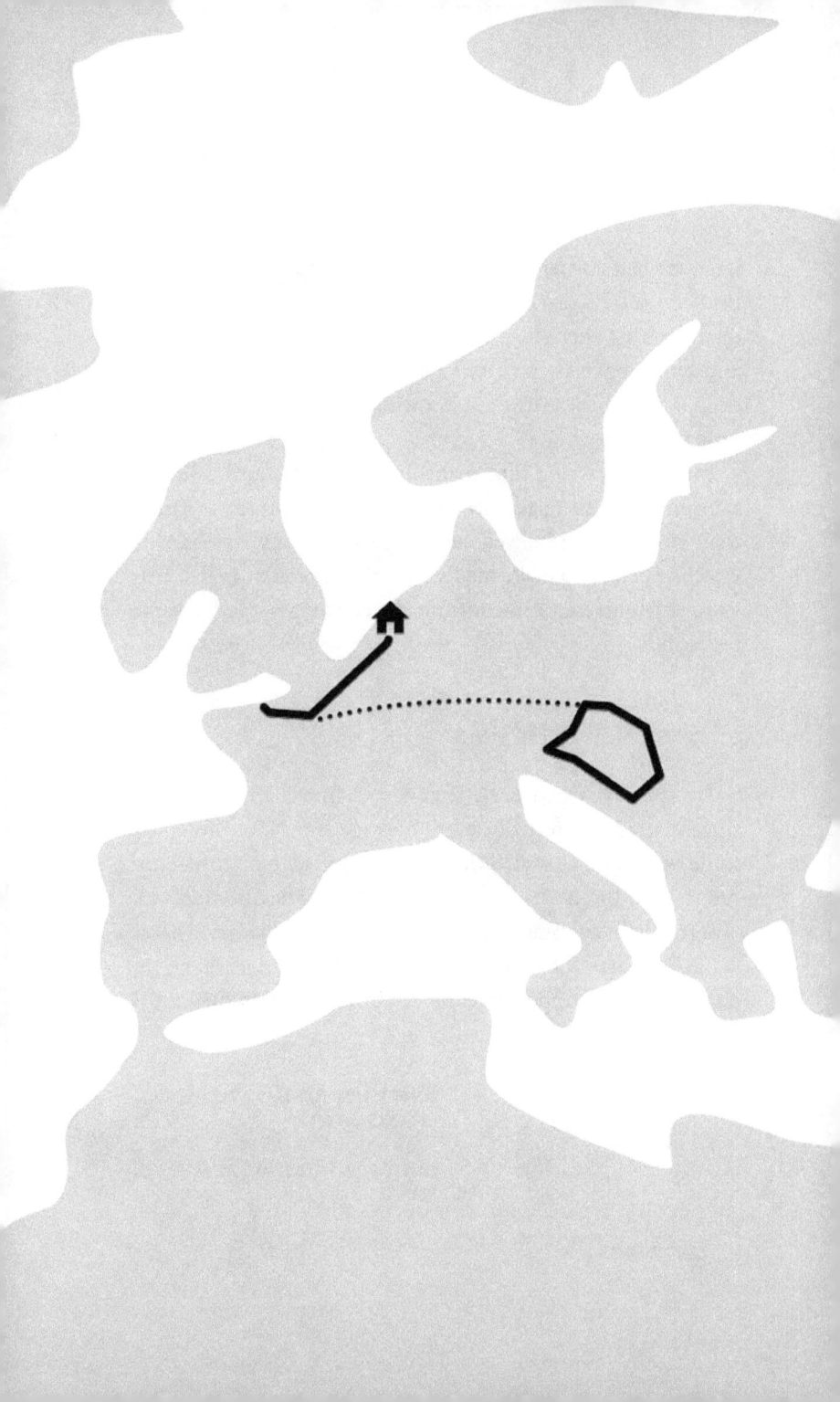

Belgium

Belgium had always been a familiar pit stop on my journeys between the Netherlands and France. Even though I wasn't disembarking this time, it was comforting to watch the land and cityscapes pass by from the bus window. Struggling to sleep, I texted the Austrian, knowing he was also awake for a little while longer.

Ever since leaving him in behind, our texts and calls had transformed into a daily ritual: frivolous and flirtatious banter that still felt solid. Even amid the ambiguity, he had an uncanny ability to make me feel like the version of myself that was gaining strength to confront my challenges. He made me feel seen.

The Austrian:
YOU MAKE ME SMILE A LOT.

He quickly texted back after I told him I wished I were there instead. Admittedly, every message from him brought a smile to my face as well. Still, I could sense it wasn't love—not yet, at least. But it was a strong connection. The question was: Was it worth investing the time and energy to discover what it could become? I weighed the risks, knowing that diving in might lead to disappointment—or perhaps something great. I decided to check.

SOMETIMES YOU HAVE TO TAKE A CHANCE IN LIFE.

FIGHT FOR WHAT YOU REALLY WANT.

LIKE WHAT?

**MOVING TO LONDON WITH YOU,
PRACTICING LAW THERE, AND
LIVING HAPPILY EVER AFTER?**

Surprised by the specificity, I pondered what that scenario might actually entail. After all, I had mentioned London as one of the places I might end up.

I WOULD FIGHT FOR THAT.

I typed impulsively, wondering if it was genuinely what I wanted, yet seeing it as an improbable—but not impossible—future.

**YOU WOULD FIGHT FOR ME, EVEN
IF I CONSIDER GETTING BACK WITH
MY EX?**

I stared at his message. Was this a test?

**NOW, WHY WOULD YOU DO
THAT?**

I asked straightforwardly, feeling a lightness in my stomach as I waited for a response. In Thailand, he had said that he was grateful he had broken free from that relationship—but still.

After an unusually long pause, he replied.

IT WOULD BE EASIER.

My immediate thought was, *Why settle for something that didn't work before—just to avoid being alone?* Was this even a choice? Even if he and I were not worth pursuing, why go backward? That comment of his made me realize that we spent a lot of time discussing our *potential* future, yet that didn't necessarily mean we believed it was a realistic scenario.

**I PREFER THE FULFILLING PATHS
OVER THE EASY ONES.**

After I hit send, I understood that this indirect remark, this insinuation, was, to a large extent, my way of showing that I was willing to fight for him.

DOESN'T MAKE IT SMART.

In the dimly lit bus, loneliness consumed me. Every now and then, streetlights and headlights shone in, but other than that, everything was dark, distant. At a loss for what to say next, I typed, deleted, retried, and typed again...the only thing that was true in my heart.

I MISS YOU.

I genuinely missed him; he had brought a profound impact into my life.

**IT DOESN'T MAKE IT ANY EASIER
WHEN YOU SAY THAT.**

I nodded, put my phone down and thought about how difficult it can sometimes be to harmonize the emotional with the practical. After a few seconds, my phone pinged again.

BUT I MISS YOU TOO.

It was still dark when the bus rolled into the Porte Maillot bus station just a little before 6 a.m. The chilly morning air greeted me as I stepped onto the streets, enveloped by the familiar and timeless atmosphere of Paris. I walked on the well-trodden path along the Champs-Élysées and into the heart of the city.

Given how deserted the streets were, I considered it prudent to reach a secure location and wait for the sun to come up. With the Place de la Concorde in sight, I made a beeline for the Louvre Museum. That's when I noticed a man walking behind me, not too close, but edging closer with every step.

At a crosswalk, I pressed the pedestrian light and hurried across when it turned green. As I reached the other side of the Champs-Élysées, I glanced around and saw the man rushing to catch the same green light.

Strange, I thought, turning my gold ring—set with thirteen diamonds—upside down so the gems faced the palm of my hand. It was an instinctive gesture; I knew it wouldn't deter someone with ill intent. But this ring was precious to me, a gift from my father on my first birthday after my mother's passing, with both of our names—my mother's and mine—engraved into the band. Protecting that memory felt like safeguarding a piece of my past.

In a split-second decision, I crossed the street again, opting for the side I was more familiar with. To my dismay, the man crossed once more. *That's not good*. I needed to vanish, to find a place where he couldn't track my steps.

I darted into the labyrinth of side streets I knew like the back of my hand, weaving through alleys before eventually circling back to the Champs-Élysées and redirecting toward the Louvre. At some point, I looked back, then around me.

He was gone.

At one of the smaller glass pyramids in the courtyard, I settled down on the edge of a triangle fountain and took in the surroundings. The square was empty and still, apart from a couple of birds pecking at dead leaves and rays of sunlight slowly creeping across the ground. There are only a few places in the world where I find this kind of homely peace, places where I feel so intimately connected that I can escape whatever turmoil might be haunting me and simply sit there with my thoughts for a while. The Louvre was one such place for me.

Around 9 a.m., Paris began to stir with life. With no specific plans in mind, I wandered the streets. The monuments, the architecture, the narrow cobblestone alleys lined with hidden cafés, and the haute couture storefronts—all of it reminded me of why I loved this city, its history, the elegance. I strolled along Boulevard Haussmann, passing by Gare Saint-Lazare, admiring the Madeleine, following the banks of the Seine, catching glimpses of the Eiffel Tower, and wandering down Avenue George V. Ah, Avenue George V—a street I dreamed of one day shopping along, sitting at a café on a charming corner by the Seine, watching the sparkling Eiffel Tower during the magical hour of twilight. A girl can dream.

By the time I started to make my way back to the Porte Maillot bus station that afternoon, I estimated that I had walked at least twelve and a half miles. The sun dipped lower, the gray tones darkening, and a quiet contentment settled in.

Paris had a way of doing that—taking the weight off my shoulders, inviting me to lose myself in the aimless exploration of its *arrondissements*, if only for a little while. This city could make me feel both small and infinite all at once.

Even as I retraced my steps, tired but content, I knew that Paris would always have a way of calling me back, always a place for me to return to.

•

Stepping off yet another bus, I spotted R, my oldest brother, waving wildly, his youngest son bouncing excitedly beside him. We hadn't seen each other in five months.

I opened my arms as I rushed toward them. If ever I needed to dive into our family history, he was the go-to person—a true history buff. With our age gap, he held a treasure trove of memories from times I hadn't experienced or was too young to recall. After a hug, he grabbed my face with both hands, kissing me on my left cheek and then my right, his warm voice mixing with the sound of his son's cheerful shouts.

He whisked me away to his home in Heuqueville, a quaint village a few miles up the coast from Le Havre. As we drove along the country road, passing all the towns *sur-Mer*, the Atlantic lay close below the famous cliffs, though not always visible from the car. Fields of golden wheat stretched across the landscape, occasionally broken by green crops, clusters of trees, or an old stone farmhouse.

We talked about everything and nothing during the drive— his latest projects, my travels, and the small moments we had missed in each other's lives over the past months. I held on to my seat as we turned onto the narrow street leading to his home. It was just wide enough for one car, yet not deterring oncoming traffic from trying to squeeze by anyway.

When we arrived at his property, his house came into view —a three-story chateau he was building brick by brick, with a tower slowly taking shape, its foundation set upon scattered German bunkers, remnants of the past. The ocean was a strip on the horizon, hidden in the night. His wife, my sister-in-law, whom I have known my entire life, greeted me at the door and led me to a steaming bowl of pasta carbonara waiting on the table.

Before retiring for the night, my brother, his family and I indulged in Dutch stroopwafels after dinner, sharing stories. The cookie's popularity was gradually spreading beyond Dutch borders. However, nothing quite compared to enjoying a freshly made, large Dutch stroopwafel straight off the hot waffle iron, with the caramel still dripping.

Laying in bed, content, I texted the Austrian, sharing about that taste of home.

The Austrian:
I LOVE THOSE.

I grinned, seeing an opportunity.

I SHOULD GIFT YOU SOME.

This was, I suppose, my way of subtly hinting at the idea of meeting again. Even if I wasn't sure of the purpose, going back to see him felt natural.

WHERE DOES YOUR BROTHER LIVE?

I dropped a pin on the map and shared my location.

1,169 KM BETWEEN US.

That message, although trivial, touched me; it struck a cord. So much so that I couldn't sleep.

In the dead of night, I tossed and turned, feeling an illness coming on as cold sweat ran down my spine. I lay curled up in bed, bewildered by the intensity of my body's reaction. Perhaps it was the cumulative exhaustion finally taking its toll, or maybe it was nature's way of telling me I needed to do something different. The unease persisted, but the urge for change felt undeniable.

I glanced at my phone again, instinctively aware of what I needed to do. With that peculiar feeling of butterflies in my stomach, I booked a plane ticket back to Austria.

The following day, my breathing was labored and shallow, my nose red and my eyes watery, but I found solace in the warmth of being with my French family.

We gathered in the living room, the kids laughing as they ran around dressed as Stormtroopers, pulling me into their *Star Wars* games. Between battles, we settled down to watch the original films on the home theater screen, the sound of lightsabers, explosions and spaceships filling the room. There's something about being with loved ones—even when feeling out of sync—that acts as a distraction for the mind, their laughter and chatter quieting the noise in my head.

To make things even better, my father drove down from the Netherlands to stay with us for a few days. Unfortunately, he still wasn't himself—coughing and showing that same shadow on his face I had noticed before, the creases more pronounced. Part of me wished he had stayed at home to rest, but I was immensely grateful that he had made the journey nonetheless. Not least because he also brought a bag filled with delicious Dutch treats, including my beloved stroopwafels. One package went into my backpack, destined to accompany me to Austria.

Days passed as we listened to my brother play the white Steinway that once belonged to our mother. We reminisced about our summers in the south of France, in the Languedoc, when we all shared the vacation house. We talked about those days—how much we missed the long dinners on the terrace, skinny dipping in the pool, stargazing, darting around the gorges, jumping off cliffs, and showering in waterfalls.

The memories of the south were warm and sun-filled, unlike Normandy, where the lack of sunshine began to take a toll on my mood. I could feel the gray coldness seeping into my spirit, draining me of the little energy I had left, making everything seem colorless and numb. As usual, when I lay in bed at the end of the day, in the dark, my mind began to race —a sort of pattern that had emerged since returning to Europe. One of those nights I exchanged messages with E, an American friend I had met in Los Angeles.

E:
OH, SO MUCH HAS CHANGED!

I'M LIVING IN FLORIDA NOW.

GOT A JOB WORKING REMOTE FOR A CALIFORNIA TECH COMPANY.

I smiled. I was so grateful for the continued support from those I had encountered along the way and really enjoyed receiving their updates. Semi-jokingly, I told him how envious I was, because the thought alone of warming up in the Sunshine State instantly made me feel better. Seconds later, he texted back a photo.

THE PLACE IS HUGE AND ALL TO MYSELF.

SO YES, COME VISIT!

Florida weather was exactly what I needed.

I WOULD LOVE TO VISIT!

WHERE IN FLORIDA ARE YOU EXACTLY?

He said he was in West Palm Beach, ninety minutes north of Miami, down the street from Mar-a-Lago—one of Donald Trump's residences. The way E spoke about the area— everything there was to do, and where he was in life—I could taste his excitement. He seemed to be living the dream.

**IF YOU ARE LOOKING FOR SUN,
YOU WILL GET PLENTY HERE.**

DON'T TEASE ME.

IF YOU SAY YOU'LL COME, DO IT.

                                    **I'LL DEFINITELY TAKE A LOOK TO
SEE IF I CAN FLY THERE SOON.**

Less than twenty-four hours later, I found myself booking flights to return to America for two weeks in April—just three weeks away. Perhaps I should refrain from making impulsive decisions at night, especially when I'm not feeling so great. Nonetheless, it was good for me to look beyond Graz. And besides, this impulsiveness had brought me so much already throughout this journey—why stop now?

I am not crazy, I am not crazy, I repeated to myself firmly on the plane. *I just don't have time for nonsense. If they can't handle my spontaneity, then they're not for me.* As these words echoed in my mind, I began to realize that perhaps this specific trip was a test, a way to quickly and definitively sever ties.

I hadn't told the Austrian I was coming, only that he would get his stroopwafels by the weekend. It felt romantic, yet I was well aware that few men could handle such a grand gesture. I wanted to be with someone who would leap with me. I wasn't sure that he would.

Drawing from my experience with the German, I vowed never to dither again. It was a simple equation: you're either with me or you're not. In this case, his hint at being with someone more convenient made it rather clear he wouldn't choose me, and that was okay. It meant I could stop dwelling on what he brought to my life and start focusing on the lessons learned, moving forward. A part of me wished I had done this when visiting him right after Thailand. But another part knew that week was its own chapter—consumed by each other, there was no past or future, only the present.

From Vienna Airport, I boarded the bus, retracing the route I had recently taken in the opposite direction, heading back to Graz. During the ride, I reminded him that the stroopwafels would be delivered to his home address that very day.

The Austrian:
NO DELIVERIES ON SUNDAYS.

His message arrived while I was walking the forty minutes to his address. I grinned and texted him back.

Sitting on the staircase leading to his apartment, I waited anxiously for him to return from brunch with his family. Then he sent me a photo—a snapshot of himself lounging on his parents' couch under a blanket.

I'M JUST GOING TO REST HERE AND
HAVE A LAZY SUNDAY.

Slightly panicked, I wondered what to do next. I couldn't linger on his doorstep all day without him knowing.

THE STROOPWAFELS ARRIVED.

HOW WOULD YOU KNOW?

I could almost sense his curiosity piquing. I took a photo of myself in front of his building, holding the stroopwafels, and sent it to him.

1,169 KM TO DELIVER COOKIES
IS NOT THAT FAR.

In the stillness of the moment, an unsettling quiet filled the air around me. I pondered the outcome of my impulsive action: Would he perceive it as absurd and simply ignore my message, or had he perhaps drifted off to sleep at last? The uncertainty gnawed at me as I glanced nervously at my feet, hoping I hadn't startled him too much.

After what felt like an eternity—in reality only about seven minutes—he came running toward me, his expression a mix of nervousness and excitement, his smile infectious despite the trembling of his hands. Without hesitation he lifted me from the staircase, pulled me close, wrapped his arms around me, and kissed me with untamed passion.

"You nearly gave me a heart attack!" he exclaimed, his eyes fixed on me. Like always, I simply smiled.

The following day, I woke up feeling exhausted from the trip and perturbed by...something. My surprise had turned out perfect—everything I had dreamed of in terms of romantic gestures. Still, a sense of unease lingered. It wasn't just the vestiges of my physical ailment; it was something in his eyes, his choice of words. Even his apartment seemed a little colder.

Sitting across from him in his kitchen, sipping cappuccino, I watched him lift his cup to his mouth. In every small gesture, it was different from the last time I was here. I didn't expect any more grand gestures—no trips to chocolate theaters or mountain cabins—but I did expect a talk, a way forward, or at least a clarification of what we were and had been since I left but stayed in touch. My intuition told me, however excited he had been to see me the day before, that that spark, that heat, was now tasteless, without flavor, without depth. I *knew* he wasn't going to leap with me and so I had to leave.

"You want to go grab dinner tonight?" I asked, swirling my spoon in my coffee.

One more day, I thought, observing.

At dinner that night at the same Austrian restaurant we had been to before—the same lady in the apron serving us, not the same glimmer in his eyes—an unusual air of tension hung between us. It had been building, compounding. All the strength, support, and the way he lifted me up had stagnated, slowed. I wasn't sure why, and I wasn't sure how to start or talk to him, but I knew there was *something*. He seemed distant, lost in his own thoughts. Finally, he broke the silence.

"I got back together with my ex," he confessed, his voice barely above a whisper as he stammered and shook his head.

"What?!" I managed to say, my tone betraying a cold calm within me.

I would be lying to myself if I said I didn't see it coming, yet I couldn't comprehend his decision—besides hinting that it was a convenient option for him, hadn't he told me many times that he didn't love her anymore? Strangely, I didn't feel angry or hurt. My first feeling was actually sympathy. Not for him, but for his ex—or should I say, *girlfriend.* She deserved better than this too.

I looked at him. He remained fidgety, shifting in his seat, his hands restless and his gaze darting away. Then, it was my turn to break the silence.

"If that is what you truly want, then it is good that I am leaving."

I wiped my lips with the red cloth napkin from my lap. I was through here. Removing myself from the equation was the only viable option at this point. Infidelity was unforgivable in my books, and I hated that by not saying anything right away, he had involved me in something I never would have chosen to be a part of.

The next morning, he drove me to the bus station in silence. There was no lingering tension between us as I said goodbye. He had become little more than a memory of the past, a comforting presence that had helped me navigate through a period of transition. It was done, but I was grateful—grateful I leapt, for I would never have to wonder *what if.*

Every time something like this happened—a rejection, not being *chosen*, finding myself alone again—it tore something from my chest, reminding me of every wound I had carried since childhood, every time I had felt discarded. Those rips, those pains, those wounds let the darkness in, dimming my light. Instead of warmth, there was cold, like a frog's skin, my eyes narrowing as the world before me came into sharp focus.

Where do I go from here? My jaw clenched, the familiar storm building—overthinking everything, barely thinking anything. I bought a ticket to Bratislava, escaping Graz. My head felt like it was going to explode; I needed to let some of it out. I grabbed my phone and texted one of my closest friends, someone who knew, who had seen that dark side and that pain, who had stood by me, rescuing me from the cold within.

C:
**YOUR BRIGHT SIDE IS STRONGER
THAN YOUR DARK SIDE.**

Deep down, I knew he was right. Yet, the hurt and pain had become such a driving force behind my accomplishments, such a relentless engine, that the light within me hadn't had a chance to emanate from a place of genuine positivity. It felt trapped, barricaded, as if keeping the light within was all I had left to protect. If I kept it safe, no one could destroy it. But by keeping it inside, in a way, had it been destroyed already?

I wondered—could I let it guide me without relying on the pain to push me forward? Could I trust it to lead the way?

I was still out of sorts when I stepped off the bus and, while trying to reach the other side of the Danube River, stumbled over some steps and fell prone on the rough asphalt. There were no witnesses to my clumsy mishap. I felt no urgency to rise. I remained there, burying my face in my hands, sobbing.

As I finally sat upright, I noticed how there were no sounds around me. The city seemed to hold its breath, its streets eerily quiet, as if it were unsure how to greet me. Suddenly, the question, "Why am I here?" hit me. I hadn't even managed to book a hostel—my credit card kept declining for some reason. So, where exactly was I heading?

After wandering aimlessly for a while, I drew some cash from an ATM and secured a night at a hostel. Upon arrival, two cheerful German girls greeted me warmly, instantly lifting my spirits. They said they were excited to exchange travel stories and asked if I needed recommendations, mentioning that they had been enjoying the city so far and that it was best to explore on foot. So when they invited me to join them on a walk through Bratislava's old town, I kept my shoes on and walked right back out with them.

This wasn't the first time that strangers had reminded me of the simple beauties, the simplicity of being alive. And I was sure it wouldn't be the last.

Strolling through the quaint, silent streets, with *Čumil*, the notorious sewer worker statue, lurking nearby, lights glowing softly, and the wind rustling through the cobblestone alleys, we stumbled upon a small coffee shop nestled against an impressive building with tall arches and intricate stonework.

Inside, the space was bright and minimalist, with clean lines and modern furnishings—a stark contrast to the imposing majesty of the neighboring structure. Curiously, the shared wall pulsed with the sound of electronic music—not from the café, but from the building next door.

"What's happening there?" I asked the barista, nodding toward the wall with a subtle tilt of my head.

"Apparently some sort of mysterious business event," she replied with a shrug. "Impossible to get in."

Outside, there were no signs of an event in progress: no lights, no red carpets, and no crowds lining up, only the deep, rhythmic pulse of music resonating through the brick walls.

We walked along the Old Market Hall, the barista's cryptic words lingering in our minds—there was an air of mystery surrounding the place. A small side door caught our attention, slightly ajar, revealing only darkness beyond. I glanced at the girls; they glanced back at me.

After a moment's pause, I pushed the door open, and we stepped inside. A few feet ahead, two long and heavy velvety drapes marked a more official entrance.

"What is this place?" I whispered to the girls, pulling the drapes aside.

A small lamp cast a warm glow on a steep staircase. As we ascended, we could hear the pulsating music growing louder and louder. At the top, a vast, open market hall unfolded before us, illuminated only by vibrant laser lights that danced in rhythm to the music. People dressed in sharp suits mingled around small, round standing tables, creating an atmosphere reminiscent of a Wall Street disco party.

Suddenly, a powerful spotlight shone on the center of the hall, casting large letters onto the floor below. Leaning over the railing, the three of us peered down to behold the word spelled out before us: "Forbes."

We scanned the event: luxury cars standing on platforms; photo booths with funky props—feather boas, colorful masks, signs to hold, and wigs to wear for social media-worthy shots; gourmet hors d'oeuvres carried by waiters in penguin suits; and a DJ on stage mixing upbeat tracks, creating an electric atmosphere.

Dressed in our casual leggings and knit sweaters, we knew we didn't quite fit the glamorous ambiance. Still, we were there, so why not check it out? We took another staircase that led to the ground floor, and just as we reached the bottom, a courteous server presented me with a fluorescent cocktail in a glow-in-the-dark glass.

"Thank you," I nodded and smiled.

The girls and I glanced around, debating our next move. Out of the corner of my eye, I saw a sharply dressed man approaching. Before he reached us, the girls darted off, but I stood frozen, nailed to the ground.

"Have you sampled some of the hors d'oeuvres yet?" he asked me in a very polite tone.

"Oh, I couldn't possibly," I replied hesitantly, feeling a little guilty at the thought. "In all honesty, I wasn't exactly invited to this soirée."

"That's not a problem at all," he replied, offering a gentle grin. "Consider yourself my guest!"

Gentlemen still exist, I thought, as I grabbed the arm he extended courteously. I glanced at the German girls, who had jumped into the photo booth, striking poses with their colorful props, while the charming gentleman—an honoree among the country's 30 Under 30 rising stars—swept me away to introduce me to others.

"So, what's it like?" I asked him. "The startup landscape in Slovakia?"

"It's exciting. Many opportunities to make a social impact, and from here, only bigger things are on the horizon."

We moved between small groups as he introduced me to innovators and thinkers, none of them questioning why I was there, and no one making me feel out of place.

The music grew louder, the cocktail-attired crowd rowdier. I looked around at all the moving lips, exposed teeth, people sipping from glow-in-the-dark glasses, gently touching elbows as jokes were made. I was both inside the circle and outside of it, like an observer in a glass enclosure, watching the rare species of ambitious minds—each one displaying their talents, vying for attention.

I floated on the edge, intrigued, as if in a different kind of zoo. With my hands against the glass enclosure of my imagination, I could see that, on the other side, anything was possible. I had started the day feeling so weighed down, but now all I wanted was to climb the ladder, follow the light. Determination was brewing, opportunities waiting.

Hungary

Wandering through Budapest's grand boulevards, I admired the Neo-Gothic and Art Nouveau buildings lining the Danube River. I stopped at a small outdoor market stall and purchased a hearty bowl of traditional goulash, its rich, paprika-infused broth warming me from the inside out.

I had to pause. My mind needed a rest and my body needed to stop moving. I reflected on the whirlwind of countries I was venturing through—going, going, going, always going. How much longer could I keep up this pace? I had to pause and re-evaluate, somehow.

A couple of days later, however, I ignored my need to slow down, choosing not to listen to myself. Wandering past the train station, I spotted a train with "Belgrade" boldly displayed on the large sign by the platform. I went inside the station and bought a ticket to Serbia for the next morning. It was the breeze of spontaneity that carried me forward, overriding any rational thoughts.

While heading back to my accommodation from the train station, my phone rang. It wasn't a video call or any pre-scheduled communication: just a call. Seeing my father's name flash across the screen, I felt a knot form in my stomach. It was a sensation I hadn't experienced in months, not like this, signaling that something was amiss.

"Dad?" I answered, my voice tinged with concern.

My father's voice sounded weak, and amidst his words, I could discern the unmistakable sound of his cough.

"I don't want you to worry, but daddy is in the hospital," he said, trying to reassure me.

Still, those words are never good. I stood in place, feeling as if the ground beneath me had shifted.

"Dad, what is it?" I asked, my voice trembling slightly.

I began nervously circling a large pillar, my mind racing with thoughts.

"It's a severe case of influenza," he replied calmly.

Influenza, a term we're all familiar with, carries a weight when spoken in full—one that feels heavier than simply saying "the flu." And with my father being a bit older, though he would never admit it, the danger felt more real.

"I'm coming home," I declared resolutely, my heart already pounding with the impulse to be by his side.

"No, no, you keep going," my dad insisted.

"Really, dad, I can come home," I tried again.

"Daughter, please follow your path," he said calmly. "I am all better now with the help of these fine doctors."

Despite knowing that I would prioritize his health and well-being, we both recognized that it was easier if I didn't come home. Our strong bond would never diminish, regardless of our physical distance. Besides, it seemed that whenever I got closer, the dynamic at home shifted, and everyone suffered as a consequence—everyone lost.

"Alright, I'll stay, at least for now," I conceded, "but I'll be home next week."

Feeling a bit lost after the call, I wandered back to the Danube and crossed the Chain Bridge that connects *Buda* and *Pest*, heading toward Gellért Hill.

Nearing the hilltop, I stumbled upon The Garden of Philosophy, where sculptures of some of the world's most renowned religious figures gather in silence, crafted by Hungarian sculptor Nándor Wagner. I circled around them, taking in the statues' serene expressions and the sweeping city views beyond the quiet greenery, until I stopped in front of an engraved stone that read, "For better mutual understanding."

This aphorism hit home, not least because of the chat I had just had with my dad and all the thoughts and emotions it evoked. It occurred to me that perhaps the reason for the tension within my family at times, and indeed the reason for so much division in the world—why so many of us struggle to set aside differences and learn from one another—isn't just because we're unwilling to open our minds. It's because part of reaching mutual understanding involves recognizing that some things aren't meant to work out. And that's okay, too. It's about agreeing to disagree respectfully. There's a lot of learning and growth in accepting that reality as well. Focus on the bonds we *can* build.

Bosnia and Herzegovina

After a few slow days in Serbia spent resting and wandering, I booked a ride in a small white van bound for Bosnia. My hosteler in Belgrade had recommended Sarajevo as my next stop. However, I was warned that the Serbian minivan service would refuse to take me into the city center.

"Politics," he said, providing no further information.

The minivan picked me up at the hostel, its battered frame rattling as it pulled up to the curb. I spotted a traveler with a backpack already seated and asked if I could sit next to him. Without hesitation, he moved his backpack to the side, his New Zealand accent breaking the tension.

"Of course. Please, sit."

His easygoing nature instantly made me feel comfortable, making the ride feel less like a covert mission and more like an adventure—though still slightly off the books, or so it seemed.

At the border, we stepped out of the van into a space that felt less like a regular checkpoint and more like an abandoned gas station, the sky a heavy gray overhead. The driver started speaking loudly, his voice rapid, almost frantic, as he engaged in what sounded like an angry negotiation with two men in uniform. Their stiff postures and the driver's intensity made me assume this wasn't a routine stop.

I couldn't understand a word of what was said, but it felt as though they needed serious convincing to let us through—and then, they finally did.

The roads narrowed, winding through the hills of the countryside, where the scars of war began to surface, casting shadows over the landscape—burnt-out homes with missing roofs, skeletal structures of abandoned buildings, and bullet-pocked walls lining the road like silent witnesses, etching a somber portrait of the region's history. The van rattled along the uneven asphalt as we passed through.

These sights were part of the lingering aftermath of the wars and conflicts that tore apart Yugoslavia in the early 1990s. It was disheartening to see, as if the devastation had frozen time, leaving behind echoes of what once was—mere remnants of shattered lives, ghostly villages where life appeared to have paused decades ago.

Among the somber scenes, the town of Srebrenica passed by—a name steeped in infamy. It was a place I had learned much about, where thousands of people were mercilessly slaughtered. Despite being designated as a safe zone under the protection of Dutch peacekeepers, part of the United Nations Protection Force, it became the site of a tragic massacre. When faced with an overwhelming assault, they found themselves inadequately equipped and outnumbered, compounded by a series of ill-fated decisions that led to this horrific atrocity.

As a Dutch citizen, I was ashamed. Out the van's window, I noticed the unmistakable blue helmets—symbols of the United Nations peacekeepers—perched on sticks amidst the backdrop of destroyed buildings. I had been lucky not to have known war in my lifetime. Here, the wounds were so fresh.

My family had stories. Some had seen similar devastation— my father, my grandparents. Stories of the resistance: hanging under trains to reach loved ones, stealing Nazi uniforms to cross borders, playing in the rubble of Rotterdam. I had seen photographs, and still today, I see them—grief-stricken faces framed by wreckage, children clutching tattered toys. Their lives tethered to a fate I had only glimpsed through a camera lens, a garden of thorns I had walked through only in my mind, through the stories of others.

"This is it," the driver said, pulling over and looking at us after the six-hour ride. "East Sarajevo Station."

"We get off *here?*" I asked.

"Yes. This is the Republic of *Srpska*—Serbian. City center —Bosnian. You take a cab," he said in a thick Eastern accent.

The capital city lay on one of the edges of the two political entities that make up the country—yet another product of the end of the war. I pondered what other ordinary aspects of life might be hindered by such divisions.

My new Kiwi friend and I shared a quick cab ride to the city center and found a charming restaurant right where the cab dropped us off. The host and owner, an older woman, guided us to a square table with a plastic tablecloth and immediately brought a basket of *lepinja*, or flatbread. One of the staff, likely her husband given how they huddled together, spoke little English but pointed at the menu, suggesting we try the traditional *ćevapčići*—succulent sausages served with a light *šopska salata* made from fresh cucumbers, tomatoes, onions, peppers, and grated cheese. A young man, perhaps a grandson no older than fourteen, sat down at our table, watching as we ate, practicing his English.

"Good, yes?"

"Delicious, thank you!" we said, as the bursts of flavor made our eyes widen.

It was as if we had stumbled into a family gathering, invited in. Their passion for the food shone through in the careful way they placed the dishes before us and the approving nods as we ate. Even with the language barrier, their warmth and enthusiasm showed me a particular kindness, I felt cared for— it was inspiring.

Parting ways with the New Zealander who had made other plans, I checked into a hostel named for Archduke Franz Ferdinand of Austria, who was assassinated a few streets away in 1914 near the Latin Bridge over the Miljacka River. This event, often regarded as the spark that ignited World War I, marked a pivotal moment in history.

The hostel was a treasure trove of art and history, its walls adorned with vintage photographs of early 20th-century Sarajevo and colorful messages left by travelers written in crayon, pen, Sharpie, and pencil. Maps depicting the divisions of the city and its historical events hung prominently, while intriguing images of key moments were affixed to the ceiling, inviting guests to look up and reflect.

Eager to learn more, I set out toward the Latin Bridge. Standing at the exact spot where Franz Ferdinand and his wife, Sophie, met their fate, I paused. The scene played out in my mind, as if I were transported back in time, watching history come to life: the motorcade's wrong turn, Gavrilo Princip's unexpected opportunity after a failed attempt earlier that day.

I gazed around the typically European street, its old-world charm juxtaposed against the weight of the past. I was struck by the significance of this unassuming location. Despite the gray weather muting the colors, it was difficult to imagine that such monumental events had unfolded here, events that would shape the course of history in profound ways.

Later that evening, as I prepared for bed and reflected on the day, I noticed a small group of young people gathered in one of the cozy, pillow-filled corners. They didn't fit the typical profile of hostel travelers I had encountered all over the world, and they spoke in a language I didn't recognize, which piqued my interest.

"Can I join you?" I asked in English.

"Of course!" replied a slender girl with a slight accent.

I took a seat beside her and the three boys in the room, who all turned out to be Bosnian students attending classes at the local university. Born just after the conflict, they had grown up in a country still undergoing painful reconstruction.

"May I ask what it was like to grow up here?" I asked, my gaze sweeping across the hostel, where the echoes of conflict seemed etched into every surface.

One of the boys leaned forward. "You know," he began, his face serious, "my grandparents and parents lost everything in the war. They rebuilt from nothing."

Another student, his voice more reflective, chimed in. "I grew up hearing all those stories, but it feels distant—like a history lesson I can't fully grasp. Yet, I can see proof of it all around me." He glanced at a large map of Europe behind him. "For us, life has been pretty normal. But our families carry that pain."

The girl, beautiful with expressive eyes and a widening smile, edged closer. "We have dreams, just like you," she said, her tone full of optimism.

I stayed up with them till four in the morning, sharing, listening. Hearing them talk about their experiences and the ongoing impact on their families reminded me how little maps and the internet actually say about a place. The truth—or at least a more unfiltered version of it—lies in the streets and with the people you meet. Through their stories, I began to grasp a sliver of what it means to be human.

Croatia

As I made my way into the city center of Zagreb, large banners promoting a famous opera bearing my name covered the streets, giving me a festive welcome. The opera itself, I knew, was tragic, yet instead of its story, I heard my mother's voice rustling through the moving banners, saying my name.

I had visited Croatia once before, in Dubrovnik, on what turned out to be the last vacation before my mother fell ill. Perhaps that was what had drawn me here. Though a different city, she was all I could think of—I saw her smile in the ecru roses at the flower stalls, reminiscent of her favorite blooms; I heard her laughter mingling with the chatter of locals, and I caught a glimpse of her at Dolac Market, handpicking ripe tomatoes and taking a bite out of a nectarine. Every step, a connection, a way of being closer.

These memories—these sightings, these feelings—reminded me of other places I had visited with my mother but never returned to: Mont-Saint-Michel, Santorini, Mykonos. They were places I held dear, where our family unit of three was all I ever needed. Cherished memories, now shared only with my father. My father... I wished he were here.

It wasn't always possible to take him back to those places to reminisce. I somehow had to protect those memories—I had *been* protecting them. Some places in the world simply weren't meant to be shared with certain others, people I didn't love. The risk of tarnishing beautiful memories with unpleasant new ones was too great. I was determined to safeguard what little I had left of my mom, no matter what.

Perhaps one day, I'll return to those places with my own child—sharing in that love, the love my mother gave me.

With my flight back from Vienna to Paris approaching in a few days, I headed to Ljubljana—my eighth European capital in just a week and a half. Europe's accessibility never ceases to amaze me. You can hop between countries with such ease. While I had always been aware of this, exploring this corner of Europe felt refreshingly new and exciting.

From Ljubljana, my journey took me back to Austria, with Graz along the route to the airport, bringing the loop full circle. I contemplated whether to make one final stop or silently pass by in the night. The Austrian made it clear it wasn't a good time for another rendezvous. I knew I shouldn't have even brought it up, after all his situation hadn't changed.

Decisively, I texted him, closing the door that somehow hadn't locked yet.

THIS IS IT THEN.

I sent the message, though *it* had already been decided when I left him last time.

The Austrian:
NO, WHY?

I WILL COME TO AMSTERDAM FOR YOU IN MAY.

A moment of weakness crept in as I battled conflicting desires. Part of me yearned to see him. But no, I reminded myself—no more safety nets. His words offered little solace. I refused to be the other woman. Besides, who knew if I would even be there in May.

A tear trickled down my cheek. Clearly, this brief contact upset me, but I couldn't pinpoint exactly why—or why I wanted to see him at all. My mind searched for any escape, the kind he had offered before, but I knew the escape I sought in him was gone, a memory. So why did this need linger, nag at me: the desire to stop in Graz one last time? Perhaps it was because I was so geographically close, so briefly. Or because I felt so close, so close to something that could have been—under different circumstances.

That was really it. I would pass silently into the night, the bus doors remaining shut, with other destinations to come.

I WON'T STOP IN GRAZ.

AND I WON'T BE SEEING YOU IN AMSTERDAM.

Netherlands

Once I reached Rotterdam via Paris, a quick thirty-minute bus ride took me to my hometown. I appreciated the comfort of knowing my father would have a bed waiting for me—he was home and much better after his brief hospital stay.

That didn't change the reality that I was once again faced with two polar opposites: feeling both profoundly welcome and distinctly unwelcome. I knew staying in that house didn't help me grow, nor did it free me from the shadows of my past —but it did give me a little time with my dad.

On the third day back "home," it happened to be election day. As with every election, whether local, national, European, or for a referendum, I worked at the polling station from 7 a.m. to 10 p.m. in my hometown, Oud-Beijerland. This was something my dad and I had always done, though at different locations, as family members weren't allowed to be stationed together to minimize fraud. Still, contributing to the country and community I had called home all my life felt good, purposeful.

There was something soothing about watching the line of people, reviewing their identification, passing their ballots, and observing everything proceed according to the law. Then, when the polls closed, counting one large paper ballot at a time—unfolding, stacking, tally marking.

In that space, amidst the organized chaos of democracy in action, even without my father physically beside me, I found warmth in our shared experience. It was a reminder of the bonds that held us together and the passions we shared.

Seeing him recovered from his recent bout of influenza— his face no longer shadowed, the creases softening—brought some relief. With that weight lifted, I was finally able to get excited about visiting my American friend, E, in Florida.

I was glad I knew where I was going, even before returning to the Netherlands. It felt less aimless, more tangible. At the very least, I could finally answer the question, "What is next?"

Before heading out again, my cousin S, who was also back in town, and I shared a cheese fondue—just like our last night in Melbourne, though nothing like our goodbye in the Thai jungle. She had just returned from Bali and was already planning her move to Ibiza—the dream she had always talked about, now within reach.

As we dipped baguettes into hot, gooey cheese, I noticed something different about her. It wasn't just in her face but in her energy—the way she cleared the table with a little skip in her step, more so than usual, and how she turned on the teapot with a playful dance.

"Did you find what you were looking for, cuz-y?" she asked, her tone light but curious. "If it wasn't in Germany and it wasn't in Austria, where is it for you?"

I nodded, thinking for a moment. "I don't think it was ever in either of those places."

S raised an eyebrow, eyes twinkling. "But you're going back to America next, right?"

"Hmhm. Just for a few weeks, maybe, to slow down and think things through."

"You'll find it, cuz-y. I believe in you."

She was one of those refuges for me, a source of comfort no matter where we were. The same was true for my girlfriend Z, the one I had taken the Siberian train with and who I last saw in Shanghai. I was grateful for both, often keeping me sane.

After finishing my tea with S, I said goodbye, grabbed my suitcase—no backpack this time—and headed to Amsterdam. I was going to spend the night at Z's apartment, who had also just returned home, before departing again in the morning.

When the train rolled into Bijlmer ArenA Station, I spotted her right away—standing firm, one hand on her phone, the other scratching her eyebrow, thinking, always thinking. Her phone disappeared into her pocket, and her face brightened when she caught sight of me.

"There's my world traveler!" Z exclaimed.

I quickened my pace and hugged her tightly.

"At least welcome me in Chinese!" I laughed.

At her apartment, just a short walk away, she brewed some tea and uncorked a bottle of wine. It was dark and late, but we had plenty to catch up on.

Cozy on the couch together, hugging pillows and sipping wine while our tea grew cold on the coffee table, we talked. Much like mine, her future wasn't exactly clear.

"So, staying here for now?" I asked.

"For now," she said, smiling. "Work, learn, save—and then I'll come up with something."

"You always do," I chuckled.

"So do you," she grinned, raising her glass to clink it against mine. *"Proost!"*

"Proost."

She studied me for a moment, her smile more linear. "You haven't paused at all yet, have you?"

I glanced down at my wine, swirling it slowly, watching the soft light catch in its deep, cherry hue, as if it might hold some kind of answer. I had become quite adept at maximizing my time, packing my days with as much activity as possible and navigating through life without pausing. But if I were to stand still, I wondered, what would happen next?

PART SIX

PAUSING LONG ENOUGH TO PROCESS

United States

Arriving at Palm Beach International Airport, the dense, salty air hit me like a wave—moist and sticky. My friend said he would be there to pick me up, and indeed, there he was, his sun-kissed blond hair glinting in the overhead lights, wearing shorts, a casual T-shirt and flip-flops. He stood next to a palm tree, a computer bag slung over his shoulder, scanning the crowd with an eager grin. When he spotted me, he broke into a wide smile and waved both arms above his head.

It was bizarre to think that our connection had begun rather out of the blue in a Los Angeles coffee shop, where we struck up a conversation that instantly clicked. Now, seven months later, hugging him on a different coast—with the travel plans I had briefly shared over coffee behind me—was another leap, trusting the kindness of people I had met along the way.

His place—a million-dollar condo on Singer Island—was the closest thing to a dream house I had ever stayed in: sunlit rooms with panoramic ocean views, a glowing Tuscan gold and white interior, sleek glass and leather furnishings, and designer throw pillows on the couch, waiting to be hugged.

E generously provided me with an entire wing to myself, equipped with everything I could possibly need—from a spacious bedroom with plush bedding to a private bathroom stocked with all the essentials, and even a balcony with a lounge area overlooking the water. This was yet another show of the generosity of strangers. This was yet another show of how you never know where each encounter may lead.

In the morning, I woke up to the sound of palm leaves rustling. I pushed the cloud-like blankets aside and stepped onto my private balcony, inhaling deeply as I took in the expansive ocean view. Palm trees swayed gently in the warm breeze; a chorus of seagulls called out, their silhouettes darting playfully against the sun-drenched sky.

It was a calmness unlike any I had experienced on this journey—a stillness tinged with the anticipation of something new on the horizon. Despite the apparent contradiction that sometimes you must slow down in order to leap forward, I sensed that I stood at the threshold of something. I just had to figure out what it meant.

After I adjusted to the time change and lightly explored the local lifestyle for a few days, E took me to Wynwood in Miami, an arts district pulsing with creativity and color. The streets were alive with murals that transformed every wall into a canvas, each piece telling a story.

E, with a heavy camera in hand, wandered ahead, capturing the scenes around us and documenting my awe as I followed. Turning warehouse corners, I would either spot his single-lens reflex camera raised in front of his face or follow the sound of his flip-flops echoing in the warm air. He was passionate, and I wondered what his creative eye saw—each click a reflection of the world through his unique perspective, a fragment of something he noticed.

At one of the many craft breweries, we paused to sit on brown, weathered leather couches, ordering a beer. Cold brew in one hand, E continued snapping photos while I observed the crowd—people working on their laptops, others waiting in line, and some chatting with friends. When I looked back at E, his large lens fixated on me.

"What are you trying to capture?" I asked. "What do you see?"

"I think I just snapped my favorite photo of you," he replied with a grin.

"Oh yeah? Just now? What did you capture?"

"A chance for the world to see you, seeing the world," he said, contemplative. "When you look at something, you really look. You see details, you take it in. It shows on your face."

"Hm," I said, sipping my apricot lager. "I think I have been told that before."

It was nice that he saw me—or at least caught a glimpse of me *seeing*, thinking. It surprised me how some of the people I had only just met, or spent a brief amount of time with, were able to see more of me than those I had known for years.

He had an appreciation for life that I recognized, but he also had the ability to challenge and expand my thinking. Somehow, in just a few days, he had become both angel and devil on my shoulder—constantly pushing me to confront my emotions and plot my next steps. Even when I agreed with him in conversation, he pushed me, believing true growth came from questioning everything, not just seeking validation.

One evening, sitting at his long glass dining room table with a glass of wine in my hand, I curled up in my chair, knees pulled close, while lights of boats on the ocean behind us flickered like fireflies. I told him about how since the day my mother passed—and even more so during my train journey through Mongolia—I had toyed with the idea of writing a book, yet I couldn't muster the right state of mind to translate the tangled emotions into words.

"Write from your perspective as a child!" he asserted.

I gazed at my wine glass. I had never considered this. It sounded intriguing, but also...

"What if I can't find the words, like I couldn't before?" I said after a brief pause.

"What do you mean?" he asked, squinting his eyes as if it would help him see the meaning.

"What if it's nothing but disjointed thoughts?" I explained. "Grief without coherence, for no one to understand."

"Just start writing without worrying about what others may think," he replied calmly.

I nodded. He was right. Though I knew my story had the potential to help others, I first needed to let it all pour out, to unlock the memories. Every attempt I had made previously had been in Dutch, but those efforts had been tinged with anger; the subject was too close to my heart, too raw, too confronting. Perhaps this time, I would write in English. That way, I could potentially approach the emotions without the baggage that comes with language.

The next morning, perched on his balcony with a cup of coffee and my notebook, the floodgates opened. Words poured forth—structured, vivid, each syllable a stab of pain. The air felt thick, my limbs heavy, but the more I wrote, the more I felt knots inside me undoing, dissolving like a paper lantern released into the night sky.

Every morning thereafter, I woke up to the light streaming through the window, most days leaving the blinds open to let the sun bathe the bedroom in a warm orange glow. I would stretch, my toes brushing against the soft sheets, and take a moment to breathe deeply, letting the morning settle in. After washing my face, I brewed a cup of rich coffee, savoring the aroma that filled the air. Then, with my notebook in hand, I returned to the balcony.

I just wrote—words, letters, sentences, questions—page after page, letting my thoughts flow freely. Even when it felt like none of it made sense, once the pen touched the paper, my thoughts transformed into clear anecdotes—moments in time, feelings and vivid experiences taking shape.

When the ink ran dry, I would pause, my coffee now cold as I stared at a fresh blank page, forcing myself not to look back at the words I had already written. I waited—waited for more to come. I tried to embrace the quiet, allowing it to guide me, hoping something meaningful would eventually flow from my pen again. There had to be more, brewing beneath the surface.

If the words didn't come right away, I felt overwhelmed and pointless, questioning myself: *Why am I doing this? Who am I doing this for?* But I wouldn't stop until my coffee cup was empty. It emptied slowly, each sip a reward for putting more thoughts to paper, releasing them from my mind.

I was transported back to my childhood, reliving the intense highs and lows all over again. I was hurting, yet a part of me felt a sense of pride in finally taking the steps to confront my memories. I knew it was necessary if I ever hoped to move forward and grow—rather than succumb to distractions and surface-level accomplishments.

Some days I dreaded making coffee and loathed sitting alone on that balcony, surrounded by piles of scribbles and anecdotes, still in my pajamas, hair a tangled mess.

Even so, with my friend nearby—my support, his condo my refuge—I pressed on. On those days, I would look out at the ocean a little longer, feel the breeze a little more intentionally, and swap the coffee for a Mimosa, reminding myself of how blessed I was to sit there to begin with—the fact that I was able to face this in paradise.

Sprawled on my bed one late morning after a long sleep, I was pleasantly surprised by a text message from a new friend from Switzerland whom I had met at a hostel in Belgrade, Serbia. He reached out after seeing a photo I shared on social media.

Q:
BACK IN THE UNITED STATES?

AGAIN?

                              I ALWAYS FEEL AT HOME HERE.

Indeed, somehow, being here resonated profoundly with my dreams and aspirations. The possibilities felt boundless—if only one dared to pursue them.

THAT'S YOUR COMFORT ZONE.

He observed astutely. Maybe he was right; the United States had become my sanctuary, a place where I felt grounded and empowered. Before I could respond, another message popped up on my screen.

**DIDN'T YOU WANT TO VENTURE
BEYOND YOUR COMFORT ZONE?**

He prodded, nudging me to reconsider my direction. His words struck a chord.

MEET ME IN BISHKEK?

I must confess, I had to consult a map to locate Bishkek and figure out where it was. Nestled in Kyrgyzstan, a country in Central Asia, it was a destination I had never even considered.

All the more reason to inquire about his plans for the trip and the logistics involved.

**I WILL SHARE ALL THE DETAILS
WITH YOU.**

THE CHOICE IS YOURS.

Gazing out of the window from the comfort of my suite in West Palm Beach, the palms, the ocean, I pondered the weeks ahead. I had a commitment to visit London and reconnect with U, a new friend from England. Yet beyond that, my calendar lay bare. An empty stretch of uncertainty—and opportunity.

A few days later, I woke up feeling a surge of energy and strength. I checked the date—April 19th. Exactly one year ago, I parted ways with my ex of six years and entered singlehood.

In hindsight, his betrayal proved to be a blessing in disguise, catalyzing a period of self-reflection and renewal unlike any other I had experienced. While there was still much ground to cover, I was certainly not the same woman I was back then.

To proudly commemorate this unusual milestone E drove me to Miami for a night of clubbing by myself. There was a time, like in the beginning of my journey, when the thought of venturing alone into Miami's nightlife would have intimidated me. Now, it hardly fazed me—in fact, it empowered me.

Stepping up to the club's entrance, I turned to the hostess in a little black dress, a clipboard in her hands.

"How many?" she asked, not looking up at me.

"Just me," I said, shrugging my shoulders.

She raised her gaze, "Girl, a woman in a sparkly gold dress like you shouldn't be here alone."

"Thank you?" I half-asked, chuckling.

"Mmhm." She shook her head with compassion.

"I'm actually celebrating one year since I broke up with my boyfriend—it set me free," I added, making a wing motion with my hands. "Being here alone felt appropriate."

"Good for you, honey! In that case, let's make sure you have the best night," she said, snapping her fingers at a guy standing nearby, who took the light coat draped over my shoulders.

I was ushered to a private table in a mezzanine VIP area, where seven male waiters stood in a row, dressed in sleek white jackets and black bowties. They bowed their heads briefly, one of them handing me a glass of champagne.

Sipping the Veuve Clicquot while seated on an elevated leather couch overlooking the dance floor, I made a solemn vow to myself: never again would I diminish my dreams to conform to someone else's reality.

As I retrieved my lightweight coat at the evening's close, my feet aching from dancing, a surprise awaited me nestled within its pocket—a note.

Alcohol holds no allure for me. Instead, I prefer the intoxication of blondes with free-flowing smiles.

I raised my eyebrows, frozen still.

I'm a professional golfer making my comeback from injury this week; not meeting you may sideline me for another six months.

I looked up, scanning my surroundings. Then I continued.

Your name is beautiful, just like you,
but how to pronounce it? I have no clue.

A soft giggle escaped me as I flicked my hair and strolled out of the radiant nightclub—by myself. I clutched the note, still amused by its audacity. The mystery man's flattery lingered in my mind, but it wasn't the words that struck me—it was the realization they triggered.

Alone, yet completely content, I walked down the dimly lit street, my heels tapping rhythmically against the pavement. His note reminded me of something I had known deep down for a while: I didn't need validation from others to know I was on the right path. I had never felt more assured that, regardless of the twists and turns, I would discover my rightful place in this world.

In terms of location, Los Angeles, New York, Sydney, and London were all contenders for the next chapter. But it was more than just choosing where to go—it was the journey itself that began to crack open my heart. The layers of reflection, the slow accumulation of moments, conversations, each memory I unearthed, and the words I had started to write helped me finally face the grief—and the resentment—that had been waiting for attention.

Sometimes, I mused, *life's challenges don't need to be solved outright.* Instead, they invite me to create space for them and, more importantly, to recognize what no longer deserves my energy.

As I lay on a sunbed overlooking the million-dollar view on my final day in Florida—the Atlantic Ocean a lullaby—I dozed off. The sunscreen on my body dripped in the humid air; my temperature rose. The distant crash of waves made way for Chopin's *Nocturne Op. 9 No. 2,* sending me into a gentle dream. First, I saw the song's sheet music on a white Steinway grand piano. Then, delicate fingers adorned with diamond rings gliding over the keys. A familiarity crept in, though I couldn't quite place it. The music continued, and a figure gradually emerged beside me on the bench, her hands still moving gracefully over the ivories.

I was getting warmer. It was within reach.

"Listen," a voice whispered over the notes.

"I am listening," I strained, holding on to the dream.

The melodies of Chopin's composition opened a chamber of emotions that had been sealed away, concealed deep within. Now, they demanded to be brought to the surface and confronted. The music grew louder, *forte*. The figure beside me had visible long blonde locks, but she didn't look at me.

"Look at me!" I yelled, but it only sounded like a whisper against the climactic sections of the piece. "Look at me!"

The music abruptly stopped, the figure coming into focus. My mother looked at me with her gentle smile.

"It is you," I cried as I tried to grab her hand but couldn't.

"Listen," she repeated softly against the silence as we sat on the piano bench together, our surroundings evaporating. She then placed her hand on my heart, and I felt it glow. "It is within you, my darling."

Consoled by her touch, my mind started racing. Everything grew darker, and then I heard it—from deep within—a cacophony of memories. It wasn't the grief of losing my mother that thundered loudest, but the emotional abuse, the shadow that had squeezed out the light. I was consumed by the torment inflicted by the woman who had taken residence in my home uninvited. It was my friend's mother. Our parents had never been close. She had arrived under false pretenses, asking to stay in our guest room and pleading that she had nowhere else to go after leaving her husband, abandoning her children. The many sympathy cards from my mother's funeral still on display, my father let her in.

A few days later I found her naked in my mother's bed, waiting to seduce my father. She wasn't expecting me to walk through the door instead. She never left—except briefly every time she didn't get her way. Whenever my father would not give her his undivided attention, *choosing her,* she simply ran away, leaving him desperate to bring her back. Her grip on him unrelenting, her claws razor-sharp and firmly embedded.

Even when I wasn't involved in their arguments, I was the one sent to find her and apologize. I was the one who gave up my father so he could have a new life, and she, a new husband. And still, she turned everyone against me, painting me as the villain, wishing I didn't exist. I was a flaw in her fantasy, the constant reminder that her fairytale with the man of her dreams—the father she had never had—was imperfect.

Our feud became notorious. To the people she knew, I was nothing more than that angry, bitter child she claimed could not accept her happiness. She worked tirelessly to isolate me, keeping away those who truly loved me while feeding lies to everyone else. I was just that grieving child, desperate to be loved by the only parent I had left. Instead, I was on my own. While they enjoyed lavish vacations, I had to stay home, cooking spaghetti without sauce because that was all I knew how to make. Even when they were there, I often sat by myself, avoiding her wrath. Her jealousy, like a hurricane, would devastate everything in its path, leaving me in the wreckage.

Her words, her actions, every instance of mistreatment and deceit were meticulously stored in the archives of my mind— and splinters in my soul. I was constantly on high alert, always analyzing and monitoring her every move, as though treading on a pressure plate, where one wrong step would trigger incalculable consequences.

Perhaps that is where my hyper-vigilance stemmed from— the time when I resorted to placing small pieces of tape on my door to detect any breach of privacy, or snapping photos of my room to ensure nothing was amiss. In an environment where a child is supposed to feel protected, such precautions became a necessity to be safe. I could never afford to let my guard down or entertain doubts about what was happening.

It brought to mind the origins of the term "gaslighting," from a story about a husband twisting his wife's reality to break her down. It echoed what I had faced—sowing doubt, undermining my sanity. If I tracked every detail, I thought, I could stay ahead. I wouldn't fall into that trap.

But who would lend credence to the concerns of a teenager? A grieving child? Surely, it couldn't be as dire as I recorded. To the outside world—teachers, friends, neighbors, even social workers—the extent of the situation was incomprehensible, and even my own family struggled to discern the gravity of the circumstances at first, sometimes overlooking the turmoil unfolding right behind them as their backs were turned.

Trauma, trauma—it echoed through the chambers of my mind, still sitting on that piano bench beside my mother. I watched it all unfold as if in a black-and-white cinema, feeling my mother's hand on my heart, unlocking the pain that had held me in its grasp for so long. I wanted to stay in this dream, yet escape it all the same. The glow at the center of my heart showed me there was still a glimmer of light left.

Like the slow dimming of a gas lamp, imperceptible with each passing day, hindsight now unveiled the shadows that had crept into my being, extinguishing the radiant light within. The brilliance I once embraced, the luminance that defined me, now flickered in the encroaching darkness. To reclaim that inner radiance, I knew I must turn away from the shadows that entrapped me.

Feeling my mother's hand pulling away, everything turned black. I slowly opened my eyes—first noticing the traces of my eyelashes, then the blurred towel I clutched, and finally my notebook lying next to me. Drenched in drops of sweat, I looked around: the palm trees were still swaying, as if nothing had happened. I buried my head in my hands. *I could never go back home.*

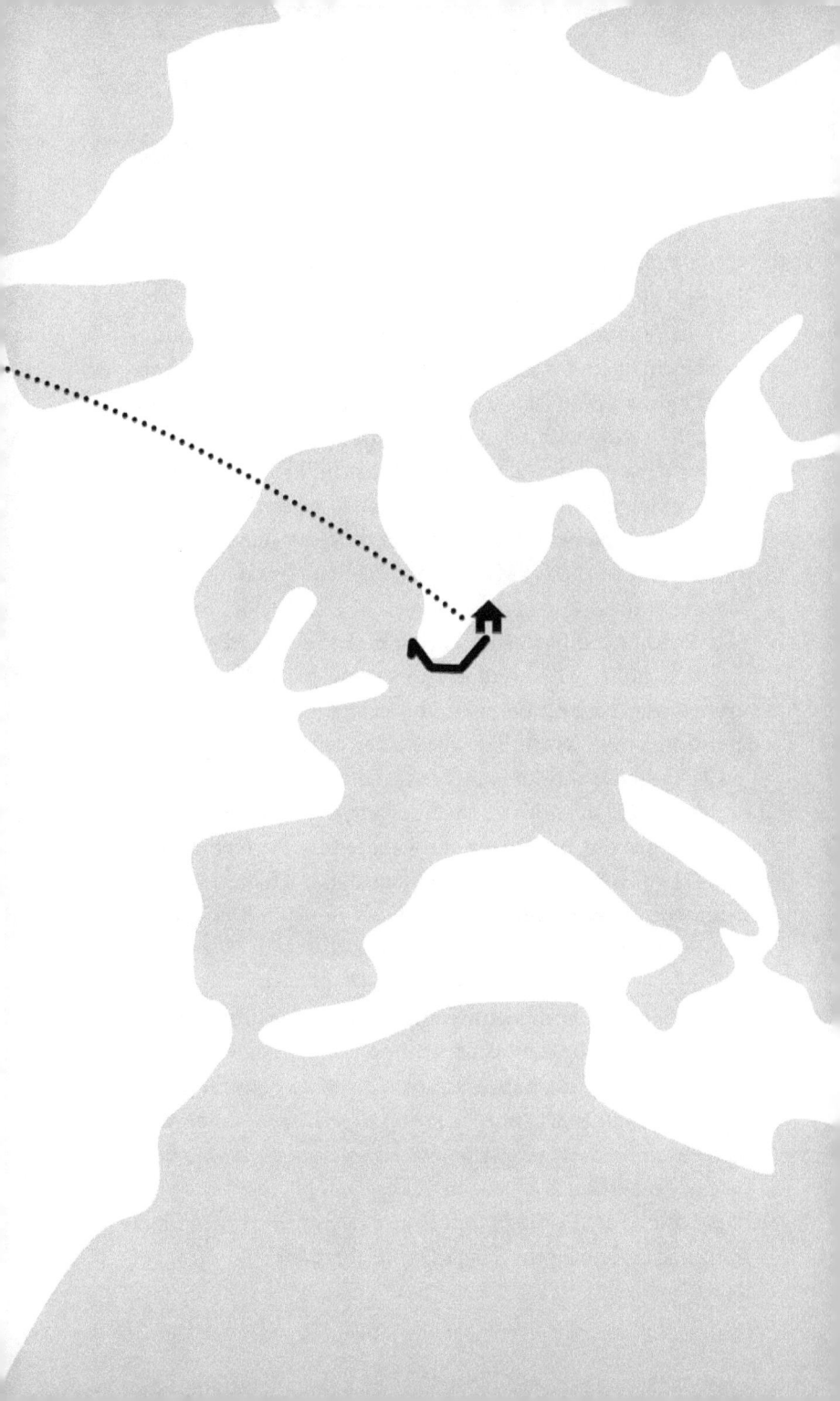

Longing for my dad's company, yet reluctant to return to his house, I chose to stay with my brother A in Amsterdam.

When I lived nearby, we were so tight—dinners, adventures in the city, laundry runs, everything. The age gap meant we didn't grow up under the same roof much, so being close felt special. Staying with him, even briefly, gave us the chance to do what we loved: walking his French bulldog through the park, indulging in his incredibly creative vegetarian cooking, and discovering hidden gems around the city—like picnicking on the roof of the NEMO Science Museum or taking a ferry across the IJ.

I couldn't complain about being back in Amsterdam. I had called it home with fondness for a few years. Yet, as time passed, my connection with the capital city underwent a transformation. Much like when I first left, returning didn't evoke the sense of belonging it once did.

If Amsterdam, with all its familiarity and excitement, felt confining at this stage of my life, where else in the Netherlands could I go? It was a question I pondered, though deep down, I knew the answer: my roots would likely be planted away from my homeland. While my Dutch identity would always be a part of me, it no longer defined where I belonged.

Speaking of Dutch identity, another of my priorities during this sojourn at home was to reconnect with friends—maybe going for a bike ride along the canals, grabbing deep-fried food from a vending machine, enjoying a *gezellige* evening at a brown café, or savoring stroopwafels, *roze koek, gevulde koek,* and all other kinds of cookies. That would have been fun, busy, and Dutch enough, but it just so happened that I had returned in time for the King's Day celebrations.

King's Day, or *Koningsdag* in Dutch, falls on April 27th and commemorates the birthday of King Willem-Alexander. It's a nationwide celebration with countless events for all ages. Streets are awash with orange, the national color, as revelers partake in street markets, live music, parades, and countless outdoor activities. With the festivities aligning closely with my own birthday, the anticipation was doubly exciting.

Therefore, when King's Day arrived, I made a deliberate effort to stay awake until midnight, marking the transition to April 28th alongside a dear friend whose birthday coincided with mine. While most others struggled to maintain their energy after a day filled with early festivities and a whirlwind of events scattered across the city—boating in the canals, hopping between apartments, and drifting in and out of bars and cafés—my birthday twin and I began a countdown to midnight at a pub.

The crowd was thinning, and most of our friends had drifted off to bed, leaving only my cousin S by our side for the final minutes of the day. In her presence, memories of our shared experiences across Asia and Oceania resurfaced. Here we were again, in the Netherlands, a place we both considered home, yet now felt disconnected from.

Despite all the colorful celebrations and the warmth of friendship, I couldn't shake the sense of displacement. It was as if the world around me had shifted subtly, leaving me standing in a past version of it, unable to fully reconnect. How could I reconcile being surrounded by love and friendship in such a beautiful country, while still standing in the shadow of unresolved parts of my past?

As we counted down to twenty-four—the floor sticky, my friend and cousin holding me tight, singing the seconds—I made a wish. I wished that wherever my future led, I would find it—that *something* I was searching for, that moment when everything would finally click, when I could stop running and start settling. And I hoped that when I found it, it would be in a place like this—surrounded by people like them. A place where its beauty would shine as brightly as Amsterdam on a spring day, but with skies always clear, free from the clouds of doubt that had been following me for far too long.

England

As I stepped into a London bar with U—a friend I had met in Salzburg, Austria—his birthday party was already in full swing. Friends cheered him on as he made his rounds, greeting everyone and introducing me along the way.

These funny, good-laughing, good-looking people—many of whom were actors—moved and talked with that ease, charisma, and resourcefulness that comes from hours spent on stage. I loved their energy. I fit right in.

His parents were no different. They immediately handed me a key to their home and gave me a room of my own, allowing me to come and go as I pleased.

U's birthday breakfast, the following morning, was just as cheerful as the evening before, cake waiting on the table. His mother hugged me with such a tight squeeze, as if I were a long-lost child and she wanted to catch me up on all the love I had been missing.

When we sat down at the table, passionate debates about her son's future quickly broke out, and he rolled his eyes in embarrassment. I giggled, observing at first, then joined in. This family had such an electric energy, continuing their days as usual—not just welcoming me, but making me feel as if I had always been there.

One of U's best friends briefly interrupted the breakfast scene—without disrupting the fun—by casually walking through the front door unannounced, taking a seat like it was the most natural thing in the world. He seamlessly dove into the lively conversation with the same passion as everyone else.

Taking sips of my tea, I soaked in the loving chaos—this was everything I wanted in a family.

During my days in London, I had a mission: to revisit the iconic landmarks and reacquaint myself with the city. Every morning, I had breakfast with U's family, then packed a light backpack and set off on foot from their house in Wandsworth, eventually catching the tube or a bus.

Big Ben, Tower Bridge, the London Eye, Trafalgar Square, Piccadilly Circus, Buckingham Palace, Oxford Street, and Harrods—all looked the same as before, each a work of art surrounded by a sea of people snapping photos, their phones and cameras seemingly more important than the company they kept. I understood the urge. I wanted to capture these moments too. Every touristy corner of the city felt like a canvas worth painting.

Pausing for a bacon, lettuce, and tomato sandwich at Hyde Park one day and watching as people hurried by and children played *footie,* I realized I had never really explored the more residential areas—Notting Hill, Camden, Greenwich—apart from the beautiful neighborhood where I was staying.

After finishing my sandwich, I hopped on the tube and headed to Notting Hill, eager to glimpse some of the chic living corners of this cosmopolitan metropolis.

Even though I was far from being a Londoner, the way I navigated the city with ease, casually chatting with locals, and even bumping into someone I knew out of the blue sparked a realization: London had the potential to be the place where I could find happiness. Indeed, out of the cities on my shortlist, London felt, and was, the closest to home. It was also undeniably the most familiar and the easiest to transition to. That seemed like a good reason to extend my stay for a little while longer.

The more time I spent there, the more immersed I became in the harmonious melody of urban life. The rush around me quickened my leisurely pace, with a variety of activities that never seemed to run out—the coquette laughter of people along the Thames, and the unusually sunny days.

I seamlessly blended into an ecosystem of people, places, and habits, meeting U and his friends or family for dinner each night, followed by game nights, pubs, or plays.

During the day, I chose one new place to visit, often writing in my journal on a park bench or a grassy stretch after lunch, following wherever my heart led me.

Somehow, being there felt like a dream—*A Midsummer Night's Dream*—akin to the captivating performances at Shakespeare's Globe under the warm light of European pre-summer evenings. Just as the characters in Shakespeare's play are swept into a forest of enchantment, lost in a whirlwind of confusion and transformation, I, too, felt as though I was navigating a world of possibilities. The confusion was finally clearing, though the transformation remained in progress. I remembered the Bard's words: "The course of true love never did run smooth." But for me, this wasn't about romantic love —it was about awakening to self-love and love for others, allowing myself to be vulnerable.

To symbolize—to solidify—this turning point I had been feeling since Florida, I returned to the shoe store where I had bought my loyal red Nikes, the ones that had accompanied me throughout my journey. There, I bought a new pair.

Though they were still red Nikes from London, walking a mile in them felt different, almost like cheating. I stopped at a bench, pulled my battered old Nikes from the box where I had tossed them, noticing a burgundy thread unraveling and a small hole forming, then slipped them back on—there were still more miles to walk in these shoes.

The night ferry from England to France docked in Calais; the bus emerged from its cavernous belly, hitting the road on the way to Lille, from where it would continue onwards to Antwerp and, finally, Rotterdam.

I watched as the French and Belgian countryside rolled by, a patchwork of fields and villages illuminated only by street lanterns and glowing window panes.

When we reached Antwerp, a young Japanese man sat down beside me, and we started chatting. He was also going to the Netherlands, planning a visit to Amsterdam and Utrecht, where he had friends. As we talked, it struck me that this time I was on the other side—I was now the local. So, just as others had passionately told me about their countries, I was now sharing my recommendations and insider tips, hoping to inspire him as much as others had inspired me.

I spoke about my beautiful Netherlands, where the fields are green, the farm animals skip happily through the expansive landscapes, and where life is enriched by small but strong communities, fresh foods, and a vault of rich history, art, and architecture. I spoke about how bakeries line their warm, crusty loaves on shelves, their aromas wafting through the air. I described how cheese farmers invite you to sample bold flavors before making a purchase. And I told him about the pleasure of savoring large, fresh stroopwafels straight off the iron at a market stall with sweet syrup oozing between the crisp wafers, all accompanied by a small paper bag of crumbs spilling over the edge—*koekkruimels,* just as satisfying as the treat itself. I had always proudly called this country mine, even when living there became suffocating. To me, the Netherlands remains one of the most wonderful places on earth.

Netherlands

When the bus crossed the border, characterized by smoother asphalt, my phone pinged, interrupting my rhapsodizing. My Swiss friend, Q, who had invited me to meet up in Bishkek, Kyrgyzstan, sent me pictures from his visit to Chernobyl in Ukraine—the site of the catastrophic disaster at the nuclear power plant in the 1980s. Looking at the photos, I admired his adventurous spirit, his eagerness to explore all corners of the globe, even places I would have never considered.

A jolt of curiosity went through me, an impulse I couldn't ignore. Without really thinking it through, I booked a flight before getting off the bus, then texted him back.

I WILL MEET YOU IN BISHKEK.

It was still early in the morning when the bus pulled up at Rotterdam Zuidplein. I took a local bus, then quietly snuck into my father's house and crawled into bed to snooze for a few hours. When I woke up, the woman in my father's life was not home, and I found him at the dining room table, reading.

"Ah, my daughter!" he exclaimed as I walked in, removing his small reading glasses off his nose.

We hugged tightly and caught up on the political initiatives around town that he was working on.

"It's a beautiful day," he said, smiling the smile of someone who just had a great idea. "How about we take the Mercedes for a drive together?"

I had fond memories of his classic 190 SL Mercedes-Benz. As a child, he was on the board of the Mercedes-Benz Club, and we always participated in old-timer tours around the country, just the three of us—he, Mom, and me. In the back of the Benz, I would watch my parents sitting together: Dad behind the mighty steering wheel in the deep red interior of the iconic long white convertible, boasting its massive three-pointed star on the nose; Mom's scarf waving in the wind, her hair tangling as we cruised down the open country roads ahead; me playing with my stuffed animals, friends joining me on the adventure.

Now, jumping into the car beside my dad felt like old times. We drove to Zierikzee, a picturesque city in the southwest of the Netherlands in the province of Zeeland—the original *Zealand*. My dad always had a knack for picking spontaneous destinations, and today was no different. He chose Zierikzee simply because it popped into his head and he liked it there.

Even over the roar of the engine and the whoosh of the wind, we chatted, our voices raised, cheeks flushed from the brisk air and the joy of being together on the open road. The sky, dotted with fluffy clouds, mirrored the scene below, where flocks of sheep grazed in the emerald-green fields beyond the swaying tall grass lining the roadside.

Dad and I loved going on adventures together. We enjoyed long walks, getting ice cream with sprinkles, and savoring a cold beer on a sunny terrace. And we talked—really talked.

We could talk for days, and we often did. I could tell him everything, even the things that weighed heaviest on my heart, the things only he could make a difference in, even when they were hard to say out loud.

"What's next for you, my daughter?" he asked as we settled onto an outdoor terrace in Zierikzee, enjoying a cold, cherry-flavored *Kriek* beer, deep-fried cheese sticks, and *bitterballen*.

"I'm meeting a friend in Kyrgyzstan."

"What's in Kyrgyzstan?" he asked.

"I don't know," I said, my forehead creasing briefly, then softening into a smile. "But I'm going to find out."

•

Besides catching up with friends and family and shopping for concealing clothes for Kyrgyzstan, the only other priority I had during those four days at home was visiting Mom at her final resting place. This is something I always do when I am home. Something that, despite being painful, also brings a quiet strength.

Sitting down on the gravel, looking at the heart-shaped pink marble headstone and the smaller stone in front of it, bearing her picture—with her long blonde hair and bright smile—I felt as though she were staring right back at me. I would then tell her all about my travels—the things I wished I could have shared with her by my side, the things I was unlocking in my heart. Her presence, even if only in spirit, reassured me that she was always with me.

At the same time, being in the graveyard reminded me of the little girl I once was, standing there in the cold on that somber February day, the day of her funeral. I remembered the twelve-year-old me, dressed in a formal dress from a school dance, covered with a coat I wore to the stables. The coat was the most comfortable fleece jacket, with some stray horsehair, but the dress was the last formal one my mother had bought me. Surely, it was pretty enough to wear to her funeral.

I looked down at the gravel beneath me, then glanced up at my mother's headstone again.

"Thank you for being a guiding light, Mom."

I wished everything were different.

PART SEVEN

CLEAR EYES ON THE ROOF OF THE WORLD

Kyrgyzstan

Darkness showed the first hints of the early morning deep blue hue when I landed at Manas International Airport. My Swiss friend had arrived two hours before me. As I walked off the plane, I immediately spotted him sitting in the waiting area by my gate, his backpack next to him.

"I can't believe you came!" Q said, jumping up.

"You think I'd leave you here at four in the morning if I wasn't planning to show up?" I replied, giving him a hug.

He felt like an old friend, a kindred spirit, even though in reality, we had only shared a few meals together in Serbia. His smile was disarming, his adventures inspiring, and despite standing in a country I knew nothing about, in the middle of the night, it felt as casual as meeting an acquaintance for a quick drink.

"So, where do we go?" I asked.

"We can take a cab to Almaty, Kazakhstan first, then circle back to Kyrgyzstan in a few days," he suggested.

Given our proximity to Kazakhstan and the early hour, we pulled out our phones and booked a hostel in Almaty, the country's largest city, just a four-hour drive away. Normally, I would argue that such a journey required a car. But, after asking around, a kind taxi driver said he could take us to the border for a "very good rate," assuring us there would be other taxis waiting to take us into Kazakhstan. He was friendly, full of life, and a real pleasure to talk to. We trusted his word and surrendered to the universe.

When we reached the border, the sky was still a deep pre-dawn blue, with only a sliver of light on the horizon. A brick security office stood nearby, while a large arch loomed over the road, guiding vehicles through. Alongside, a long, high-gated walkway stretched out for pedestrians crossing on foot.

We got out of the car, leaving our driver behind, and started walking. On both sides, military officers critically examined our red passports. Within an hour and a half, our passports had been stamped three times: arriving in Kyrgyzstan, leaving Kyrgyzstan, and arriving in Kazakhstan.

As we left the checkpoint on the Kazakh side and walked toward a rest stop, the sun began to peek over the horizon, and the fenced-in walkway came to an end.

"It's all about the experience!" I said cheerfully.

Kazakhstan

There were indeed taxis waiting for us on the other side. Driving from Korday to Almaty, we already caught a glimpse of what this land had to offer: undulating green hills dotted with wildflowers, red poppies and yellow daisies lining the road, framed by the towering snow-capped Zailiysky Alatau mountains, their peaks fading into a sunrise painted in the same bright colors as the blooms below.

At the hostel, scarcely occupied, the receptionist welcomed us with cookies, hot tea and clean towels. As I worked out the exchange rate to settle the bill, I couldn't believe the nightly rate—it was so affordable that I could live there for a year on what I would spend on a month's rent in the Netherlands, if not longer.

I sat down on my bunk bed and scanned the room. Ten neatly spaced beds lined the walls, each with a small personal drawer tucked underneath and covered with soft, quilted bedding in muted tones of pink and blue, while an itchy rug kept my feet warm against the cool wooden floor. Suddenly, my phone rang. It was a video call from the German.

"What are you doing?" he asked, sounding concerned.

"What do you mean, what am I doing?" I replied, slightly annoyed.

"I am worried about you," he said, his eyes nearly burning through the screen.

There was something about his voice that soothed me in a familiar way—yet it also upset me. He had been a constant presence in my life for almost this entire journey, even after I left Germany a couple of months ago. But why? Why did he care so much?

"In my opinion," he continued, "you need to find a place to settle and something to keep you busy all day long, so you're not always thinking about traveling."

"You don't get to have an opinion," I snapped back quickly.

"That's fair, but please be safe," he concluded.

In silence, I stared at my feet, my toes playing with the fringe of the rug. I understood what he was saying, and I knew he wasn't the only one who thought I needed to settle down.

I wasn't just going to settle—especially not just because it was expected or because it was what people did without ever asking why. Besides the hurt I was leaving behind, I didn't want to be born in one town, go to school there, work there, marry there, have kids there, and find my final resting place within the same square mile. That wasn't for me—not when there was a whole world out there, with places where I felt more connected, more grounded, and where I could grow in a single year more than I ever could in that small, comfortable, safe, beautiful town.

Maybe one day that town, or country, would call me home. Or maybe another town would, or a sprawling metropolis, or even a remote cabin in the woods. Perhaps it would be a community that rooted me, or maybe it would be someone special—a person I would want to build a life with.

For now, I didn't just want to exist—I wanted to live fully, to explore every corner of life that pulled me. I wanted to really get to know myself through a diversity of experiences, to grow through new perspectives, and to love life with intent, depth, and an unapologetic passion—free from the whispers of what anyone else thought I should do.

I had to keep going, at least until I knew in my heart it was time. When I decided what was next, it would be on my terms, and it would be exactly what I wanted it to be.

Recharged by a brief nap at the hostel, we restarted our day with a long walk that ended at sunset in Panfilov Park—a central and historic location in Almaty.

The park features several important sites and memorials. The Eternal Flame, which burns in dedication to the soldiers who fought and died during World War II, and the colorful Zenkov Cathedral, a Russian Orthodox church recognized as one of the tallest wooden buildings in the world, are two of the park's most prominent landmarks.

Standing there, surrounded by the gentle rustling of trees and the golden light fading into the evening, we paused, taking it all in. The monuments loomed large, demanding respect with their sheer stature, as though the park were an open-air museum. The ground was spotless, every corner meticulously maintained, and only a couple of other visitors quietly passed through.

The magical purple sky started to turn dark and ominous as a storm began to brew. Q and I quickly ran back to the hostel, making it just in time to avoid the downpour that followed. Other guests—from the United States, England, and France, as well as an ethnic Uyghur native to the Xinjiang region of China (or, as we learned to call it, East Turkestan in Inner Asia)—also returned to shelter. We sat together in the dining room, eating *shelpek,* a sour cream dough flatbread, drinking tea, and chatting.

Listening to the steady rhythm of raindrops against the windows, punctuated by the rumble of distant thunder, we gathered around the flickering candlelight. Every now and then, a flash of lightning illuminated the room, casting fleeting shadows on our faces. The mood was peaceful yet charged, the kind of intimacy only shared during a storm. We broke pieces of the warm *shelpek*, its soft, tangy texture mingling with the sweetness of the tea.

Conversations drifted easily between us. The American had visited U.S. military bases and found himself captivated by the local way of life and the tapas-style food. The Englishman, a writer, had monetized his musings, giving him the freedom to continue wandering. The Uyghur man, with quiet reverence and sparkling eyes, introduced us to the complexities of East Turkestan—a name unfamiliar to most at the table. He spoke of a people without a land to truly call their own, swallowed by larger nations.

In that small room, breaking bread, finishing our tea, it felt as though we were unearthing pieces of history and humanity, peeling back layers of what we thought we knew in order to understand the unknown. The more we spoke, the more we began to question if borders really defined us.

We defined ourselves by the nations that claimed our lands, but the Uyghur man anchored his identity in the people he belonged to, not the land taken from him. It was a moment to step outside our own borders, our own reference frames, and glimpse a detail of the world we knew nothing about.

In the morning, I lay in bed, reflecting on the sliver of peace that was gradually clearing my mind. My reflection was abruptly disturbed when I learned that my American friend T, whom I had met in Thailand, had lost his mother.

Just a few months ago, I had hoped with every fiber of my being that he would never have to experience such a loss—but cancer had prevailed once again.

We had bonded over shared experiences, and now I felt a deep compassion for him, knowing exactly how he felt. I emphasized that he could always reach out to me if he wanted to talk about her, to keep her memory alive. Together, we could navigate this shared pain, even though we didn't know each other that well. Feeling alone in our grief, yet connected —alone, together.

T:

**I WILL DEFINITELY NEED YOU IN THE
COMING YEARS.**

**TO UNDERSTAND HOW YOU HAVE GOTTEN
THROUGH CERTAIN PARTS OF THE YEAR.**

The truth is, I didn't really know how I got through those difficult times. But by talking about it, I found solace in sharing happy memories during dark moments. That's what I always tried to do—think of happier times, honor traditions from the past, and follow in my mother's footsteps, doing things she enjoyed and things we used to enjoy together.

But as I considered the message I had just received, I realized that every milestone, every tough moment of my teenage years, was spent with the woman in my father's life, leaving little room for us, as a family, to honor my mother. That first December month without her, my name had already been erased from the family Christmas card. Many holidays that followed were spent with the new woman's family, not mine —people who didn't like me and made no effort to hide it.

For a short while, I had my maternal grandmother in my corner, sharing our tears, disbelief, and frustration. Frail but fierce, she always offered me a shoulder to cry on. Then she died too. She was my last grandparent, and with her gone, my support system was shrinking, leaving only my godparents and two older brothers by my side. But the lingering toxicity in my home made it increasingly difficult for anyone to breathe. As a consequence, I often went to go see *them,* and rarely under normal circumstances. It was always me fleeing home— running from the destructive chaos, while searching for love elsewhere, desperate to spew out the fire building inside me after every argument, hoping that venting would still my trembling hands. In the end, maybe it was anger and agony that got me through the hard parts of grief, not so much love.

I shook off my thoughts—it was already 10 a.m., time to get up. Q and I had breakfast and walked back to Panfilov Park to continue the tour. An army of pigeons—I dare say hundreds-strong—flew around the monuments, the buildings, landing on rooftops, coming back to the ground to peck.

In the square in front of Zenkov Cathedral, children played with tiny automated luxury cars, while horses clicked their hooves on the concrete as they pulled carriages, and lovers strolled by, hand in hand. Somehow, at least in my mind, the pigeons and their fluttering wings tied it all together.

"Magnificent, huh?" a man said in broken English from behind me, while Q was wandering around, taking pictures.

"Yes," I nodded at him, understanding that he was referring to the pigeons, then turned back to watch the birds.

"Good fortune and peace," he said philosophically.

When I turned around to respond—the man was gone.

"What's up?" Q asked when he saw me looking around.

"I'm not sure," I shrugged. "Let's keep walking."

Soon, heavy clouds began to take over the already gloomy sky, signaling another storm brewing. Everything darkened around us—gray asphalt deepened to black. We rushed back to the hostel. This time, however, the storm caught us. The wind picked up, sending grains of sand swirling and staining the air a dusty brown.

Suddenly we heard a loud bang. Turning around quickly, we saw a jet of brass-colored water shooting up higher than the trees with great force. It was erupting from the middle of the sidewalk we had just walked on, just seconds earlier. A water pipe had probably burst.

"That could have been bad," Q said.

I had no words. I just stared at the powerful stream while two police officers ran toward it.

Good fortune and peace.

On our last day in Kazakhstan, Q and I joined forces with a new American acquaintance from the hostel. O was a young, medically retired U.S. veteran, traveling indefinitely, and able to live comfortably for years on the strength of the U.S. dollar in these parts. Together, we hailed a taxi to Big Almaty Lake.

While I knew little about the lake or the surrounding peaks, I trusted my new friends, as I had done on so many occasions before. I no longer needed a reason to go see something. I wanted to see the things I wouldn't have thought of by myself. I loved lakes, I loved being in the mountains—that was enough for me.

The taxi left the city, ascending a narrow mountain road, flanked by thick snowbanks, until we reached a small red-and-white gate, marking the entrance to Ile-Alatau National Park.

A soldier was standing there, alone. We stepped out of the car, and as I handed him my passport, he glanced at my feet and chuckled. Patches of snow dotted the ground around my fashionable T-strap sandals. It was a silly and unremarkable episode, but to me, it seemed like I had finally started to loosen up after all those months—no longer trying to be prepared or plan everything—taking life as it came, taking things in stride.

"The car stays here," the soldier said sternly as we cleared the checkpoint.

"Huh?" Q raised an eyebrow.

"I'll wait," the taxi driver replied, pulling the car into park.

I glanced down at my sandals, my bare toes wiggling, and burst out laughing. "Not a problem!"

O pulled a harmonica from his brown vest, brought it to his lips, and began playing as we started the fifteen-minute walk up a narrow asphalt road.

Eventually, we reached a viewpoint, where Big Almaty Lake spread out below us—vast and deep, its matte aquamarine waters framed by near-black spruce trees, contrasting sharply against the snow-covered peaks of higher altitudes. Nestled in the Trans-Ili Alatau mountains, the northernmost range of the Tian Shan mountain system, the waters of this natural alpine reservoir not only captivated the eye but also served as an essential source of drinking water for the region.

In the crisp mountain air, the cloud-filled sky muted the landscape to shades of black, white, and brown, making the lake's color stand out. Nature's enduring power and beauty.

The scene was still and silent, with nothing in sight but a lone picnic table and a large rock further down the slope. We descended a little closer to the water's edge, the chilly spring air biting at our skin—and my toes—sharpening our senses.

The lake grew larger with each step, the view more colorful, the peaks higher. When we reached the rock, we stepped on top, side by side, and threw our arms skyward in synchrony, the Swiss, the American, and I, partly in celebration of just being there and partly as a way to physically embrace the vast expanse before us.

I stared at the mountains, the water, the trees, and the slowly shifting blue sky. It was odd in a way, but just looking at the landscape—attentively, calmly—made me feel lighter. Many a time in my travels, I had sensed the effect that the sheer beauty of nature could have on my state of mind and spirit. How it could hush my worries and redirect my perspective.

Here, it was no different. Past worries and future hopes faded away, and I was left with that minuscule, impalpable and indescribable sensation that, despite everything, we were all free.

Kyrgyzstan

The same taxi driver who had dropped us off at the border a few days earlier was waiting for Q and me when we returned to the crossing. After we texted him our arrival time, he was ready to take us to Bishkek, the capital. With his loud and funny demeanor, he felt more like an uncle giving us a ride than a taxi driver, keeping the journey lively.

As we approached the city, I couldn't help but notice the lingering Russian influences, particularly on signs, even as we moved further away from Russia. The remnants of the Soviet era were still visible, and while I was slowly getting better at recognizing some words, the hodgepodge of Cyrillic letters mostly remained a mystery.

At the hostel, we met two other travelers—P, a French girl, and G, a Dutchman. We started talking, and at some point, G suggested renting a car to explore the region together, splitting the cost. A nearby lake caught our interest, and we were also eager to explore Tajikistan, more specifically, driving along the Pamir Highway all the way to Wakhan National Park, where Tajikistan, Afghanistan, and Pakistan converge.

So it was settled. In the morning, we went to the Tajik embassy to apply for a visa, which would be ready for pickup the next day. Afterward, we rented a car and set off for Issyk-Kul—a saline lake in northeastern Kyrgyzstan that was once a major hub on the Silk Route, connecting East and West.

Before we left, the rental car agent advised us to bring essential supplies, such as water, snacks, and fuel, because amenities were sparse in certain areas. He also warned us about the possibility of the police stopping us, not for a genuine reason, but as a means to extort money. Said and done: only fifteen minutes into the trip, we were pulled over.

Two police officers stepped out of their vehicle and slowly made their way to our car, faces impassive but watchful, heavy guns strapped to their waists. The air inside our car thickened with unease. My Swiss friend, ever smiling, rolled down the window as they approached, hoping his calm demeanor would diffuse any tension. The Dutchman sat beside him in the driver's seat, bolder but quiet for the moment, hands resting on the wheel. The officers started speaking, their language unfamiliar—perhaps Kyrgyz, though it sounded Russian.

"English? Permits?" one of them asked, his accent thick and clipped. Before we could respond, he tapped on his phone. "Tolk," he said, summoning a translator.

"Yes," Q confirmed, handing over our paperwork.

P and I sat in the back, exchanging nervous glances, neither of us daring to speak. The officers didn't seem angry, more indifferent—going through the motions of something they had probably done many times before. They said little, just pointed at our car papers, shuffled through them without care, and muttered to each other.

When a translator finally answered the phone, the purpose became clear: they weren't interested in our explanations or clearing things up. They wanted money. The accusations were vague—something about the car, a line in the rental papers, questions about where we were headed. The pauses between their comments felt calculated to unsettle us.

"Problem," one officer said, rubbing his thumb and index finger together in the universal gesture for money, making it clear that the solution would come at a price.

Despite having done nothing wrong—at least, not that we knew of, or that they specifically told us—the unspoken threat of a jail cell, or at least hours of bureaucracy, loomed in our minds. We handed over a wad of cash, none of us willing to push our luck. As the officers pocketed the money and waved us off, P finally broke the silence.

"That could have been worse," she muttered, her face pale, though she tried to laugh it off.

G shook his head, gripping the wheel tighter as we pulled away, while Q smiled, his eyes glistening. I stared out the window, watching the officers disappear.

Twenty minutes later, two new officers pulled us over. It was the same routine—calling the interpreter on the phone, giving vague reasons, mumbling, rifling through our papers, and taking our money. G shook his head more aggressively this time, Q smiled less intrigued, and P and I exchanged glances in the backseat, watching our wallets grow thinner.

Back on the road, we couldn't help wondering: Were we too polite? Too respectful? Too easily intimidated? Given that this was already the second run-in in what could potentially be many encounters with the police, we felt the need to regroup and rethink our approach. When we spotted a building with what looked like the word "café" painted on the facade, we stopped.

Inside, it might as well have been a wedding: flamingo velvet chairs spread across the room, silver tableware carefully placed on shimmering pink tablecloths, and pearl-encrusted candle holders. Even the menus had English descriptions, which was great, for a change, to know what I was ordering. The waitress didn't speak English, but she eagerly pointed to the menu with us as we made our choices. Then, with hips swaying in excitement, she darted off, thrilled that we—the only guests— had come in. We were equally thrilled to enjoy a hearty meal.

While waiting for our orders, we counted our cash.

"We're going to run out real quick at this rate," P said with narrowed eyes, referring to the bribes.

"But we're not doing anything wrong; it's fine," G pointed out nonchalantly.

"That doesn't matter much," Q said mockingly.

"It really doesn't," I agreed.

After a brief pause, I added, "Maybe we have to change our strategy. Mix things up. If they don't know what language we speak, can they extort us without understanding?"

We all looked at each other, sitting in thoughtful silence, contemplating the risks and rewards of our potential plan. It was a delicate balance between maintaining our principles and navigating the corrupt system. After more discussion, we came to the conclusion that sometimes, survival on the road meant adapting to the circumstances—even if it meant bending the rules we held dear, such as respecting law enforcement.

For the next three hours, we didn't see any more police—only mountains, hills, and the occasional solitary man on a mule carrying freshly cut grass. Then, we spotted two small children by the side of the road, walking with determined yet sluggish strides, lugging small backpacks.

"We have to give them a ride," G said as he slammed on the brakes and rolled down the window.

"English?" he asked the children.

"Yes!" they answered excitedly in unison.

"Where are you going?" Q chimed in.

"Home!" they said with the same enthusiastic tone.

I opened my door, and they hopped in with beaming faces, hugging their backpacks tightly on their laps as the four of us squeezed into the back seat, crammed together.

The kids came alive even more when they heard the pop music playing from the speakers. G grinned, glanced at them through the rearview mirror, and turned up the volume. They giggled, swaying to the beat.

"Did you come from school?" I asked the boy next to me.

He suddenly nodded shyly and replied, "Thank you!"

"Thank you! Thank you!" the other boy echoed, bouncing with excitement as he pointed at the car's speakers. "Music, music, music!"

Their home, a small village of single-story farmhouses and shipping containers repurposed as stables or sheds, was much farther than we expected—at least a fifteen-minute drive away. I started to grasp how common it still is in many parts of the world for people, including these children, to walk long distances for daily necessities. It also made me more mindful of the small acts of kindness that can make a big difference in someone's day.

In the morning, bright sunlight revealed the surroundings of our hotel—a rectangular, motel-like building perched on the shore of Lake Issyk-Kul, overlooking a small beach and the dark saltwater. Disheveled buildings lined the streets, but not a soul was in sight. There were no restaurants, only a gas station with a convenience store, adding to the eerie stillness that made us feel as if we should speak in whispers.

After a picnic from our convenience store haul, we set off by car to see more of the lake and the area around it. Most buildings we passed seemed abandoned. If it weren't for one horse tethered by a long rope near what looked like a barn, I would have thought no one lived there. Indeed, each time we briefly got out of the car, all we could see were horses and goats grazing in long, rolling fields; all we could hear was the rustling of the wind in the tall grass, the creaking of a rusty swing at an abandoned fairground. We could have been the last people on earth, surrounded by the remnants of a world slowly being reclaimed by nature.

Driving west, we left the Ring Road around Lake Issyk-Kul and continued northwest, eventually reaching the Burana Tower—one of Kyrgyzstan's most iconic landmarks. Located near Tokmok and perched atop the remains of the ancient city of Balasagun, now a grassy plain dotted with gravestones, this 11th-century brick construction was still standing. Next to it there was a small museum, showcasing archaeological findings such as coins, pottery, and tools that offer a glimpse into what life was like for the people who once lived in the region.

Inside the narrow tower, we climbed a dark, steep, winding staircase to reach the top—an ascent that would be far from ideal for anyone with claustrophobia. Originally estimated to stand one hundred fifty feet tall, we stopped at around eighty feet, as centuries of earthquakes had reduced it to this height.

My legs shook as we emerged through the opening where the steps ended, relieved not to have encountered traffic on the way up. The panoramic view of the Tien Shan mountains and the plains before them was undeniably beautiful, but I found myself preferring the perspective from below, admiring the tower's Tetris-like details rather than standing atop it. Yet, as I stood there, high above the ground, gazing at the fields and farmland stretching out in a 360-degree view, I reflected on how long this building had stood and how many people had climbed these steps—people from long ago, with lives and stories so different from mine.

I thought about how small the world sometimes feels and how immense it actually is. No book or online search could illustrate this dichotomy, or help me make sense of these contradicting sensations of vastness and intimacy, distance and accessibility. Only by feeling the pulse of the place—just as my own pulse reminds me I'm alive—I could see where I was in relation to it all.

Back in Bishkek that night, after a quick stop at the Embassy of Tajikistan to collect our visas, we exchanged our car for a four-wheel-drive Ford Ranger and prepared to set off on our road trip along the Pamir Highway. Unfortunately, only three of us would continue on—Q had to fly back to Switzerland. It felt bittersweet since he had nudged me to come here.

"Remember, it's all about the experience," he said as we parted ways.

As he caught a taxi to the airport, I was once again weighed down by that familiar mix of appreciation and sadness—a nagging knot in my stomach that always came with saying goodbye to someone dear. Goodbyes felt like a Christmas card garland, each card a snapshot of a connection, strung together one after another. Some were like those from distant relatives, barely remembered faces from a great aunt's birthday, while others—like my Swiss friend—were cherished, tucked away in a special box, treasured forever, surrounded by memories of people who had made a lasting impact. He had unveiled this part of the world to me, and I was committed to embracing every opportunity it offered.

•

The Pamir Highway, also known as the M41, is one of the most famous and scenic routes in Central Asia. Stretching roughly seven hundred and fifty miles, it runs from the city of Osh in Kyrgyzstan to Dushanbe in Tajikistan. The road traverses the Pamir Mountains—a remote and rugged area often referred to as the "Roof of the World" due to its extreme altitude, including some of the highest peaks in the world, many exceeding 23,000 feet—forming a junction between several mighty mountain ranges, like the Himalayas, the Tian Shan, the Karakoram, the Kunlun, and the Hindu Kush.

Driving out of Bishkek, we headed south with nothing but a jerry can of fuel in the truck bed and a couple of maps and dictionaries scattered across the dashboard. No set plans, just the open road ahead. Our only preparation had been a warning: the roads would be rough, the altitudes high, the weather unpredictable, and infrastructure sparse.

"Did you check the travel advisory for Tajikistan from our Ministry of Foreign Affairs?" the Dutchman asked me from behind the wheel.

"I haven't," I replied, a little taken aback that I hadn't even considered it. "What does it say?"

"To remain alert, stay away from demonstrations, and there is a risk of serious crime against foreigners," he paraphrased, matter-of-factly.

"Ah, how comforting," I said, watching the road stretch ahead into the unknown.

"Right!" he chuckled. "And there's also no Dutch Embassy, so if we get in trouble we have to contact the Embassy of the Netherlands in Kazakhstan or go to the Embassy of Germany in Tajikistan."

"That's good to know…"

"Probably. And there was also something about landmines in border regions," he added nonchalantly.

"Landmines?!"

"Well, we better be careful then!" P said from the backseat, echoing my thoughts.

It was hard to imagine any kind of violence against tourists when we were being pulled over by police officers every twenty minutes and handing over money every time. Though perhaps that was a form of violence—a silent, non-physical violence that leaned closer to theft. In any case, the next time I would take the wheel, I decided that I would try something different when they pulled us over.

After two hours, the Too-Ashuu mountain pass beckoned us, its jagged peaks towering over a two-lane road that clung to the steep northern face in a series of switchbacks and hairpin turns. We began our ascent in lush green valleys, but as we climbed, the landscape shifted; the green fading to the stark white of snow. Trucks crawled up the steep grades, forcing risky passes on the narrow, winding road. Flocks of sheep often blocked our path, herded by people on horseback, their saddles packed with bags, pots, and pans. Even cyclists pedaled along, tents strapped to their bikes, defying the harsh climb.

At the top, nearly 10,000 feet above sea level, the infamous Too-Ashuu tunnel gaped ahead, its dark maw so close to the mountain's peak that it made me wonder why they had built it here at all, so high and remote. We entered the one-point-seven-mile stretch, the oppressive darkness swallowing the car as our headlights strained to cut through the thick, damp air.

The tunnel walls seemed to close in, their rough surfaces gleaming faintly, and the distant pinprick of light at the exit felt like a far-off hope rather than an end in sight. But soon enough, we made it through, emerging into the daylight.

Descending the continuously winding road on the other side, I took the wheel from G, the landscape shifting to softer hills. Mountains pierced through low-hanging clouds on the horizon, and the sun became more vivid as as we made our way down. With my sunglasses resting on my nose, I gazed out at the barren slopes, shadows stretching like veins across the land. This wasn't like the tree-covered, towering Alps I had known in Austria or the dramatic peaks of New Zealand. These mountains breathed differently—smoother—their presence quieter but no less imposing.

Just as we rounded a sharp bend and went down a steep slope, enjoying the view, there it was, disturbing our silent reverie—another police car. One officer sat behind the wheel, the other stood by the side of the road with a walkie-talkie in hand, and of course, he signaled for us to pull over.

"Okay, friends, this is it. Let's give them every language we know," I said before rolling down my window.

"*Hallo, officier!*" I called in Dutch, flashing a cheeky smile as he stood outside our car window, peering in.

Looking at me with piercing eyes, he spoke something that I assumed was Russian. I caught the word *machina*, meaning car, but, unsure of the rest, I just stared back at him, smiling.

He spoke again, this time more assertively, demanding me

to get out of the vehicle. I stepped out onto the asphalt and closed the door behind me, then followed him to the police car just five feet away. The officer busily gestured with his arms, pointing at our car.

"Excusez-moi?" I said in French, slightly tilting my head.

The officer continued speaking in Russian, then grabbed his phone and asked, "English?"

I signaled to my friends in the car, and they rolled down the windows, chiming in with a mix of Dutch, French, English, and a little German, Spanish, and Russian, while I shrugged at the officer. He looked at his partner, then back at me, then back at my friends in the car, his brows furrowed.

He walked to the front of his car and slammed his hand on one of the headlights. I suspected he was saying I should have had my headlights on, even though it was broad daylight. Yet, given our previous experience with law enforcement, I wasn't sure if he was making it up or if it was an actual law.

Regardless, our strategy this time was to confuse them with a mix of languages, hoping they would eventually give up trying to communicate their demand for money.

"Machina, machina." The officer slammed his headlight a few more times, then continued speaking, walking to his door and pointing through the open window at the headlight switch next to the steering wheel.

"Ah! *Machina!*" I exclaimed, stepping toward the police vehicle, now pretty certain he was asking me to turn on my headlights.

I leaned in and touched the switch through the window.

"Da? Nyet? Da? Nyet?" I repeated, saying yes and no while miming turning the lights on and off.

He looked at me, perplexed; his partner laughed as if it were a skit. My reasoning was simple, even if risky: they would either throw me in jail or think, "Ah, she tried to understand; let her go."

The officer continued speaking in Russian, more relaxed this time, throwing a quick smile to his partner.

Then, out of the blue, one word I could understand clearly: "Go."

I squinted, as if to double-check I had heard it correctly, then pointed to our car.

"*Da,*" he said firmly, frowning. "Go!"

Afraid he might change his mind if I stalled, I jumped back in the car, turned the headlights on and drove away. Once we were out of sight, we all burst into laughter.

"We didn't have to pay!" G shrieked.

After driving through endless stretches of desolation, we spotted what appeared to be a restaurant—more a charming rest stop—with a thatched canopy covering a seating area for less than ten people. Two stone blocks served as tables, and there were no walls, overlooking a gleaming, motionless lake.

We stepped into the grass, where a small hut next to the seating area served as the kitchen. A fire crackled nearby, colorful pots and pans hung from a tree branch, and the scent of simmering spices wafted toward us. We settled onto a large rectangular stone platform, its surface cool but covered with a woven blanket, and ordered rice and bread to share, excited for a taste of the local cuisine. It was a subtle, romantic embrace of self-love, savoring each spoonful of spiced rice with focus and intention. In that distraction-free space, I finally began to appreciate myself and the way I focused on the present.

By the time we left the restaurant, the lake was catching the colors of the setting sun, and the temperatures were dropping. We had agreed to keep driving until we reached Tajikistan, which was still nine hours away, and although the car had a rather powerful heating system, we wanted to limit fuel consumption to make it last. This was yet another instance that reminded me how spontaneous I had been, not planning or preparing. P was the only one who had thought to bring a sleeping bag, and she kindly lent it to us, so we could take turns resting in the back seat.

Passing by Osh, Kyrgyzstan's second-largest city, we decided to stop for provisions. Given the late hour, most shops were already closed—only a small convenience store had its "Open" sign flickering. Though there was no fresh food, the shelves were stocked with snacks—sweet and savory—and at this point, we took what we could get.

The man at the cash register smiled at us; that kind, inviting smile one receives when the other person notices you're a foreigner. I smiled back at him, nodding slightly in greeting.

As we browsed the shelves, pointing at packages of chips, dried noodles, and cookies, an older woman suddenly emerged from the back of the store. She walked toward me, holding what looked like a very large sausage.

"Kolbasa?" she asked with a smile, offering me the sausage.

I had seen enough Russian menus by now to know that *kolbasa* meant sausage.

"Spasibo," I said, expressing my gratitude.

The man at the cash register didn't charge us for the sausage when we paid—it was indeed a gift.

When we left the shop, P turned to me, still processing the exchange.

"Did they just give that to us?"

I nodded, reflecting on how this gesture transcended words. It felt as if the older woman had read the weariness in our eyes. Perhaps it was the universal language of kindness—a gesture of hospitality that spoke volumes to weary travelers far from home. It reminded me that sometimes a simple smile or a shared moment of understanding could bridge the gap between strangers, making the world feel a little less daunting, a little less lonely once more.

There was already enough sunlight illuminating the landscape when we neared the Tajik border. The more we drove, the fewer gas stations we saw, so when we spotted one in Sary-Tash, we immediately pulled over. The place had only two pumps, and a man on horseback stood guard. Looking at the somewhat surreal scene, I was struck by the juxtaposition of past and present forms of transportation, with the sleepy farm town slowly awakening against the timeless backdrop of the majestic Pamir Mountains.

Leaving Sary-Tash, two men pushed wheelbarrows laden with grass toward the town, their silhouettes etched against the snow-capped peaks. A final stretch of narrow, straight road lay before us, leading into the mountain range that marked the border between the two countries. Though the road had been paved, potholes and bumps riddled the asphalt, rattling the car. We couldn't decide whether it was better to speed over them or drive slowly to avoid the worst of the cracks.

G, at the wheel, found going around the holes inefficient.

"I'm going to try another way," he said, flicking on the 4x4 and pressing the gas.

The vehicle surged forward, bounding over the uneven ground as we bumped in our seats.

"*Oh, non, non!*" P exclaimed from the backseat.

I clutched the hand grip with my right hand, holding on to the seat with my left, as the car bounced continuously, its suspension emitting a squeaky sound. G kept gaining speed.

Then, one of the potholes blindsided us, sending the car high in the air.

"Aaaah!" I shrieked, my head colliding with the roof.

Thank goodness for our seatbelts, which kept us from being completely tossed about.

Slightly dazed, I looked around: my phone flew off my lap and wedged between the seat and the door, water spilled over the armrest, and the map flapped wildly in the air.

"Stop, stop, stop," P urged.

"Stop!" I echoed. "We need to reorganize!"

Finally, G slowed down and stopped.

Before opening the door, I glanced in the side mirror to see what had launched us.

"Oh no," I murmured, perplexed. "Oh no, no, no, no."

"What is it?" G asked.

"It's ours..." I mumbled. "It's leaking!"

"What is leaking?"

"Fuel!" I exclaimed, opening the door and walking to the back of the truck. "All the fuel!"

Both G and P followed my gaze, seeing the long trail of diesel we had left behind. It ended in a large bump in the road.

"Check the car," P said.

The fuel level on the dashboard still showed full, but after a shock like this, who knew if things were working correctly. The car likely didn't expect to dump all its fuel in mere seconds. I knelt by the side, peering underneath, trying to spot where the fuel had leaked from.

G scratched his head, glancing around.

"Maybe we should call someone."

"No service," P said, holding up her phone.

"Then we flag someone down," he retorted.

I stood up and circled the car, scanning our surroundings—the empty road ahead, the open fields, and the long trail of spilled fuel behind us, marking our path.

"We could walk back to Sary-Tash," I suggested. "Maybe we can call the rental car company from there."

"Can we still drive it?" P asked.

We exchanged glances, panic creeping in as we kept circling the car. Then, we noticed movement on the horizon.

Around half an hour later, a car approached from the Tajik border, a *Lada* filled with border patrol soldiers. They pulled up beside us and rolled down their windows. Unsure if they had spotted us or if it was mere coincidence, we tried to communicate with them. P pulled out a little dictionary from her pocket and attempted to explain the situation, with loose words and hand gestures.

Some of the soldiers chuckled, but one of them got out of the car and began to inspect the truck.

"*Machina, machina, nyet, nyet, nyet,*" he muttered, then got back into the *Lada* and they drove off.

"What do we do now?" P said, confused, as we watched the car disappear.

We sat by the side of the road, staring at the car parked in the middle of the lane, as if watching it long enough would somehow reveal what to do next.

Half an hour later, another *Lada* arrived, filled with more soldiers. They had a working phone, and we called the rental car company, explaining the situation. They guided us on what to look for underneath the car to diagnose any damage— nothing was found. Even some of the soldiers volunteered to inspect the vehicle. But despite the dramatic trail of diesel on the road, no one could find any holes.

Finally, just as the soldiers were about to leave, G noticed something.

"Look!" he called out. "It is even dripping here!"

P and I joined him by the rear, and as he opened the truck bed, the three of us gasped.

"It is the jerry can!" we said in unison.

The busted jerry can lay empty in the truck bed by our luggage, with a large crack in it. Twenty liters, just over five gallons, of diesel fuel had poured out of the car and soaked our belongings, including my only warm denim jacket.

The soldiers left, laughing at our quandary, as we took a moment to collect ourselves, realizing we were probably fine to continue. I walked away from my friends, the adrenaline still coursing through me.

I sat down on the cold road, cross-legged, in front of the truck, the fuel trail behind me, a stretch of bumpy asphalt ahead, surrounded by dry green fields and the waiting, snow-covered mountains at the border. My mind and heart—jittery, shocked, scattered—seemed to somehow contrast with the morning air—still, tranquil, whole. I breathed in and closed my eyes as if all alone on the Roof of the World.

No Man's Land

After passing the Kyrgyz border checkpoint, we entered No Man's Land—a stretch of arid land and rocky outcrops, with steep cliffs flanking either side, threatening to send us tumbling if we strayed from the road, patches of snow frozen in the shade.

A row of stern-faced soldiers lined us up as we exited our vehicle at the Tajik checkpoint. They held Kalashnikov assault rifles and scanned us up and down as if we were criminals or prizes for ransom. There seemed to be no system or structure to their actions; they snooped around, asking us questions, knowing we couldn't understand them, testing us, and trying to find an opening to get what they really wanted—or what it felt like they wanted—money.

We handed over our GBAO permit to drive the Pamir Highway, along with our passports and rental car documents. One soldier took our papers inside a modest cabin, and we hesitantly followed to the door. Inside, some of the soldiers sat at a small square table, indifferent in their thick uniforms.

I glanced around: bare walls, no heater, animal skin blankets, a deck of cards on a shelf, no kitchen. I wondered how much time they spent there, on the edge, waiting for travelers to pass through. The soldier holding our documents squinted and came in close—so close I could almost feel his breath on my skin. He spoke words I didn't understand, gripping the papers tightly as if waiting for something in return, something that made it worth giving them back.

"*Kolbasa?*" I said, suddenly remembering the sausage given to me the previous night.

One of the soldiers at the table looked up.

"*Kolbasa?*" he repeated.

I signaled that I was going to the car, my hands raised to show I meant no harm. Another soldier kept his hand on his Kalashnikov as I reached for the sausage in the back seat.

"Here," I said, offering it to the soldiers.

As if struck by a bolt of happy lightning, the soldiers smiled and burst into raucous laughter. They snatched the sausage from my hand, speaking loudly as a pocket knife appeared from one of their uniforms. Without hesitation, they started cutting it up and passing it around. Whatever tension there was in the air, it suddenly dissipated.

"Aah, go, go!" the soldier holding our passports and papers said, handing everything back to us with a stamp.

Tajikistan felt deserted at first, with crumbling buildings and small yurts scattered through empty towns, where cows, yaks, and goats roamed freely. Forty minutes after leaving the border post, driving south along the Chinese border, Karakul Lake stretched out beside us. Still isolated, but introducing the first splash of color to the landscape's earthy tones. The lake's name, "Black Lake," contrasted with its shimmering waters, reflecting deep blues and greens, mirroring the sky and the peaks encircling it.

As we stepped out of our car, the crisp air tightened its grip on our lungs. At an elevation of about 13,000 feet, the low oxygen forced me to be more mindful, more deliberate with each inhale. The stillness of the surroundings—occasionally broken by the distant call of a bird or the gentle rippling of the lake—was almost hypnotic.

Walking along the shoreline, we noticed a fascinating phenomenon: ice heaving. The ice below the lake's surface expanded and contracted with the shifting temperatures, causing it to push upwards and create intricate, jagged formations along the edge. These ice heaves—glistening in the sunlight—were like nature's sculptures, emerging from the depths as if the lake itself was breathing.

Continuing our journey south toward Murghab—the highest town on the Pamir Highway—I closed my eyes and dozed off, letting the rhythmic hum of the engine lull me into a light sleep. When I awoke some time later, we were pulling over to the side of the road near a clay building where cows lay in the sun and three people stood chatting. As it turned out, they were also travelers—a Swiss couple driving from Dushanbe to Osh in a *Lada*, and a young man from Bosnia cycling along the same route. It was exciting, and even a bit unexpected, to meet other foreigners in such a desolate place. They were the first people we had encountered since crossing the border, and that alone was reason enough for my friends to pull over, eager to see anyone. It was a relief to have a conversation with people we could understand.

"How far is Murghab?" I asked before we continued on.

"This *is* Murghab," said the Swiss man.

We looked around. Crooked telephone poles and small livestock pens dotted the landscape, while a few scattered homes, yurts, and dilapidated structures stretched across the wide, windswept plain. It wasn't quite what we had expected.

"Go to the Pamir Hotel," the Bosnian man advised before we drove off. "They will take care of you."

A little further down the road, the Pamir Hotel rose taller and more imposing than the other structures, its high window panes reflecting the clouds. Considering the remoteness of the area, having a hotel like this was quite remarkable. We were greeted with warmth and ushered to a cozy corner filled with pillows in a window nook, where they served us tea, potatoes, tomatoes, and bread. I was so absorbed in the taste of the food that I nearly bit my fingers.

After the meal, I wandered up a staircase, clutching my diesel-soaked denim jacket under my arm, hoping to find a bathroom. Upon entering, my eyes widened at the sight of communal showers. Without hesitation, I kicked off my red Nikes and turned on the water, letting the drops fall at my feet as I shoved my jacket beneath the stream, trying to rinse off the fuel. The water cascaded close to my face, and an irresistible urge pulled me in. I plunged my head into the running water, clothes still on.

As my hair dripped onto my shoulders, I heard the door open. An older woman in a blue dress and white apron looked at me, puzzled. Almost instinctively, with a motherly gesture, she motioned for me to hand over my jacket, which I trustfully placed in her care. She retrieved a wooden washboard from a supply closet and began scrubbing it clean while I sat on a crate, wringing out my hair and watching her help me, gratefully nodding in appreciation.

Back on the road, still without a phone signal, we relied on an old map to take us to a place called Rabat Sasök-Kul'. From there, we had two options: go straight to Khorog, the capital city of the Gorno-Badakhshan region, or to keep driving south to the Wakhan Corridor and the border with Afghanistan.

As darkness began to fall, we spotted a small tent beside a lake called Sassyk-Kul, right where our map indicated Rabat Sasök-Kul' would be. Assuming the split in the road was nearby, we pulled over and turned off the car. We didn't have a tent, but if there was someone in a tent, perhaps this would be a good enough spot to park for a while and close our eyes in the car. I shifted in the front passenger seat, trying to get comfortable, but the longer we sat, the more eerie the shadows between the mountains seemed. The more I strained my eyes to see, the more movement I detected—real or imagined.

And of course, I had to pee. Leaving the car was the last thing I wanted to do. I held out as long as I could before finally reaching for the handle. The second I cracked open the door, the screeching car alarm shattered the silence. I froze, hand still on the door, while G behind the wheel quickly silenced it with the keys.

"Sorry," I whispered, as if lowering my voice could undo the noise we had made.

"Will you be okay out there?" he asked.

"I'll be quick."

I closed the door and squatted next to the car. The only light came from the full moon and from stars twinkling high above like distant eyes. I felt watched, not alone—some presence lingering in the night—so I hurried to finish and got back inside. In my seat, the thick smell of diesel fumes engulfed me, making my head throb. I stared through the windows, every shadow putting me on edge. A disorienting cocktail of sensations: altitude sickness, the fumes burning my nostrils, and the view of nothingness outside, knowing—or suspecting—that the Taliban lurked just beyond the border.

Besides ghosts and radicalized Islamists, a more concrete and immediate issue troubled us—the cold. We tried to fight it by huddling together beneath the single sleeping bag, but the frigid air seemed to penetrate every gap and crack, seeping into our bones. At some point, unable to take it anymore, G turned the key in the ignition. The car's heater brought both physical and emotional warmth, but as it hummed, we wondered if that was a good idea, whether it was worth the risk of running out of fuel or battery without knowing where the next diesel pump was, or when the next car would drive by.

We crept forward in the car, thinking the battery wouldn't run out if we kept driving slowly, attempting to keep the heater going. Once we reached the split in the road, we turned left toward the southern border. Since we didn't want to arrive before sunrise, every time we warmed up a little, we stopped the car and turned off the heater, waiting patiently. Each time, the cold crept back faster, our breath visible in the air as we discussed what to do, with no one able to sleep. We repeated the cycle—creeping forward in the night, the heat a brief reprieve, followed by the silent return of the cold.

Dawn's first light revealed the dramatic contours of the mountains, casting long shadows across the valley known as the Wakhan Corridor—a narrow strip of territory in northeastern Afghanistan that extends to China, separating Tajikistan from Pakistan and Pakistan-controlled Kashmir. The peaks, dusted with snow, glistened in the soft, early sunlight. We found a place to pull over and stepped out.

Standing there on the rocky edge, gazing at the gorge, my dress dancing in the gentle wind along the mountain road, the fears and discomforts of the night began to dissipate. Even with the distant, muffled sounds—pops or bangs, similar to those I had heard while firing rifles in Indiana—hidden among the sheer walls of rock. I was calm, confident. Was this it? Had I pushed my boundaries enough? Crossed enough borders?

The sun kissed my skin as I fixated on the landscape; all else disappeared. My arms, my legs, my core—everything felt engaged, as solid as the rocks surrounding me. I could almost see the puzzle pieces shifting against the backdrop of the mountains—flashbacks of anxieties, memories, and pent-up pains starting to make sense, finding their place, one move at a time. My shattered heart was finally beginning to bring the shards to a place of healing, the cracks filling with all the kindness I had encountered, the lessons I had learned, the appreciation for the little things, and the validation I had received to mend what was broken inside me. Was I ready to reach the finish line, my finish line—that elusive feeling I had been searching for but still couldn't quite put my finger on?

Questions swirled in my mind as my gaze remained fixed on the barren peaks, their hypnotic blue and white hues. The gorge carved its way through, as if to show with determination and strength—chip away and a path will form. But what path? What else could I possibly search for on this endless road? I had been terrified I might never get that feeling—the one I knew I would recognize when it came, the feeling that would say, "enough is enough, this is what you're going to do."

"Manon? Are you ready to continue? We need to reach the next town before nightfall," a voice with a French accent broke through my loud moment of silence.

"Yes," I replied, wondering what other choice I had but to keep moving forward.

Afghanistan
(Sort of)

"This is it," G said, hitting the brakes abruptly.

P and I looked around, puzzled, not seeing anything other than rocks and sky, while G pulled out our map.

"This is what?" I asked.

"Afghanistan," he said triumphantly, a grin spreading across his face.

We all pressed our noses against the map, trying to double-check his assertion. We had been told we would cross in and out of Afghanistan on a few occasions—unofficially, as no one would set up a border security checkpoint in a place where the only road runs along the border, east to west. From here, in this rough terrain, there were no visible roads leading south.

"Huh," I agreed, looking at the map and tracing the snake lines with my finger until I found the familiar curve of the road. "We really are here."

Out of the car, the rocks crunched under my feet. My body was there, my eyes scanning the place, but my mind traveled back in time, imagining when people migrated by simply packing a bag and walking, sometimes for months, searching for the perfect spot to build their community, long before ships crossed oceans and airplanes soared the skies. I wondered if, in some ways, we were not all that different—searching for something, moving forward, without fully knowing where we would land.

I refocused on the scene before me—just barren, jagged rocks, and the road curving back into Tajikistan up ahead. Before getting back into the car, I paused to listen to the silence of the mountains, with not even the Panj River's murmur audible yet.

Once the river came into sight, it drew a much clearer border, separating us from Afghan soil and, from that point forward, confining us to the Tajikistan side of the water. The river's presence made this stretch more habitable, with small villages and mud-brick houses scattered along the banks. As we drove slowly along the rough, narrow road, we spotted a fisherman wading in the river on the Afghan side, holding a fishing pole.

Then, suddenly, a Tajik soldier appeared out of nowhere, crossing the road in front of us, and firing a warning shot, screaming at the fisherman. The fisherman glanced up briefly, calmly, before retreating to his shore, stepping backward carefully. We kept driving.

Further toward Ishkashim, the scenery transitioned into lush greenery, with patches of farmland lining the river's edge and terraced fields stretching up the slopes, dotted with small brick houses. Our travel guidebook mentioned a homestay nearby—a place where travelers could stay with local hosts in their homes.

Turning onto a dirt road, we followed a small sign that read, "Homestay" in English and spotted a stone wall surrounding a farm nestled at the dead end of the turn.

"This must be it," P pointed to a gate in the wall.

"I guess we should knock?" I said, climbing out of the car and walking up to the wooden gate, then knocked and waited.

After a few minutes, a man peeked his head over the wall, observing us.

"Hello, sir," P said softly, sticking her hands out of the car and pointing at her travel guidebook. "We were hoping to eat something—are we at the right place?"

The man stood there for a moment, his posture curious, scanning the car and us with sharp eyes before slowly pushing open the gate and making his way toward us.

"Or do you know where we should go?" I jumped in.

His face softened into a gentle smile, a sparkle flickering in his eyes as we waited, hoping he understood what we were asking.

"You sleep, I cook," he said when he finally spoke, gesturing for us to follow.

My friends got out of the car, and we grabbed our small backpacks before trailing behind him into the courtyard.

Colorful blankets swayed on a washing line, strung between two gnarled trees, while mismatched pots and tools cluttered the stone pavement. He shouted something toward the house, and a slender boy appeared briefly, only to disappear again.

Without a word, the man led us into a cozy, carpeted room, where rich purple and red velvet pillows were scattered around a round stone table. Moments later, the boy returned, placing three cups of water in front of us.

"Rest," the man said softly, his expression full of care, the kind you get from someone who recognizes your exhaustion and wants to take care of you.

After they left the room, we sank into the pillows on the floor with deep sighs and closed our eyes for a little while. I must have dozed off almost instantly, unsurprising given how tough it had been to find sleep in the car the past few nights. It was in moments like these—feeling safe and sheltered—that things came into perspective.

"Eat," I heard the man's voice in my slumber.

When I opened my eyes, unsure how long I had been out, the round table between us was filled with berries, potatoes, and tomatoes, alongside a large pot of tea with an intricate floral design in deep green and gold accents. Berries, potatoes, and tomatoes seemed to be a recurring trend in these regions.

While this wasn't fine dining, there was something about the way the boiled potatoes melted in my mouth, the juicy tomatoes quenched my thirst, and the sweetness of the berries burst on my tongue like a decadent dessert.

When we left, I looked at my wallet. This man had been so kind and all I had to offer were currency bills in return, which felt woefully insufficient to repay his hospitality. I was so grateful for the chance to recharge, for the food he shared, and for the rest that went beyond my body to soothe my mind— sheltered in the confines of his stone-walled farmhouse.

We drove on, curving north toward Khorog. Sheep herders and their flocks shared the road with us as we passed through a town where more terraced fields climbed the slopes, framed by towering snowy mountains. The bright green fields, with their neatly farmed rows, stood in stark contrast to the gray and beige of the dusty road and the low stone walls lining it.

Children were playing with a ball in one of the fields, running around where a rocky path wound its way up. Intrigued, we pulled over—about halfway between Ishkashim and Khorog—a perfect moment to stretch our legs.

The local children, with their rosy cheeks and curious eyes, waved as we approached, their screams and chatter a cheerful counterpoint to the serene landscape. As we drew closer, they came running with their hands tightly clasped, as if holding something precious.

A small girl, no older than seven, with curly brown hair and a beanie on her head, stopped in front of me and opened her hands. Inside, rough gemstones in various shapes and sizes, resembling rubies, gleamed.

"I find," she said softly, her hazel eyes wide as she looked up.

I remembered reading about the ancient spinel mine at Kuh-i-Lal. *We must be close,* I thought, as I crouched down, trying to engage with her about these treasures.

"They're beautiful," I said, as I met her at eye level.

Two little boys appeared beside her, and she clutched the stones tightly, saying something in their language before all three of them dashed off.

As we walked the winding path up the slope, my friends and I could still see the children playing. Their clothes were worn, but their laughter echoed off the rocks, filling the air with a sound as comforting as a Sunday morning.

"They seem so joyful, even without all the things we think we need," I whispered as we took in the sight.

We all stayed silent, then turned and made our way back to the car.

By the time we reached Khorog, darkness had settled. Our bulky vehicle seemed completely out of place as we crawled through the pitch-black narrow streets, searching for our hostel. Suddenly, our headlights illuminated a large iron gate marking a dead end.

"Is this it?" I asked.

"I don't think so," G replied, scanning the surroundings for a way out. "I took a wrong turn."

He tried to turn around, but the car was too large. Then he tried to back up, but the curve in the narrow street was too difficult to navigate in reverse. We sat there for a couple of minutes, the car in idle, discussing how to get out, where to go. Some curious residents began to emerge from their homes, watching as G inched backward, trying not to scrape the walls.

P and I got out to help, attempting to guide him. Now, at least ten people had gathered—mostly men, some women— chattering among themselves and observing the scene. Finally, a young man dressed in all white stepped forward.

"Help," he said with a nod.

We gratefully accepted what we assumed was an offer of assistance. With exaggerated arm gestures, I tried to explain that if his neighbor could open their gate, we would have enough room to make the turn and leave. The man nodded a few times, then hurried off.

Finally, the iron gate creaked open. An older, gray-haired, bearded man stepped out, and one of the other spectators, who spoke some English, offered to translate our request to use his yard to turn the truck around.

"Yes," the man said, giving us a friendly nod.

We all sighed in relief as G maneuvered the truck while we stood by, thanking everyone profusely. With the nose of the white Ford pickup truck now facing the right direction, we jumped back in, this time with the correct route to the hostel.

●

I brushed the hair out of my face as I rolled over in my small but cozy bed at the hostel. It had been days since we last slept in a real bed. I shared a room with P, and we chatted while staring at the imposing natural stone walls surrounding us. She was petite yet fierce and I was glad to have her by my side.

"Pretty amazing, isn't it?" I said, feeling utterly relaxed.

"The only thing that would make it even better is finding a laundry machine," she chuckled.

That's when I remembered all our luggage, mostly hers and G's, was still soaked in diesel fuel. Since our accident, the only thing I had been able to somewhat clean was my denim jacket —and even that could use another wash.

We packed up all our clothes and took it to the hostel's laundry. As they washed, I ventured off to see if there was any internet connection available. My family had no idea where I had gone to and I hadn't been in touch for days.

I wandered across a spacious courtyard, dense with trees, passing sparsely scattered seating areas, while heading toward the hostel cabins. My eyes flicked to the Wi-Fi signal bars on my phone, watching them strengthen and drop as I moved.

Spotting some rocky steps carved into the mountainside, I noticed a girl coming down, phone in hand. When I reached the third uneven step, the signal peaked, so I decided to call my dad from there. The three-hour time difference with the Netherlands meant I should be able to reach him.

"Where are you, daughter?"

"On the border between Tajikistan and Afghanistan."

"You are *where*?" he asked, widening his eyes. "How did you get there?"

"Rented a car and drove," I said with a smile.

"Of course you did," he replied, smiling back.

Even though the conversation was short, it felt good to hear his voice, to be reminded of his love and support. Yet the geographical distance, amplified by the isolation of where I was, sharpened the gap between our realities. It was as if I lived two parallel lives: here, a traveler navigating solitude and uncertainty, searching for healing and finding my way; and there, a daughter anchored in familiarity and, even with the wounds of the past, safety.

I then skimmed a few Dutch news websites on my phone. Coincidentally, the first headline I saw read: "Afghanistan Confirms Death of Taliban Leader in U.S. Air Strikes."

I looked up at the sky. I was far enough from the airstrikes, yet I felt close enough—or closer than I had been before—to put myself in the shoes of the people here and consider what it must be like to live in an area of such unrest, where life and death loomed under a cloud of man-made fear.

•

Somewhat in a rush, after a quick meal and a visit to a bazaar, we left Khorog and got back on the Pamir Highway, taking the route straight back to Murghab—the road we would have taken if not for our detour along the Afghan border.

It was a gloomy day, with low, thick clouds hanging above and patches of snow scratching the ground. It felt as if we had landed on the moon, floating over the road weightlessly, with only the occasional cyclist jolting us back to reality.

After not seeing another car for hours, we saw what looked like a Soviet era version of a Volkswagen van parked by the roadside. As we approached, we noticed a single rope stretched across the road, held by a small wooden pole on the other side, blocking our way.

We stopped the car, somewhat curious, somewhat anxious, suspecting that someone had set up shop here to charge a toll. Not a lucrative business in these remote corners of the world, it appeared. At least, not today.

Carefully, we walked up to the van, and a man, hearing us approach, stuck his head out of the door. He spoke to us in what we assumed was Tajik, but we didn't understand him—only that he sounded excited to see us.

"Come, come," he said in broken English, waving for us to step inside his van.

"Maybe we shouldn't g—" I started, but G had already followed him in.

"Sit, sit!" the man continued excitedly, offering us food that looked like goulash.

We couldn't possibly accept; we had to keep moving. The man raised his hands, gesturing that it was fine, then checked our permit to drive the Pamir Highway and asked for money, which we handed over without debate. He then jumped out of his van and happily lifted the rope for us to pass.

Not pressing our luck, we quickly got back into our car and started driving. In the rearview mirror, I watched as the van disappeared into the distance, the single rope spun across the road once more.

The clouds looked dark and threatening, and the sun had already dipped behind the mountains when we stopped for food—more potatoes and tomatoes—at the familiar Pamir Hotel in Murghab. Reason would tell me it was wise to spend the night, safe, warm, and protected. Yet I had a flight to catch out of Bishkek in two days, and even though a part of me didn't care about catching it, I also knew that continuing on gave me the greatest chance of making it.

"I am fine to keep driving." G broke my internal debate.

"I don't know," P said, shaking her head.

And I genuinely didn't know. Rationally, we should not drive through the night—especially considering how scared I had been when we did. Existentially... Existentially I almost wanted to face that fear again, as if I had to live through it once more—feel it in my core—in order to conquer it.

"Let's do it," I heard myself say aloud after a few seconds.

And so we did.

As luck would have it, the weather worsened. By the time we neared the Tajik customs office ahead of the Kyzyl-Art Pass, small snowflakes landed on our windshield, and the mountain pass rose in front of us. The stillness and cold emanating from our surroundings made the hairs on the back of my neck stand up. The shadows of occasional yurts were the only sign of life, and the sole light ahead came from the post of Tajik soldiers guarding the border.

"This was a terrible idea," P murmured as we rolled down our windows at the barricade.

A soldier waved us through. Between two small buildings, we stopped the car and waited for instructions. Another soldier approached, signaling to hand over our passports, visas, and permits. We glanced around. From one of the buildings, a line of six or seven soldiers now emerged, each carrying a Kalashnikov, their fingers resting on the triggers, their faces set in a stern, intimidating expression.

"Out, out!" one of them commanded, lining us up.

Snowflakes fell on my face, the thin layer of snow under my feet illuminated by the border post's spotlight. I looked at my friends, standing stiffly in line, their eyes scanning the soldiers, shivering uncomfortably in the cold.

"Drugs?" a soldier asked, looking each of us in the eye.

We remained silent, frozen, staring back at him.

"Cocaine! Cocaine! Cocaine!" he shouted, touching his nose, frowning, then saying something to another soldier near him, who slightly raised his Kalashnikov in response.

My stomach cooled, and all I could think of doing—indeed all that the three of us did—was shake our heads, firmly.

Two soldiers began inspecting our vehicle while another grabbed our passports and permits and disappeared into a small cabin. We just stood there, for what felt like an eternity, watching the soldiers rummage through our belongings and the snow slowly building around us, melting into my shoes.

"*Nyet* permit!" one of the soldiers declared as he stood in the doorway of the cabin where he had taken our documents.

I exchanged glances with my friends again. Those words we understood, and yet they didn't make sense.

"You have it right there," G insisted, pointing toward the building where our papers had vanished.

"*Nyet,*" the soldier repeated, stubbornly.

My mind raced. Were they saying we couldn't pass, or that we didn't have the permit we had just handed over?

"*Da!*" I exclaimed, but the soldier shook his head.

I'm not sure what possessed me to do what I did next, given the circumstances, but I carefully moved toward the building, keeping the row of Kalashnikovs in the corner of my eye.

"Permit," I said, signaling inside.

My friends shuffled behind me as we all moved toward the door. Through the opening, we saw a small table over the soldier's shoulder.

"*Da!*" P said excitedly, spotting our permit next to our passports on the table.

Were they really trying to charge us for a permit we had just given them?

"*Nyet* permit," the soldier repeated, blocking the doorway.

"*Da* permit!" we chorused, pointing behind him.

P raised her hands and tried to slip past him. Surprisingly, he didn't stop her from entering the cabin and snatching the permit off the table just a few feet away.

"Permit," she said, raising the paper in front of his face.

"Okay," he replied, shrugging his shoulders.

He handed back our passports, then signaled to the others, who cleared out and closed the car doors.

"Okay?" G said, scratching his head.

"Let's go," P nudged him as the path forward cleared.

I followed without another word.

The Final Frontier

No light pierced the thick storm clouds; large snowflakes fell, and the headlights cast an unsteady gleam, often more blinding than the darkness itself. Steep cliffs flanked us as we crawled along the narrow, treacherous road, gravel sliding under the wheels. We had no control—nothing to grip but my backpack, my sweaty hands clamped tightly around it.

G, the only one who dared to drive in these conditions, exuded a terrifying confidence. Yet I knew he must be as scared as the rest of us. Every turn elicited soft shrieks.

"Slow down!" P pleaded, her voice trembling with fear.

"Slower," I echoed, gasping for breath in the thick air.

But how much slower could he go?

In the backseat, I unbuckled my seat belt, sliding from the right to the left seat, always keeping the cliff on the opposite side, gripping the door handle, ready to jump.

"Stop. Stop. Stop," P and I said in unison.

The car came to a halt, snow swirling angrily around us. We sat in the middle of the mountain pass, the road at its highest point—14,042 feet above sea level.

We sat there, hoping the snow would relent, allowing us to continue. Part of me wanted to curl up in a fetal position, close my eyes, and hope we would be okay when I opened them again. But another part of me was fueled with energy, my eyes straining to see, irises widening, pupils dilating, hoping to discern the path—the path to the other side, the path to clarity.

A Kyrgyz soldier waved us through the fence, entering the border station on the other side of the mountain pass. We handed over our permits and passports once more. I watched the documents pass from hand to hand. I knew their game by now. They weren't going to fool or rattle me any further.

After fueling up in Sary-Tash, we kept driving, hoping to cover the one hundred twenty miles to Osh, near the border with Uzbekistan, in three and a half hours. We drove toward the dawn of a new day. The road stretched out like a ribbon cutting through rough terrain. Little by little, the clouds drifted away, revealing first a dazzling array of stars, then a fiery sunrise—as if the mountains were erupting. I listened to the hum of the engine and, when we pulled over to stretch our legs or switch drivers, to the rustle of the wind.

I could almost feel the finish line—not just of our trip, but of my journey. I had wondered if I was ready to see it, to feel it, as I overlooked the Wakhan Corridor a few days earlier. My savings weren't depleted yet; I had no deadlines to meet, and there were no external forces pushing me to stop. Instead, there was this pull, coming from within, catching me off guard. It wasn't a physical homecoming but a spiritual one, like my mind was being drawn toward something inevitable, like a moth to a flame.

Sulaiman-Too—a World Heritage Site within the city of Osh, named for Solomon—has long been a beacon along the Silk Road, its distinct five peaks visible from afar, guiding travelers for centuries—millennia, even. This ancient sentinel also has been a place of mystery. Petroglyphs are scattered across its ridges, and numerous caves and ancient sites of worship testify to the mountain's spiritual history. Pilgrims have ascended its heights for countless reasons: seeking blessings, marveling at the endless views, even hoping for increased fertility. When it finally came into sight, I knew that was where I had to go; for me, still feeling that pull, that intuition, the only way was up.

As the minarets of mosques around us began their midday call to prayer, we found a spot on a sharp rock formation off one of the mountain trails and sat down. The melodic sounds reverberated all around, creating an ethereal symphony that filled the air. We sat and listened, thankful for the distance we had covered on the Pamir Highway and content to be this far up Sulaiman-Too's slopes, allowing us to look back at the road we had traveled.

When the air returned to silence, G animatedly gestured, his excitement spilling over as he described how each challenge of the past few days felt like shedding layers of doubt, fueling the confidence he already possessed. P chimed in, her voice warm as she expressed her appreciation for the opportunity to push her limits alongside us. We talked through everything that had happened, all we had felt, and what we believed was next for the three of us—both of them eager to return home yet already dreaming of new adventures.

Once the conversation subsided, we embraced the quiet, each of us taking a moment to ourselves. We listened to the murmur of hikers on the trails and observed the city of Osh, the Fergana Valley, and the mountains we had admired from the road. My mind began recapping the events of the past two weeks in Central Asia, the past thirteen months since deciding to leave home, and the past eleven years of my life without my mother, along with the questions of what it all meant. I had been running away from confronting my feelings and inner demons for so long, burying them deeper. I had drowned my grief and anger in positive things, always thinking that was the only way—the right way—the way not to become a victim of circumstance. But to truly do that, I had to take the time to look at myself in the mirror first, and let it all in. I had to understand it, for *it* not to haunt me later. Somehow, by distancing myself from all I had known, revisiting difficult memories, and writing about them, I was finally beginning to do just that.

It didn't feel solved, completed, concluded. Would it ever be? Could it be? But I did feel like I had found a crucial piece of the puzzle, something I had needed all along: the courage to confront and look into my own depths. And when I did, what I saw were scars. Scars from not being chosen. I had begged my father to choose me—not forever, but at first, to get through our period of mourning together. And by refusing to choose, he chose her. She had also made her choice. She chose *not* to be a figure of support, but instead to claim my father entirely for herself. There were wounds from moments so subtle they seemed trivial in other peoples' eyes, compounding over time, widening the scars. Their reasons difficult for me to articulate, but their cumulative impact causing deep psychological harm. The little girl on the receiving end—often trembling, lashing out, countering with a sharp tongue—always played defense against the seasoned bully.

I am not that little girl anymore. I chose to want something different. I was going to find a place that was all mine—a place she would have no part in. I would not invite her to my wedding. She would never be a grandmother to my child. My life's achievements would only be celebrated with the people I loved, barring *her* from ever having the opportunity, the power, to hurt me again. The missed opportunities to choose kindness, now her cross to bear. Kyrgyzstan's Sulaiman-Too, my proverbial *Mount Doom*—I had to throw the Ring into the fire.

It took me countless Greyhound buses, many thoughts of pink trees standing tall with beautiful confidence, feelings of loss, love, anxiety, happiness, determination, a very long, very cold train ride, climbing mountains, savoring food, meeting new people, total and devastating heartbreak, a breaking point of the soul, intense loneliness where I was never really alone, spontaneous airfares, delicious encounters, meaningful conversations, a journey by car on the Roof of the World, pushing boundaries, crossing borders, gaining confidence and courage, while being vulnerable, in order to truly see, envision things, with eyes wide open. The world has many faces, but at its core, it is kind and welcoming, diverse and encouraging. Through the world, I saw, I would always have a choice. Not just to decide to travel and figure myself out, but the choice to shape my future into whatever I wanted it to be. Everything that was a part of me was no longer wearing me down. Where was I going? I knew where I was *not* going: I was not going backward. I was no longer allowing negative energy into my life as I had for far too long.

There is still residue from that pain—some things might never heal, some things might never be forgiven. But by now it was clear that whatever I did, wherever I went, my main focus had to be letting in the light; my mother's light—the light that shone through me, the light so many people I met had seen in me and had written about in my journal. I had to keep that light alive, the spark that made me, *me*. No storm could blow out my candle; nothing could ever extinguish my flame.

As the afternoon call to prayer echoed, we realized we had been sitting there for at least four hours. There was no way I would make it back to Bishkek on time for my flight in the morning, unless I would fly, instead of drive, out of Osh. All of a sudden, there was no desire to miss my flight, no need to linger. I saw clearly—this is the end. I *will* choose, I *will* settle.

I looked up at the clear blue sky, then at my friends, uttering the following words with an ease and lightness that surprised me, but no longer scared me:

"This is it. Drop me off at the airport?"

Epilogue

California—the golden coast, where sandy beaches meet swaying palms. Cities rise tall, mountains tower higher, and hills roll into sprawling vineyards crafting bold new wines.

Touching down in Los Angeles, I felt my journey had come full circle. After leaving Kyrgyzstan, I connected with the very actor I had mentioned in Sydney—the lead in one of my favorite romantic comedies. He appreciated my travels and reached out to share more, reinforcing my belief that anything is possible. Originally from Australia, he had been traveling in Hawaii and living in LA. Our conversation reignited my thoughts about the City of Angels, the place where it all began, and the United States had long been my longing. It felt right—like tying the final knot and sealing the promise of what I had set out to accomplish.

This place had the raw nature of New Zealand, the diverse food scene of Australia, the upscale flair of London, the sun-soaked beaches of Florida, and the unapologetic zeal of New York.

I dove headfirst—not into the Pacific, but into opportunity itself. Nothing was out of reach; dreams had no ceiling. I couch-surfed through the Hollywood Hills, Downtown LA, Santa Monica, and Manhattan Beach, tasting every corner of this vast, ever-changing metropolis.

Ocean View Park—an invitation. Two bicycles gliding along the boardwalk: me and the actor who inspired me to be there, someone who had taken the leap to make his dream a reality.

I found my community. People who *believed*, like I did: dream big, and dare to follow. I immersed myself in LA's creative scene; I colored outside the lines every single day. Starting from scratch, with nothing but ambition and a relentless drive —drive that emerged from my light. I slept under desks, hoping one day I could call this city home.

Maybe it already was. Friendships flourished, new routines took root, a trundle bed in Palms opened up long-term with roommates who quickly felt like siblings, and the city finally became mine. It liberated me, wiped clean the past, silenced the ghosts in my head.

And then I wrote a book about losing my mother—from a child's perspective—pushing for transparency around illness and loss, so no child would ever feel the ache of words left unsaid, while they still had the chance to speak them.

And just when I stopped searching for love to complete me, love found me.

I married the guy who didn't flinch when I packed my suitcase before we even talked about moving in together. The one who showed up in different cities to surprise me—instead of the other way around. The one who was standing, leaning against his car, at the end of a Greyhound bus, holding flowers.

And then I became a mother myself. The deep-rooted pain I once carried turned into an impenetrable wall, vowing to shield my daughter from the same sorrow.

Every Sunday, we watch Formula 1 together.

The kindness of the world
reveals itself in countless ways and places,
especially when you find yourself in unfamiliar spaces
where you are not yet known.

Acknowledgments

It took years to write this book, to make sense of my scribbles, thoughts, and all the layers of emotion woven into this story. Writing about deeply personal topics is exposing. For me, the journey itself uncovered light, but it was the writing that truly allowed me to piece it together. Unfortunately, my situation is all too common; I'm certainly not the first to face it. However, by opening up about my journey, I felt less alone, and I hope that by doing so, others know they are not alone either. I often hesitated, pausing for long stretches, fearful of hurting anyone. Many conversations with my family ensued—raw, difficult, and navigating that delicate line between love and resentment, bringing us closer and deepening our understanding.

I am forever grateful to my father for his endless patience and willingness to listen—grateful for the long talks while looking at landscapes or sharing lengthy car rides, for allowing me to lay my heart bare, even when it hurt. Thank you for helping us find our way together and for being my rock, always.

To my brothers: one, who briefly joined me on this journey, sharing his wisdom and understanding of what it takes to finish such a waterfall of words; the other, for his spiritedness and for always having a steaming pot of cheese fondue ready when I needed it most. I am grateful for both of you and for the steady, unconditional love that has kept me grounded.

To my godparents, who stepped in when my mother was diagnosed with cancer and have been there every step since—through anything and everything. You are my pillars, the extra set of parents every child should be so lucky to have.

To my husband, my confidant, who gave me the space and support to dive into the depths of my soul for days and nights —thoughts wandering, head aching—enduring the specific kind of torture that writing sometimes is. For offering me stability, sparking critical thinking, embracing fiery debates, letting me keep the Christmas tree up for three months to reclaim lost holiday cheer, and, most of all, for giving me the feeling that I finally belonged.

To Olivia, my *Livylove,* my *Livylou,* who gave me back the joy of mother-daughter time. From the moment I became pregnant, you inspired me to finish this story. Throughout our first year, during those long, sleepless nights, you kept me company as I typed out another chapter and another, your big blue eyes gazing up at me while you lay on my chest, finally bringing this story to completion. I love you endlessly.

To my friends, my fellow travelers, you know who you are. The many people who stood by my side, who believed in me, who opened up their homes and treated me like family.

Even those who put me through trials I never wanted to endure contributed to my growth and resilience.

And finally, my editor, who shepherded me through the final stages, encouraging me to go mile deep and inch wide. Thank you for helping me find clarity in every line and depth in every chapter, as we covered every last bit of ground.

For all of you, I am grateful.

This book was first published on February 1, 2025,
twenty years since my mother's passing.

Trudie Rinsma
12 juni 1951 - 1 februari 2005

Thank you for shining your light.